THE LIFE AND TEACHINGS
of
TSONGKHAPA

THE LIFE AND TEACHINGS

of

TSONGKHAPA

Edited by

ROBERT A.F. THURMAN

Translation by

Sherpa Tulku
Khamlung Tulku
Alexander Berzin
Jonathan Landaw
Glenn H. Mullin
Robert A.F. Thurman

LIBRARY OF TIBETAN WORKS & ARCHIVES

ISBN: 81-86470-44-1

Published by Library of Tibetan Works & Archives, Dharamsala and
printed at Indraprastha Press (CBT), 4 Bahadur Shah Zafar Marg,
New Delhi-110002

Reverence to the
Guru, Mañjughosha !

Contents

viii

Publisher's Note

Since the opening of the Library of Tibetan Works & Archives a decade ago, a number of Tibetan texts had been translated by our Research and Translation Bureau and brought out in print as part of our publishing program. Several of these were by or centered upon the life of Lama Tsongkhapa (1357-1419), an important teacher who had been born in eastern Tibet and later spent many years travelling from one monastery or yogis hermitage to another in search of the various lineages of the Buddhist teachings. His studies and practice explored the full range of Hinayana, Mahayana and Vajrayana doctrines as found in all the schools of Buddhism then extant in the land of Snow Mountains. Studying with almost four dozen masters from all traditions of Tibetan Buddhism, the order established by him was in fact the first attempt at combining all Buddhist lineages in Tibet and the first appearance of what might be called "indigeneous Tibetan Buddhism"; for the earlier traditions in existence at the time were mainly rooted in a specific Indian master, such as the Nyingma with Padma Sambhava, the Kagyu with the masters Tilopa and Naropa, and so forth, whereas Tsongkhapa's tradition was to represent a synthesis of the several dozen most important schools of early fourteenth century Tibetan Buddhism. The eighteen volumes of writings that had issued forth from his pen were to act as a major inspiration in Tibetan cultural history, ushering in a renaissance of religious prose and poetry. His effects upon art, architecture and folk culture were a natural product of his creating festivals such as the Great Prayer Festival of Lhasa; and by the specific artists and craftsmen he used in his building and restoration work as mentioned later in *A Short Biography*.

In the spring of 1979 Prof. Robert Thurman of Amherst College, Mass., visited Dharamsala on a sabatical. Prof. Thurman is indeed one of the Western world's foremost scholars concerning the life and works of Lama Tsongkhapa, and the LTWA was most pleased when Prof. Thurman accepted our request that he collect together the various monographs by or related to Tsongkhapa that the LTWA had previously published in English translation, and to complement these with any of his own works that were as of yet unpublished.

The text of "A Short Biography" is based on an oral teaching by Geshe Ngawang Dargye as translated by Khamlung Tulku and Sherpa Tulku, compiled by John Marshall and edited by India Stevens. It has been revised and re-edited for this publication by Michael Richards and Kevin Garratt. It was first published by the LTWA in 1975 as *A Short Biography and Letter of Je Tzong-k'a-pa*.

"Song of the Mystic Experiences" of the first chapter of this anthology, as well as the first three items in chapter five, were translated by Glenn H. Mullin and Losang N. Tsonawa in accordance with the commentaries of Geshe Ngawang Dargye, Gen Sonam Rinchen and Geshe Losang Tenpa. They were first published by the LTWA in 1978 as *Four Songs to Je Rinpoche*.

"Lines of Experience", "A Letter of Practical Advice on Sutra and Tantra" and "The Prayer of the Virtuous Beginning, Middle and End" were translated by the team Sherpa Tulku, Khamlung Tulku, Alexander Berzin and Jonathan Landaw in accordance with the commentary of Geshe Ngawang Dargye. The first of these was originally published as a monograph by the LTWA in 1973, and then reprinted in 1974 in a revised edition. The second originally appeared under the title *The Graded Course to Enlightenment* (Statesman Press. New Delhi, 1971) and in a revised edition under the title "A Brief Exposition of the Main Points of the Graded Sutra and Tantra Course to Enlightenment" in the text *A Short Biography and Letter of Je Tzong-k'a-pa* (LTWA, Dharamsala, 1975), with reprintings in 1975 and 1976. For this, their third edition, all three of these works have been retranslated by Alexander

Berzin, with the assistance of Ven. Amchok Rinpoche, Librarian at the LTWA in *A Letter of Practical Advice on Sutra and Tantra.*

The remaining works in the collection have all been translated by Prof. Thurman, some in the earlier years of his work with Tibetan literature and some—notably the "Supremely Healing Nectar Garland"—specifically for this collection. The Library is most appreciative of the spirit of thoroughness with which Prof. Thurman approached the subject.

Although Lama Tsongkhapa is one of the most important figures in Tibetan religious and philosophical history, very little material by or about him has appeared in English to date. It is hoped that this small effort will contribute in some way to the Western world's growing knowledge of Tibet, her culture, philosophy and religion, and the figures of Tibet's past who inspired and influenced the trends of Tibetan thought.

Gyatso Tsering
Director
LTWA, October 1981

Editor's Note

This anthology of some of the important works of the great Dharma Master Tsongkhapa Losang Drakpa (1357-1419) is presented for the general reader and practitioner of Buddhadharma to give him an introduction to the life and profound teachings of that great Lama. Most of the translations contained here were done same time ago, and published as pamphlets and xerox-manuscripts. Mr. Gyatso Tsering requested me to gather these translations together, adding some explanatory notes and translating newly some special pieces that round out the collection. It was decided from the beginning not to attempt to impose any standard terminology or even transliteration system on the works done by different translators, leaving each with his own style and taste. The keynote of the anthology is to grant access to the useful *Teachings* themselves.

The book is divided into five parts. The first begins with a short biography drawn by Geshe Ngawang Dhargye from a number of traditional sources, notably Khaydrub's *Haven of Faith.* This biography is supplemented by Tsongkhapa's own *Song of Realization,* a spiritual and educational autobiography, and Jamyang Choje Tashi Palden's *Song of The Mystic Experiences,* a record of his visionary experiences.

The second part presents Tsongkhapa's teachings on the *Stages of the Path to Enlightenment (Lamrim),* including the quintessential summary given in revelation by the Bodhisattva Mañjushri, the briefest version written by the Master himself, and a lucid version of the overall path written in a personal letter to a close disciple. It concludes with a prayer for the accomplishment of the path.

The third part gives Tsongkhapa's enlightenment-poem, his *Praise* (to Shakyamuni for His Teaching) *for Relativity*, written on the morning of his attainment of realization; as well as his middle length version of the cultivation of wisdom through transcendent insight.

The fourth part shows his lyrical and mystical side, including praises of the two emblematic Bodhisattvas, Mañjushri and Maitreya, a descriptive prayer for rebirth in the pure land of Amitabha, and a dialogue between the great Nying-ma Master Lhobrag Khenchen Namkha Gyaltsen and the Bodhisattva Vajrapani, in the presence of Tsongkhapa himself.

The final part includes three praises of Tsongkhapa, written by his disciple Khaydrub, the Seventh Dalai Lama, and the Eighth Karmapa Lama, respectively. The entire collection concludes with the famous invocation of Tsongkhapa, *Lord of Tushita's Hundred Gods*.

Special thanks must be given to His Holiness the Fourteenth Dalai Lama, the clarity and inspiration of whose Presence being instrumental in getting most of this work done; to Yongzin Ling Rinpoche, who clarified a number of points in my own translations; and to Demo Locho Rinpoche, who saved me from a number of bad mistakes. And of course, my original thanks are always due to my first Teacher, who introduced me to the wonderful teaching of Tsongkhapa, the Venerable Geshe Wangyal.

Thanks are also due to the translators and teachers who contributed to the various works collected here, especially to Glenn Mullin who got me moving on it, and to Gyatso Tsering, the dedicated and able Director of the Library of Tibetan Works & Archives, who saw it all through to completion. In spite of all this excellent help and inspiration, I am sure there are errors still undetected, at least in the works of my own, for which I alone assume responsibility, inviting others to contribute criticism and improvements toward an eventual final edition of Tsongkhapa's works, the scholarly task I have set myself for this lifetime.

Robert A.F. Thurman
Ashok Niwas, Dharamsala, Wesak Moon; May 29, 1980 and
Woodstock, Dharmachakra Day; 1980

PART I

Life, Liberation and Accomplishments

The first chapter in this part, "A Short Biography", was taught by Geshe Ngawang Dhargye in Dharamsala at the Library of Tibetan Works & Archives, translated in the main by Khamlung Tulku. Its major source is Khaydrub's *Haven of Faith,* the standard short biography that is usually printed at the beginning of Tsongkhapa's *Collected Works.* I have a complete translation of this work, which will be forthcoming later in this series. It is included here essentially to give the reader an idea of the many-sided marvel of the life of this great Scholar, Saint and Teacher-Sage.

The third chapter is included to show, in Tsongkhapa's own words, the extreme breadth and depth of his education and experience, as well as his own sense of gratitude to Mañjushri, his final Guru. I translated this myself.

The fourth chapter balances the picture of his vast learning with a sketch of the richness of his mystic experiences, the catalog of his visions sounding like an iconographic encyclopedia.

❖

A Short Biography

The great Nyingma teacher, Lhodrag Khenchen Namkha Gyaltsen once asked the Bodhisattva Vajrapani to describe the qualities of Lama Je Tsongkhapa; but since these were innumerable, Vajrapani was unable to do so. To hear the complete biography of the Lord Tsongkhapa would take at least a year. This brief exposition has been compiled merely as an introduction for English speaking readers.

Tsongkhapa, popularly known as Je Rinpoche, was born in 1357, the year of the Bird, in the Tsong Kha region of Amdo Province, in eastern Tibet. His father, who was bold but unassuming, energetic yet taciturn and reserved, was constantly in thoughts of the Doctrine and recited the *Expression of the Names of Mañjushri* each day. His mother, a guileless and very kind woman, was always chanting the six-syllable mantra of Avolokiteshvara—Om Mani Padme Hum. They had six sons, Tsongkhapa being the fourth.

During the time of Buddha Shakyamuni, Tsongkhapa, in a previous incarnation, was a young boy who offered the Buddha a clear crystal rosary and received a conch shell in return. The Buddha then called his disciple Ananda to him and prophesied that the boy would be born in Tibet, would found a great monastery between the areas of Dri and Den, present a crown to the statue of the Buddha in Lhasa and be instrumental in the flourishing of the Doctrine in Tibet. The Buddha gave the young boy the future name of Sumati Kirti, or, in Tibetan, Losang Drakpa.

All this occurred exactly as the Buddha had prophesied. The conch shell that the Buddha had given the boy was unearthed during the building of Ganden and, until 1959, could still be seen in Drepung, the largest Monastery in Tibet. The crown still rests on the head of the Buddha in Lhasa.

Over a thousand years after the passing of Shakyamuni Buddha, further prophesies relating to Je Rinpoche, were given by the Lotus Born Guru, Padma Sambhava. He predicted that a fully ordained Buddhist monk named Losang Drakpa would appear in the east near the land of China. He said that this monk would be regarded as being an emanation of a Bodhisattva of the greatest renown and would attain the Complete Enjoyment Body of a Buddha.

During the Year of the Monkey, which preceded his birth, his parents had unusual dreams. His father dreamt of a monk who came to him from the Five peaked Mountain (Wu-tai-shan) in China, a place particularly associated with Mañjushri. This monk required shelter for nine months which, in the dream, his father gave by accommodating him in their shrine room for that length of time.

His mother dreamt that she and one thousand other women were in a flower garden to which a boy dressed in white and carrying a vessel came from the east while a girl dressed in red and holding peacock feathers in her right hand and a large mirror in her left came from the west. The boy went to each of the women in turn and asked the girl if she would be suitable. The girl repeatedly rejected them until the boy pointed to Tsongkhapa's mother, whom she indicated as the perfect choice. The boy and girl then purified Tsongkhapa's mother by bathing her and when she awoke the next day she felt very light.

In the first month of the Year of the Bird, Je Rinpoche's parents again had striking dreams. His mother saw monks coming with many different ritual objects, saying that they were going to invoke the statue of Avalokiteshvara. When the statue appeared, it was as big as a mountain yet, as it approached her, it diminished in size, finally entering her body through her crown aperture.

Tsongkhapa's father dreamt of Vajrapani, who, from his own pure realm, threw down a vajra, which landed on his wife.

Just before giving birth, his mother dreamt of many monks arriving with offerings. When she inquired about their purpose they replied that they had come to pay their respects and gain an audience. Simultaneously, the boy in white from her previous dream appeared and pointed to her womb. With key in hand he entered it and opened a box, from which came the golden statue of Avalokiteshvara. This statue was stained, and a girl in red appeared and cleaned it with a peacock feather. This dream symbolised that Tsongkhapa would be an emanation of Avalokiteshvara as well as of Mañjushri. The same morning, Tsongkhapa was born without causing any suffering to his mother. At the time of his birth an auspicious star appeared in the sky.

These portents were ample evidence of the birth of someone remarkable. In this respect Je Rinpoche's birth resembled that of the Buddha.

Prior to these events, Tsongkhapa's future great teacher, Choeje Dondrup Rinchen, had been in Lhasa and had learnt that on his return to Amdo, he would find a disciple who was an emanation of Mañjushri. After Tsongkhapa's birth, he sent his chief disciple to the parents with a protection knot, some relic pills and a letter of greeting.

At three years old, Tsongkhapa took the layman's vows from the Fourth Karmapa, Rolpay Dorje, and received the name Kunga Nyingpo.

When Tsongkhapa's parents invited Choeje Dondrup Rinchen to their home, the Lama brought horses, sheep and a huge amount of gifts which he gave to Tsongkhapa's father. When the Lama requested the father to part with his son, the father was delighted at the prospect of his child being with such a great teacher and allowed him to leave with the Lama.

Before taking the novice vows, Tsongkhapa, received many tantric initiations and teachings, including the Heruka empowerment, and was given the secret name of Donyo Dorje. When he was seven, he fulfilled his yearning to take the novice vows; receiving them from his teacher. It is here that he was given the name of Losang Drakpa, that, forty years later, was to become the most talked about and controversial nom de plume in Central Tibet.

Tsongkhapa attached greater importance to guarding his vows than his eyes or his own life. He had entered the mandalas of Heruka, Hevajra, Yamantaka and other deities before receiving ordination and was even performing self-initiation meditations upon Heruka when he was only seven. Before self-initiation is allowed, a major retreat of the specific deity must be completed.

His eminent teacher took care of him until he went to central Tibet at the age of sixteen. Before the statue of Shakyamuni Buddha in the Lhasa Cathedral, he offered prayers to enable his completion of all the stages of sutra and tantra in order to mature and lead other trainees to enlightenment.

Choeje Dondrub Rinchen proffered advice in poetical form to the effect that Tsongkhapa should first study and master the *Ornament for the Realisations (Abhisamayalamkara)* and then approach the other four great treatises. The Lama further suggested Tsongkhapa's lifelong choice of meditational deities to whom he should make offerings and with whom he should feel perpetually inseperable. The following deities were to be cultivated accordingly: Yamantaka for the continuation of his practice; Vajrapani for freedom from interruptions; Mañjushri for increase in wisdom and discriminating awareness; Amitayus for long life; the three Doctrine Protectors for the availability of prerequisites while practising; and Vaishravana, the Six-Handed Mahakala and Dharmaraja for protection.

On his departure, his Master came with him as far as Tsongkha Kang from where Tsongkhapa went on alone, walking backwards with his hands folded at his heart and reciting the *Expression of the Names of Mañjushri*. When he reached the line. "Those who do not return to cyclic existence do not come back," he had tears in his eyes for he realized that he would never return to Amdo.

Travelling with Denma Rinchen Pel, in the autumn of the Year of the Bull, (1357), Tsongkhapa arrived at Drikung, a five day journey from Lhasa, where he met the head Lama of the Drikung Kargyu monastery, Chennga Choekyi Gyalpo by name. This great Lama was his first teacher after leaving his original Master, and tutored him on various topics such as the Altruistic Mind *(bodhicitta)*, and five sections of the *Great Seal (mahamudra)* during his stay at the monastery. He also met the great doctor Konchog Kyab who taught him the major medical treatises and, by the time he was seventeen, he had become an excellent doctor. Thus his fame was already spreading even in the early years of his study.

From Drikung, Tsongkhapa went to the Choedra Chenpo Dewachen monastery in Nyetang where he studied with Tashi Sengi and Densapa Gekong. Furthermore Yonten Gyatso taught him how to read the great treatises and continually helped him with the *Ornament for the Realisations.* Within eighteen days he had memorized and assimilated both the root text and all its commentaries, and soon mastered all the works of Maitreya Buddha. He then gained a complete understanding of the *Perfection of Wisdom (Prajña paramita)* at great speed and with little effort. His teachers and fellow students with whom he debated were astonished at his knowledge and, after two years of studying the *Perfection of Wisdom,* he was recognized, at the age of nineteen, as a great scholar.

That year Je Rinpoche debated at the two biggest monasteries of the day in Tibet: Choedra Chenpo Dewachen and Samye. He now became very famous in U-tsang, the central province of Tibet and undertook an extensive tour of it. First he visited the great monastery of Zhalu, where the renowned translator Khenchen Rinchen Namgyal, a direct disciple of the founder of the monastery, gave him the Heruka initiation. He went on to Sakya, the centre of the Sakya tradition, in order to debate further on the major treatises and there by increase his understanding of them. But on arrival, he learned that most of the monks had gone to debate at the distant Karpu pass so instead he went to Zhalu and met the great Lama Demchog Maitri, who initiated him into the Thirteen Deity Yamantaka practice. Later he returned to Sakya but the debaters had still not returned so this time he went to Sazang and met the great Sazang Pandit Matt, who gave him extensive teachings. Returning a third time to Sakya, he was able to take the required examinations on the *Perfection of Wisdom.*

He then continued on his travel around the other monasteries of U-tsang, engaging in more and more debate. There are many stories concerning the miraculous visions of those present at these places, as well as Tsongkhapa's ever-developing great realizations and insights.

Je Tsongkhapa continued with many other required debates on the systems of tenets and the five major treatises at various monasteries. As he had a great admiration for Nyapon Kunga Pal whom he met at Tzechen in U-tsang and from whom he received many discourses, he went to him and requested instructions on the *Perfection of Wisdom*; but this master was unwell and referred him to his disciple, the Venerable Rendawa, Je Rinpoche developed tremendous respect for Rendawa's method of teaching the *Treasury of Knowledge* and its auto-commentary. Tsongkhapa asked many searching questions on certain points to the amazement of his teacher, who was sometimes unable to answer immediately. This master had innumerable spiritual qualities and Tsongkhapa later came to regard him as his principal teacher. Their relationship became such that simultaneously they were each other's Master and disciple. He also received teachings on the *Middle Way* (*Madhyamika*) philosophy from Rendawa.

Tsongkhapa composed a verse in honour of Rendawa and would often recite it:

> Mañjushri, Lord of stainless omniscience,
> Avalokiteshvara, mighty treasure of immaculate love,
> O Rendawa Zhonnu Lodro, crown jewel of Tibetan sages,
> At your feet I make this request,
> Grant protection to me, a fly seeking Liberation.

Rendawa replied that this was more applicable to Tsongkhapa than to himself and so adapted the verse as follows. This is now regarded as Tsongkhapa's mantra:

> Avalokiteshvara, mighty treasure of immaculate love.
> Mañjushri, Lord of stainless knowledge,
> Vajrapani, destroyer of all demonic forces,
> O Je Tsongkhapa, Losang Drakpa,
> Crown jewel of the sages of the Land of Snow,
> Humbly I request your blessing

During the autumn and winter he received many teachings on the *Entrance to the Middle Way* by Chandrakirti, who also wrote an auto-commentary to it. He then returned to U-tsang, where the great translator and metaphysician Jangchub Tsemo, was to give teachings in Lhasa on the five major treatises.

On arrival in Lhasa, Tsongkhapa went straight to him and requested teachings. However, this old Lama was in delicate health and intended to leave soon for an area south of Lhasa. Tsongkhapa was not satisfied with the short discourses he received so returned to Nyetang to become the student of the great scholar of *Monastic Discipline (Vinaya)*, the Abbot Kazhiwa Losal, at whose feet he studied the root texts of *Discipline* and of the *Treasury of Knowledge*, as well as many related commentaries. By the time he left, his depth of understanding surpassed that of his teacher. He memorized a commentary on the extensive root text of the *Discipline* at the daily rate of seventeen Tibetan folios which is thirty four pages.

While reciting prayers with the other monks, he had complete and effortless single-pointed concentration on insight meditation. However, he remained dissatisfied and continued to search for further teachers and teachings. Surely we can derive inspiration from such rectitude considering that he had memorized, for example, over twenty thousand verses of the extensive *Perfection of Wisdom Sutra*.

During that winter a troublesome backpain developed and he thought of returning to Rendawa in U-tsang but the bitterly cold weather forced him to stay at Nanying where he gave his first teachings. Scholars had asked for teachings on *Knowledge (Abhidharma)*, or metaphysics, and in particular on Asanga's *Compendium of Knowledge* which composes the Mahayana Abhidharma. He also wished to re-study the *Treasury of Knowledge* written by Vasubhandu, which is a compilation of Hinayana Abhidharma. Tsongkhapa studied the higher tenets; and although it was his initial encounter with this text, he mastered it on first reading and gave perfect teachings.

From there he went to Rendawa, who was at Sakya and for eleven months taught the *Compendium of Knowledge*.

At this time he himself received teachings on Dharmakirti's *Commentary on the Compendium of Valid Cognition*, as well as various texts such as the *Entrance to the Middle Way* and the transmission of the *Sutra on Discipline*.

While at Sakya he also received an explanation on the *Root Tantra of Hevajra* from Dorje Rinchen. This lama also taught him a method by which to cure his painful back.

In the company of the master Rendawa, he left for northern Tibet and spent the spring and summer at the monastery of Choeday. Here Rendawa wrote his commentary to the *Compendium of Knowledge* which he later taught to Tsongkhapa upon the disciple's request.

At this time, many people from Tsong Kha were coming to Lhasa with gifts from his now wealthy family and brought with them many letters from family and friends imploring him to come back. Reading these on his return to Lhasa, Je Tsongkhapa considered going back but realised that return would necessitate a break in his studies with the consequence of failure in his drive to help sentient beings. Thus he stayed and wrote to his mother instead, enclosing a self-portrait which spoke to her when she opened it. From childhood he had always possessed a strong sense of renunciation and later on even refused an invitation from the Emperor of China, who had requested his services as Imperial Tutor.

Tsongkhapa went into retreat for a few months and in between sessions studied the *Commentary on the Compendium of Valid Cognition*. This text contains four chapters, and when he reached the second, he realized the profundity of the work and developed the greatest respect and admiration for Dharmakirti, whilst deepening his conviction in the Buddha and his teachings.

He then returned to Tsang to debate, traveling to Narthang where the Tibetan woodblocks of the Buddha's actual teachings (the *Kanjur*) and of the Commentaries (the *Tanjur* were kept. Here he met the great translator, Donzang, author of a critique to the *Commentary on the Compendium of Valid Cognition* which he taught to Tsongkhapa. They also debated on the two sets of *Knowledge* and on the *Discipline*.

He received teachings on the technical aspects of poetry from the Translator Namkha Zangpo and then returned to Rendawa for further elucidation on the five major treatises: the *Middle Way* philosophy, *Logic, Knowledge, Perfection of Wisdom* and *Discipline*. He especially concentrated on the *Entrance to the Middle Way* and from the Abbot of Narthang, received instruction on the *Six Works on Reason* by Nagarjuna.

Having further refined his dialectical skills, he and Rendawa
returned to Sakya where he took examinations on four of the five
treatises, omitting the *Perfection of Wisdom,* which he had previously
covered. Tempers are sometimes short during a debate, but he always
remained calm and spoke with amazing mastery.

Tsongkhapa practised simplicity and lived without affluence or
great comfort. People felt over-awed before meeting him, but once in
his presence were happy and relaxed. He would treat all questions
with equal respect. Many of his disciples attained enlightenment in
one lifetime.

By this time people realized that Tsongkhapa was an exceptional
person who had taken birth by choice in order to help the sentient
beings. His pure morality gained him the greatest respect from all
sides and his devotees in U-tsang were now legion. It is certain when
he took the vows of a fully ordained monk, or Bhikshu, for there is
nothing to substantiate the commonly accepted thesis that he was
twentyone. However, at a monastery just south of Lhasa, the Abbot
Tsultrim Rinchen and a group of Bhikshus were present at the
ordination ceremony. This was conducted in accordance with the
tradition of the Hinayana, which requires the presence of ten bhikshus
and an abbot when ordination is given in a place where the teachings
are flourishing, technically called a central land. If the ordination is
not held in such a place, then at least five bhikshus and an abbot
should attend. In either case, the presence of two elders is essential.
One reads from the *Sutra on Discipline* and the other questions the
candidate concerning his suitability for the monastic way of life.

After ordination, he returned to the great Lama at the Drikung
Kargyu centre and while the two were engaged in lengthy conversation
the elderly Lama was overcome by tears, wishing that he too could
have practised so intensively in his youth. He later told his disciples
that both he and they had merely received higher rebirths whereas Je
Tsongkhapa received a stream of realisations even in his youth. He
received many teachings froth the Lama on such topics as tantra, the
Six Doctrines of Naropa, the works of Je Phagmo Drupa (who was one
of the foremost disciples of Gampopa) and the teachings of the founder
of the monastery.

By this time, Tsongkhapa had received from this Drikung Kargyu master all the teachings that Marpa had given to two of his four sons: Milarepa and Ngogchu Dorje; the other two 'sons' being Meto Chenpo and Tsultrim Dorje Wang. In addition, Tsongkhapa was constantly developing spiritual qualities and reading all the texts and commentaries available.

At thirty-two, he travelled to Tsay Gungthang where he commenced writing a commentary on the *Perfection of Wisdom Sutra*. He synthesized all twenty-one Indian Commentaries relating to the *Ornament for the Realisations,* for Maitreya's text is itself a commentary to the *Perfection of Wisdom Sutra,* and called his work *Legshay Serteng (The Golden Rosary of Eloquent Teaching).* The translator Tagtsang, who had previously disputed many of Tsongkhapa's viewpoints, was amazed by this commentary and showered praise on the text and its author. He wrote, "As your sun of wisdom rises, my flower of arrogance disappears."

Tsongkhapa and his chief disciples travelled to Lhasa and started a fasting retreat near the statue of Avalokiteshvara. One evening, he told the disciple, who was his scribe, to observe his dreams that night. The acolyte did so, and dreamt that two conch shells appeared in the sky and then descended into his lap, where they merged. He blew this conch, which gave forth a deep resonance. The dream symbolised that Tsongkhapa's teaching would flourish.

After this retreat, he visited Nyethang once more and gave many discourses on the *Middle Way* and the other major treatises. He decided to study the *Kalachakra Cycle* and received the relevant teachings from Thubten Yeshe Gyaltsen, who lived near Lhasa. This teacher also imparted the relevant instructions on astrology and mandala construction.

He now started giving tantric initiations and the teachings related to such practices; especially the permission of Saraswati, a female deity of wisdom, whom some took to be his particular protectress. The instructions that he conferred ripened and liberated many disciples.

While staying at Moenkar Tashi Dong, just south of Lhasa, he taught the biographies of the great accomplished beings of the past. Je Tsongkhapa was requested to teach in the tradition of Geshe Shatonpa and others who had dealt with as many as eleven volumes during the period of teaching. He promised to do so and went into retreat for twenty days to prepare. His idea was to commence the discourses on the first day of the Tibetan month, but as so many people wished to attend, he deferred until the fourth to give them time to arrive. In the interim, he gave some teachings from the lineage of Marpa and Milarepa, and thereafter proceeded to teach not just eleven, but seventeen texts in three months. Each day was divided into fifteen sessions between dawn and dusk and the texts covered were as follows: *Commentary on the Compendium of Valid Cognition, Ornament for the Realisations, Treasury of Knowledge, Compendium of Knowledge, Sutra of Discipline,* the latter four works of Maitreya, the five texts by Nagarjuna, *Entrance to the Middle Way,* Aryadeva's *Four Hundred Stanzas* and Shantideva's *A Guide to the Bodhisattva's Way of Life.*

All these texts and their commentaries he taught from memory, explaining their use of profound logical analysis and expounding upon them, in great depth; yet he still continued concurrently with his own daily practices. For example, he carried out many self-initiations daily into the mandalas of various deities such as Yamantaka.

From here, he went to the south for a very intensive retreat in the practice of Heruka in which he did the self-initiation each night. In the Kargyu tradition, great emphasis is placed on the *Six Doctrines of Naropa* and the *Six Doctrines of Nigu,* both of which deal with breathing and mystic heat meditation. After tremendous practice, in which he engaged in eight hundred rounds of heat meditation daily, he developed both powers.

The summer was spent with his Sakyapa teacher Rendawa. They resided together and mutually gave many initiations on the hill where the famous Potala palace was later to be built. Rendawa then returned to Tsang, Tsongkhapa returned to Kyomo Lung, where he gave discourses on the *Kalachakra Cycle,* the *Ornament for the Realisations* and *Entrance to the Middle Way.*

He decided to concentrate on the four classes of tantra and searched once more for a teacher, even though he had been giving initiations himself since the age of seven. He left for Tsang to discuss his plans with Rendawa and on the way, at Rongrub Choelung, Abbot Dragpa Shenyen Rinpoche gave him many initiations. Each of the four Tibetan sects has a standard set of initiations and permissions with respect to the practice of the lower divisions of Tantra and the Rinpoche conferred part of such a set. Two of Tsongkhapa's disciples had received many discourses from Lama Umapa Pawo Dorje, who now requested Tsongkhapa, via the disciples, to give the initiation of Saraswati. This Lama as a young shepherd in eastern Tibet had received visions of Black Mañjushri. Tsongkhapa asked him for the teaching of Mañjushri Dharmachakra, but was unable to receive it at the time, since he was determined to see Rendawa.

One night Tsongkhapa dreamt of Choekyi Pel. In his dream, he asked the lama how many times he had received Kalachakra teachings from Buton Rinpoche. The reply was seventeen, which he subsequently substantiated on meeting Choekyi Pel in person. At that time, the living tradition of Kalachakra was in danger of extinction.

He arrived in Tagten, meeting Rendawa and two other teachers, Dragpa Gyaltsen and Choeje Kyabchog, and together the four gave many discourses. He received teachings from Rendawa on the *Guhyasamaja Tantra,* called "The King of Tantras", and Rendawa advised him to concentrate on the teachings of the Three Baskets, or Pitakas, the *Discourses, Knowledge* and the *Discipline.*

He returned to Lama Umapa Pawo Dorje to receive the Mañ jushri Dharmachakra teaching and a commentary on *A Guide to the Middle* Way and thereafter, due to military activity in the area, he practised intensive meditation in a cave. Afterwards he set off to meet Nyento, a learned scholar and practitioner of Kalachakra, who was also a disciple of Buton Rinpoche. On arrival he found that this great Master had already finished teaching the first chapter of the *Kalachakra Tantra* Tsongkhapa first presented him with a yellow scarf, the colour symbolising accomplishment of the Completion Stage yogas, and the next day offered blue and green brocade, the colours being auspicious regarding the Development Stage yogas. In their ensuing conversations the Master told Tsongkhapa that his predispositions would enable him to reach the pinnacle of the Completion Stage of that practice, and proceeded to give him the external, internal and secret Kalachakra teachings.

One night during this discourse Tsongkhapa dreamt of the Nyingma Lama Kyungpo Lhaypa, seated on a great throne, a crown on his head and bell and dorje in hand, repeating the word "karmavajra", the Sanskrit form of Tsongkhapa's mystic name. Je Rinpoche was overjoyed and determined to go to Zhalu where this lama lived. Another night, he dreamt of the same Lama who had at his heart many circles of mantras. The image was so vivid that Tsongkhapa could read them all individually. Consequently he journeyed to Zhalu to meet this Lama, who proved to be identical to the figure in his dreams.

From this master Je Rinpoche received a complete set of standard initiations into the three lower classes of tantras. Later he embellished the walls of the temple where these initiations were conferred with gold leaf as an act of devotion to the master. He also here received the teachings that this Lama held on the *Heruka Tantra* in accordance with the three traditions of the Mahasiddhas Luhipada, Ghantapada and Krishnapada.

Not only should the trainee have impeccable devotion for the master, as exemplified by Tsongkhapa's actions, but the master in turn should be willing to fully teach such a receptive vessel. After every initiation, in order that psychic attainment be transmitted, this lama would always say that he had received the material from such and such a teacher who had been completely willing to instruct.

Tsongkhapa and Lama Umapa Pawo Dorje left for Lhasa in the Year of the Monkey for Gawa Dong, the seat of the Second State Oracle, located about three miles from Lhasa. In Lhasa Cathedral they paid their respects to the large statue of Shakyamuni Buddha which had been made during the Buddha's lifetime and consecrated by him in person.

This sacred image had been brought to Tibet via China, in the seventh century A.D. by the first queen of King Srongtsen Gampo. They offered some prayers before the statue and then returned to Gawa Dong for intensive retreat.

During the retreat Tsongkhapa received many tantric lineages including the special teachings on Mañjushri Dharmachakra. Although he experienced visions of Arapatza Mañjushri, the most well-known of the five aspects of Mañjushri, he spoke of these to no one but Khaydrub Rinpoche, who was one of his chief disciples and, after Je Rinpoche had passed away, was also his biographer. Henceforth, Mañjushri and Tsongkhapa became teacher and disciple. From this time onward Je Rinpoche was able to question Bodhisattva Mañjushri on any topic.

After this retreat, many thousands of people came for teachings. Mañjushri advised him to enter another intensive retreat, but Lama Umapa felt that it would be of greater benefit for sentient beings if he gave discourses. Thus in spite of Mañjushri's exhortations, he carried on teaching for some time out of respect to his guru. However, secretly he felt that it was vital for him to master the import of Nagarjuna's profound view and that scriptures and teachers were unable to provide him with these. What was required, he felt, was intensive meditation. Therefore after teaching for a short period he announced, that he would soon enter a retreat. Lama Umapa chose to go to eastern Tibet and Tsongkhapa escorted him to Lhasa, where they stayed in one of the small rooms on the upper floor of the Cathedral and engaged in long discussions.

Tsongkhapa then returned to Kyomo Lung and taught until winter. He then left for Wolka Choelung a few days journey south of Lhasa, in order to enter meditation. When in the Lhasa Cathedral, he had asked Mañjushri how many disciples to take with him into retreat. The reply was eight, and he chose four from Central Tibet and four from the two eastern provinces.

The retreat was to last for four years. During the first phase, both master and disciples undertook intensive generation of spiritual energy and purification of the obscurations in order to demonstrate the indispensability of such practices from the outset. Je Rinpoche personally performed three and a half million full-length prostrations and one million eight hundred thousand mandala offerings. Indeed, his prostrating form wore an impression in the floor of the temple;

and at the conclusion of the mandala offerings his forearm was raw and bleeding.

While the nine were engaged in prostrations, they recited the names of the thirty-five Confession Buddhas, which are found in the *Discourse on the Three Heaps of the Doctrine,* and eventually received a vision of a golden Maitreya. The next vision was that of the Medicine Buddha, Bhaishajyaguru, and by this stage, their insights and spiritual qualities had increased to an extraordinary degree. After they had carried out many self-initiations into Thirteen Deity Yamantaka Mandala they received a vision of Nageshvaraja, King of the Nagas, who is one of the thirty-five Confession Buddhas. Tsongkhapa subsequently wrote a detailed commentary describing the visions.

The first Tibetan month is known as the Month of Miracles, for the Buddha competed with six non-Buddhist masters in a contest of miracles from the first to the fifteenth. On the New Year's day after the retreat, they went to the temple of Dzingji Ling where there is a statue of Maitreya. They found this to be in very poor condition, and Tsongkhapa wept on seeing it thus cracked and covered with bird droppings. In order to repair it they all sold all their possessions, except their robes. However, as this was insufficient to make significant repairs, they made offerings to Vaishravana, the Wealth Deity, and lit a lamp using butter that they had been given by a passing monk. Mañjushri himself blessed the work and as a result many people came and offered both financial and physical assistance. Everyone involved in the restoration took daily Mahayana precepts and they were all careful to ensure that their speech during the work was prayer rather than mundane chatter. This work upon the Maitreya statue was the first of Tsongkhapa's four major deeds.

Soon thereafter, Tsongkhapa wrote down two prayers composed and given to him by Mañjushri: a praise of Maitreya and a prayer for rebirth in the pure realm of Sukhavati.[1]

Tsongkhapa and the eight disciples then travelled south of Lhasa to Nyaello Ro, where they spent five months meditating in the mountains. Here they gained many insights and Tsongkhapa gave a large number of discourses on topics such as *Discipline.* They had a vision of Mañjushri surrounded by a concourse of not just Bodhisattvas, but also Mahasiddhas like Naropa and Tilopa and great scholars like Nagarjuna and Asanga. Tsongkhapa made little of such experiences and did not mention them. Mañjushri predicted that by following the teachings of these Bodhisattvas, Tsongkhapa would be able to benefit the living beings immeasurably. Mañjushri also manifested to Tsongkhapa in the aspect of Yamantaka, and after that reappeared as the youthful Mañjushri, his sword handle at his heart and its tip at Tsongkhapa's chest with a stream of nectar flowing down the blade. Thus Tsongkhapa experienced utter bliss.

The Nyingma Lama Lhodrag Khenchen Namkha Gyaltsen invited Tsongkhapa to his residence at the Lhodrag Drawo Monastery to answer some questions for him. When they met, the Lama saw Tsongkhapa as Mañjushri and Tsongkhapa saw him as Vajrapani. When he was seventy the Khenchen had a vision of a white goddess who had told him that he would meet a man indistinguishable from Mañjushri and closely linked with Saraswati. The goddess had also noted that there was a karmic connection between Je Tsongkhapa and the lama spanning their past fifteen lifetimes. That evening Tsongkhapa requested the Khenchen to give teachings on guru-yoga and during these he had a vision of Vajrapani.[2]

The oral teachings of the Kadam tradition coming from Atisha had been passed to Atisha's chief disciple, the layman Dromtonpa. He in turn passed on the lineage in three distinct lines. The *Textual Kadam Lineage* was given to Geshe Potowa and emphasised the need for a thorough comprehension of the meaning of the Buddha's actual words in their entirety, not omitting even a single word or syllable. The Kadam *Lamrim* Lineage was given to Gampopa and places reliance on Atisha's *Light on the Path to Enlightenment. The Guideline Instruction Lineage* was given to Geshe Chen Ngawa, the disciple of Geshe Sharawa and depends on the transmission of oral instructions, especially those Atisha obtained from Guru Suvarnadvipa. This included the lineage of Shantideva's *A Guide to the Bodhisattva's Way of Life*, that Atisha had travelled to an island near Java in order to receive.

Only the latter two lineages were taught to Tsongkhapa by this Nying-ma master, for he had already received the first one elsewhere. The Khenchen dreamt that he was told to receive Shantideva's *Compendium of Training* from Mañjushri, so he asked Tsongkhapa for this instruction. On Tsongkhapa's head he witnessed Maitreya Buddha; on his right shoulder, White Mañjushri; on his left, Saraswati; and he saw many Doctrine Protectors as well. Tsongkhapa and the Khenchen gave each other reciprocal teachings, and this kind of mutual teacher-disciple association quickly became the pattern in Tsongkhapa's relationship with his various masters.

At this time Tsongkhapa was considering going to India to meet Nagabodhi and the great Mahasiddha Maitripa, for he desired further elucidation on Middle Way theory as well as the tantric teaching on the illusory body, which is one of the highest stages in the tantric path. So he checked his dreams that night, and beheld he and his disciples, dressed in robes, sitting on Vultures Peak at Rajgir where the Buddha had taught the *Perfection of Wisdom Sutra*. Tsongkhapa discussed his plans with Khenchen Namkha Gyaltsen, and the Lama said that he would consult Vajrapani. The reply was that if Tsongkhapa went to India, he would develop great renown and probably become the abbot of one of the monasteries there, but Vajrapani advised Tsongkhapa to remain in Tibet because it would be of greater benefit both to sentient beings generally as well as to his direct disciples, some of whom had already attained the Mahayana path of preparation. Furthermore, the heat in India would prove unbearable for some of the Tibetans. The present Junior Tutor to His Holiness the Dalai Lama, Kyabje Trijang Dorje Chang, has said that we have this Nying-ma Lama to thank for such works as Tsongkhapa's *Great Exposition on the Stages of the Path* because Tsongkhapa might otherwise have gone to India and been lost to Tibet.

For six months Tsongkhapa stayed at Nyan studying the *Great Exposition of the Stages of the Teachings* by Geshe Drinlay, which is a text on the stages of the path *(Lamrim)*. Contrary to popular belief, this literary form was neither the creation of Je Rinpoche nor of Atisha but originates from the Buddha himself. Tsongkhapa derived innumerable insights from this particular text and would other incense in its honour. He also gave a variety of other teachings while in Nyan.

Tsongkhapa had now gained complete understanding of all the five paths and perceived the need to compose a text for the benefit of future practitioners. He planned to write in accordance with the works of Nagarjuna and Atisha, taking guru-yoga as the foundation of the path and proceeding onwards to meditative quiescence and penetrative insight, the very heart of all meditation. He also planned to compose a similar graded text explaining the stages of tantra. The basis for the former project would be the *Light on the Path to Enlightenment*.

From Nyan, Tsongkhapa and thirty others went on a pilgrimage to Tsari, a sacred place of Heruka. This site is only visited once every twelve years during the Year of the Monkey It is in a very primitive area inhabited by extremely wild peoples. Here Tsongkhapa had a vision of Maitreya, who told him that he was propagating the Doctrine in the same manner as Buddha Shakyamuni had done. The cave in which he experienced this vision can still be seen there.

Tsongkhapa then went into retreat on the *Kalachakra Tantra* which contains the "six branched yoga." Again he had a vision of Kalachakra, who said that he would become a second Dharmaraja Chandrabhadra, the famous king who received the Kalachakra system from Vajradhara; the form in which Buddha conferred the highest tantric teachings.

Tsongkhapa gave many ordinations and discourses on the *Discipline* for he was a very strict practitioner in that respect and would never transgress even the minor rules of a monk.

He received a vision of Saraswati, who told him that he would live only to fifty-seven, and until then he should maximize his work for the Teachings and sentient beings. Because of this he offered Prayers to the eight-armed Ushnishavijaya, a female aspect who is one of the three long-life deities. His disciple Tokden Jampay Gyatso approached Mañjushri regarding the possibility of lengthening Tong Khapa's life, and the reply was affirmative.

Mañjushri told Tsongkhapa in a vision that it was no longer necessary for him to ask for further advice regarding the correct view of emptiness since he himself now had extensive insight into it. He advised Tsongkhapa to teach in accordance with the standpoints of Nagarjuna and Atisha. Je Rinpoche travelled to the south of Lhasa to stay for the summer, and there he met Gyaltsab Dharma Rinchen, the great scholar and debater from the Sakya tradition. Gyaltsab Je wanted to debate with Tsongkhapa and first encountered him while the latter was giving teachings. Gyaltsab even had the temerity to climb onto Tsongkhapa's throne, but as he listened to the discourse, all of his questions were so perfectly answered that he realized his grave error, got down from the throne, offered three prostrations and humbly sat with the listeners. Later on Gyaltsab Je was to become well known as one of the foremost disciples of Tsongkhapa.

Tsongkhapa then returned to Wolka Choelung, the scene of his four-year retreat, this time to undertake an intensive one year retreat in which he concentrated upon the Middle Way schools of thought in greater detail. During this period he received a vision of Nagarjuna with his five chief disciples known as the "Holy Father and Sons", Buddhapalita, one of the sons and also the author of a famous composition by the same name, placed his text on Tsongkhapa's head to give him inspiration and blessings. The *Sustaining Buddha* is the best commentary to Nagarjuna's *Fundamental Stanzas on the Middle Way* and the very next day while Tsongkhapa was perusing the eighteenth chapter of this commentary, he gained complete nonconceptual understanding of emptiness. He then composed a text in praise of the Buddha's teachings on the interrelationship of all phenomena. This text, popularly called *Essence of the Eloquent,* and also the text *In Praise of Relativity,*[3] mention how he was unable to restrain tears whenever he thought of the Buddha's kindness in teaching the *Perfection of Wisdom* at Vulture's Peak.[4]

After intensive practice, many retreats and a great deal of meditation, Tsongkhapa received visions of many deities. He also constantly sought Mañjushri's advice on his choice of abode and a study material.

He travelled to Wolka and spent the winter and spring teaching the monks the enormity of the altruistic attitude and the profundity of emptiness. He accepted an invitation to spend the rainy season retreat to the south of Lhasa, after which he came back to Lhasa at the request of Namkha Zangpo and stayed on the Potala Peak giving many discourses. Thereafter he travelled to Gawa Dong.

For tantric practice, extraordinary devotion to the tantric master and flawless moral discipline are necessary, especially to keep the very easily broken tantric pledges. Tsongkhapa taught the *Fifty Stanzas on the Master,* written by Ashvagoṣa, who had initially been a non-Buddhist but who had changed his faith after defeat in debate by Aryadeva and thereafter was known as Acharya Vira or Aryasura. Je Tsongkhapa also taught a text on the root tantric vows and Asanga's *Bodhisattva Levels* as well as writing commentaries to them.

Rendawa had so far remained in Tsang but now came to meet Tsongkhapa at Gawa Dong where they gave many teachings to each other, Tsongkhapa made elaborate offerings to Rendawa in connection with his practice of guru-yoga.

They both considered doing a retreat at Reting, the monastery that had been founded by Dromtonpa. The great Kadam geshes had stayed there, and a special tradition of group retreats had originate at this monastery. Thus, it seemed to be an ideal environment for such activity.

Reting is a place of beautiful juniper forests located three day' journey by horse to the north of Lhasa. It was here that Tsongkhapa wrote the *Great Exposition of the Stages of the Path* as well as many commentaries. Just above the monastery was a large rock in the shape of a lion where Tsongkhapa sat with a scroll painting of Atisha by him. This painting was still in the monastery in 1959. First he made entreaties to Atisha and received a vision of all the lineages from the Buddha to his own teachers. The vision continue for one month, giving Tsongkhapa the chance to put forth many questions. Finally all the lineages dissolved into Atisha, Dromtonpa, Geshe Potowa and Geshe Sharawa. Thus, Tsongkhapa was able to have prolonged discussion with these great lamas. Then the latter three Masters absorbed into Atisha, who gave Tsongkhapa a blessing by placing his hand on Tsongkhapa's head.

After this vision Je Rinpoche completed the *Great Exposition* as far as the section on penetrative insight.[5] At this point he hesitated, feeling that in future such teachings would be beyond anyone's comprehension. However, Mañjushri appeared and bade Tsongkhapa both to finish the work and to write a small and medium exposition on the stages of the path for those whose aptitude was not commensurate with the presentation in the *Great Exposition*. The eight great Doctrine Protectors also requested him to continue with this work, and it is a tribute to his humility that such great names were not included in the colophon where it is customary to mention those who have requested the teaching. In fact he wrote only the name of one of his disciples there.

Meanwhile Rendawa had been discoursing on some of Nagarjuna's tantric writings. Tsongkhapa gave many teachings using Asanga's work, the *Hearer Levels*, which includes a section on meditative quiescence, and at this time many people staying in the surrounding mountains developed samadhi. Rendawa and Tsongkhapa also clarified points of issue concerning certain tantric practices.

They were then invited by the great Lama Jamkawa to stay some time at the main Drikung Kargyu monastery. So they went there in the spring when the great translator Kyabchog Palzang was in residence. Tsongkhapa was now about forty. There he received instruction according to the Kargyu tradition on the *Six Doctrines of Naropa* and a special oral teaching on the *Great Seal*.

The master Yonten Gyatso invited Tsongkhapa, Rendawa and Kyabchog Palzang to Namtze Deng, a monastery of six hundred monks, where they spent the rainy season retreat with their host as sponsor. Tsongkhapa gave an elaborate discourse on the *Discipline* so lucidly that it is regarded as the second of his four greatest deeds. He also gave teachings on *Pramana* and the *Middle Way*.

After the retreat Rendawa left for Tsang and Tsongkhapa went to Reting where, ensconced at the lion shaped rock above the monastery, he completed the *Great Exposition*. Kyabchog Palzang had particularly urged the completion of this work.

Tsongkhapa now decided to teach tantra and so sent twenty-five of his disciples to Kyabchog Palzang for initiations before he started. He was concerned that many people who had taken Bodhisattva vows from him and from countless other masters did not know how to guard their vows properly. Therefore, he wrote a commentary on the moral discipline chapter of Asanga's *Bodhisattva Levels*. There are two distinct lineages with respect to taking these vows, one of which derives from the above text, whereas the more well known one is from *A Guide to the Bodhisattva's Way of Life*. In both cases the vows are identical.

Je Tsongkhapa wrote a commentary to the *Fifty Stanzas on the Master* to reinforce the paramountcy of such devotions in the tantric vehicle. He then taught the *Great Exposition* in its entirety to Kyabchog Palzang who thereafter went to U-tsang with the text while Tsongkhapa stayed and gave teachings on this remarkable composition. He spent the Month of Miracles at Reting making offerings, after which he returned to Lhasa.

Until his time little value was given to the study of dialectics and epistomology; but Tsongkhapa's discourses provided the necessary impetus for people to realize the enormous importance of these subjects as an indispensable tool in the quest for enlightenment. Khaydrub Rinpoche noted that people were able to appreciate this because of Je Tsongkhapa's infinite kindness which would be difficult to repay. At the request of Miwang Drakpa Gyaltsen, Tsongkhapa spent the next rainy season retreat at Wonde Chenteng where he gave many discourses.

At Wolga Jampa Ling he taught all the stages of the highest tantras as well as the *Great Exposition* and then entered a strict retreat with a few disciples. During this retreat he composed a commentary to Nagabodhi's *Ordered Stages of the Means of Achieving Guhyasamaja*, Nagabodhi being a disciple of Nagarjuna.

One of the most difficult parts of tantra is the Guhyasamaja teaching on the illusory body. Here Tsongkhapa confidentially told several disciples that he had clearly understood and mastered these teachings some ten years earlier and affirmed his intention of explaining how to actualize such a body. Complete understanding of this ensures the attainment of Buddhahood in one lifetime.

Following many requests, he wrote the *Great Exposition of Secret Mantra,* the sequel to his previous *Great Exposition* dealing with the path from the point where the previous text finished up to resultant enlightenment. He also composed a text on the method of attaining enlightenment as found exclusively in the practice of Yamantaka. In all facets of the practice his concentration was single-pointed and uninterrupted. During meditation he was completely oblivious to all disturbances around him.

South of Lhasa at Jangchub Ling he taught both *Great Expositions* after which he went to the area near Lhasa where Sera monastery now stands. Close to the site was Choeding hermitage where he had spent many rainy season retreats. After completing a retreat there, he taught the *Guhyasamaja* and *Heruka Tantras* and gave general discourses on the completion stage of the other tantras.

Nagarjuna's *Fundamental Stanzas on the Middle Way* is very difficult to understand, and Tsongkhapa, now almost fifty, was requested to write a commentary to it. During the composition he would invoke Mañjushri, and seed syllables would appear in the air around him. Once the wisdom letter *AH* appeared and descended onto a nearby rock, leaving an impression that could still be seen in 1959 in one of the Sera gardens. Je Rinpoche prophesied that a large monastery producing many sages would be constructed at that spot. Sera Monastery was duly built there by one of his disciples, Jamchen Choeje who also went to China as the Imperial Tutor in Tsongkhapa's stead.

Tsongkhapa foresaw interruptions if he remained at Choeding, so he departed for the peace and solitude of Raka Drag. Soon afterwards a party of Chinese officials and ministers arrived at Choeding, but in the absence of Tsongkhapa, they proceeded on to Lhasa. Miwang Dragpa Gyaltsen met these dignitaries who requested his services in obtaining an audience with Tsongkhapa. So he travelled to Raka Drag to inform Tsongkhapa of the situation.

Je Tsongkhapa came to Lhasa where the ministers presented him with a letter from the Chinese Emperor requesting his presence in China that he might teach, but Tsongkhapa replied that his advancing age and his wish to stay in retreat precluded acceptance. The officials went back to China with his reply and some images of the Buddha for the Emperor while Tsongkhapa returned to Raka Drag.

Tsongkhapa then commenced writing the *Essence of the Eloquent, An Analysis of Interpretive and Definitive Teachings,* which differentiates between the interpretive and definitive teachings of the Buddha. He went to Choeding and stayed for two years, giving teachings on his stages of the path texts.

After the rainy season retreat Miwang Dragpa Gyaltsen invited him to spend the winter at Kyimay Drumbu Lung, and he travelled there with an estimated five hundred to one thousand disciples; many of whom were great scholars. He gave many discourses on the *Stages of the Path,* the *Heruka Tantra* and other tantric systems during his stay.

On leaving Choeding, he conceived the idea of and decided to inaugurate the Great Prayer Festival, asking two of his disciples to prepare many offerings for it; however funds were lacking because he always gave away whatever he received. Henceforth, he kept everything he was given solely for use in the festival.

The two disciples gathered many artists to both wash with perfumes and paint the statues and walls of the Lhasa Cathedral. In 1409 Tsongkhapa was fifty-two, and during the final evening of the Year of the Mouse eight thousand monks assembled for the first Great Prayer Festival which ushered in the Year of the Bull. An enormous offering ceremony commenced at midnight with Tsongkhapa presenting a crown of fine gold to the statue of Shakyamuni Buddha, which he consecrated, thus fulfilling the Buddha's prophecy. This is the third of his four major deeds.

Tsongkhapa also presented a jewelled silver crown to the statue of Avalokiteshvara. This statue was destroyed by the Chinese after 1959 though some Tibetans managed to salvage three of the heads, two of which are now on display in the Cathedral at Dharmasala in India. Je Rinpoche made copious offerings, including a huge silver begging bowl which he presented to the Buddha statue. He also robed and crowned many of the other statues in the Cathedral.

Large amounts of food were offered and later distributed amongst the poor and destitute. The multifarious events of the festival, which lasted twenty-one days, would take many pages to describe even in broad outline. Each day gold was applied to the face of the Buddha statue, and on the eighth and fifteenth the bodies of all the statues were painted with gold.

During the festival Tsongkhapa gave many teachings on both sutra and tantra, including a discourse on Ashvagosha's *Birth Tales*. This teaching is still given annually in Dharamsala on the fifteenth of the first Tibetan month by His Holiness the Fourteenth Dalai Lama. The power and clarity of Tsongkhapa's discourses wrought beneficial change in many people who also saw great accomplished beings of the past appearing in the sky. Tsongkhapa had now become celebrated as an author and teacher of great renown.

At the close of the festival his disciples concluded that it would be unwise for him to continue his peripatetic lifestyle. Hence, they offered to build him a monastery wherever he chose. He prayed in front of the Shakyamuni statue and examined his dreams, concluding that such a monastery should indeed be built, and he chose Nomad Mountain (Drogri) as the site. This was, in fact, the very spot cited in the Buddha's prophecy. He decided to call the monastery Ganden— in Sanskrit, Tushita—the abode of Maitreya Tsong Khapa went to the site with one of his disciples, Gendun Drub, who was later posthumously recognized as the First Dalai Lama, appointing two others to take charge of the construction.

Many gave donations, and many volunteered their services in the building of the monastery. The main temple and over seventy other buildings were completed within a year. The monastery was built in accordance with the rules of the Discipline laid down by the Buddha, so there was a preliminary survey of the site for future dangers and a check to make sure that there was no infringement of land ownership. In the following year, the Year of the Tiger (1410), Tsongkhapa went to Ganden and gave instruction on the *Stages of the Path*, discourses on the *Guhyasamaja Tantra*, on Asanga's *Compendium of Knowledge* and explanations of difficult dialectical points.

Not only did he compose a host of commentaries to such texts as the *Guhyasamaja Tantra*, but on careful consideration of the list of

Tsongkhapa's discourses and teachings, it would also appear that he must have spent his whole life discoursing. Yet from the point of view of his daily practice it seems that he spent his life in meditative retreat. But on reading his literary output, it would seem that he could only have read and composed texts. His Holiness the Dalai Lama feels that Je Rinpoche's greatest feat was to have done all three.

Signs now appeared suggesting the onset of considerable health problems from his fifty-seventh year onwards. Therefore, when he was fifty-five his disciples requested him to perform special practices in the extensive Yamantaka system in order to transcend these auguries. Together with thirty disciples he went for a Yamantaka retreat during the winter and spring after which Khedrub Rinpoche and many other disciples performed long-life rituals for their master's well being.

When fifty-six, he taught extensively, telling his disciples not to forget such instruction, for his ability to continue teaching was uncertain. His disciples' mounting concern impelled them to offer still more prayers and mandalas, and it is said that every longevity practice possible was carried out for his benefit.

In Tsongkhapa's fifty fifth year, the Year of the Dragon, he and many disciples entered an intensive retreat on the seventh day of the eighth month, and during it the disciples offered fervent prayers for his long life.

During the eleventh month he felt unwell, and though no sickness manifested, he was unable to sleep. Khaydrub Rinpoche and the future First Dalai Lama carried out a wide range of rituals and offerings to the Doctrine Protectors in order to safeguard their master's life.

He frequently entered long periods of single-pointed concentration until one day while out walking, he said that he felt much better. From his throne he urged his disciples never to separate themselves from total altruism or from meditation on it, and while seated there, he had a vision of the Buddha, Conqueror of Interferences. The Buddha approached, then dissolved into him filling him with renewed strength and vigour. He was temporarily cured and his disciples rejoiced.

In the following year he accepted Miwang Dragpa Gyaltsen's invitation to spend the rainy season retreat at Wongyi Tashi Dokar where he gave many discourses. After this sojourn he returned to Ganden and composed a commentary to Luhipada's system of *Chakrasamvara* (the *Heruka Tantra);* a commentary to Chandrakirti's logical analysis of the completion states of the highest tantras; and the commentary known as the *Four Commentaries Combined* on the *Guhyasamaja Tantra.*

At this juncture he decided to erect a special temple where tantric rituals could be carried out privately since the uninitiated are not permitted to see artifacts such as the mandalas. In the Year of the Sheep (1415) the construction of this hall at Ganden commenced. He was fifty-eight at the time.

Two years later in the third month of the Year of the Bird (1417) artists and sculptors congregated at Ganden to make a statue of Buddha Shakyamuni. This was to slightly exceed the dimensions of the one in the Lhasa Cathedral. The artists were commissioned to make gilded copper three dimensional mandalas relating to the thirty-two deity *Guhyasamaja,* the sixty-two deity *Heruka* and the thirteen deity *Yamantaka* practices.

During the fabrication of these, miraculous manifestation occurred, and effulgent symbols of various deities, possessing an inherent sheen and luster, came forth from the moulds and were often surrounded by rainbow light. The consecration ceremonies were performed, thus completing the construction of Ganden's main hall and the various figures contained therein. This is held to be the fourth of Tsongkhapa's major deeds.

In the Year of the Dog (1418) when Je Rinpoche was sixty-one, he gave extensive discourses and wrote a commentary on *Entrance to The Middle Way.* His complete works fill eighteen large volumes.

Four of his disciples one day witnessed him losing a tooth, and each of them asked if he might have it. Je Tsongkhapa's choice fell on Khaydrub Rinpoche, whom he likened to Mount surrounded by rings of golden mountains. However, the three did not relent so Tsongkhapa elected to satisfy everyone. He took back the tooth, placed it on the altar and then proceeded to make offerings, perform rituals and recite prayers. The tooth transformed into the Youthful Mañjushri from whose forehead came a white relic pill the size of a plover's egg, from whose throat came a red one and from whose heart, a blue one. Thus, everyone was satisfied. The manifestation became the tooth once more, which was returned to Khaydrub Rinpoche.

In the Year of the Hog (1419) Tsongkhapa's disciples invited him to the hot springs at Tolung. From Ganden Tsongkhapa first went to Lhasa and made offerings and prayers, then journeyed on to the hot springs where he gave teachings to those assembled there. On a previous visit there he had leant against a rock, and his body had left an imprint that still can be seen. Here he also received a vision of the Sixteen Great Arhants. Thus, Tolung was included on the itinerary of the Lhasa Lower Tantric College during their annual one-month stay at Ganden.

Tsongkhapa then went on to Drepung at the invitation of the founder, Tashi Palden, and gave a variety of discourses on material like the *Stages of the Path,* the *Six Doctrines of Naropa* and *Entrance to the Middle Way.* Those present saw rainbows appear in a clear sky, which they took as an indication of his impending death. About two thousand of the roughly nine thousand monks present were holders of the *Tripitaka,* the three baskets of the sutra teachings. Tsongkhapa privately requested a sculptor to fashion a large silver image of Buddha Vairochana.

During a teaching on the root text of the *Guhyasamaja Tantra* which contains seventeen chapters, Tsongkhapa unexpectedly halted at the end of the ninth, saying that he would break there. This was a most unusual occurrence, and again people felt it to be an indication that he was preparing for his passing away. It is considered auspicious to leave a teaching unfinished if departing somewhere to ensure that master and disciples will meet again and continue the teaching in this and future lives. Before he left Drepung, there was a minor earth tremor and the appearance of more rainbows.

From there he went to the Lhasa Cathedral to make comprehensive prayers and offerings with the wish that the teachings might endure for the benefit of all sentient beings. He prostrated before leaving the Cathedral, which also was unusual because it is only done in such circumstances when return to that place will be impossible for a long time; he said that he might be unable to come again to the Cathedral.

He was invited to Choeding hermitage by a disciple whom he instructed to build a large monastery there. This came to be the famous Sera Monastery, and Tsongkhapa went to the site of the future monastery to conduct a Confession Ceremony in order to strengthen the links between Master and disciples. He also taught the root tantras of *Guhyasamaja* and *Heruka*.

From there he returned to Ganden, stopping on the way at Dechen at the invitation of a government official. He suggested that Dechen Monastery should be rebuilt and that the monks should harmonize their practices of the *Discipline* and *Tantra* following the method introduced into Tibet by the great kindness of Atisha. He presided at an elaborate consecration ceremony and stated that he would be unable to return to conduct another when the reconstruction was finished. In addition, he donated many things to furnish the monastery.

Back at the main hall in Ganden, he offered a massive ritual cake then concluded the rite with many prayers from the *Stages of the Path* tradition. Together with the assembly of monks gathered in the hall, he dedicated the accumulated merit for the benefit of all sentient beings and finally recited the *Prayers for the Pure Land* and other auspicious verses. Afterwards, in the room, he expressed satisfaction at being back in the monastery far removed from trivial affairs. That night he developed a back pain so many monks gathered for prayers. It was the Year of the Hog and Tsongkhapa was sixty-two.

The next day he admitted he was in pain though it was not immediately obvious. He gave his hat and robe to Gyaltseb Je and proffered advice to his disciples stressing the importance of not drifting away from an altruistic state of mind.

He continued to perform self-initiations and four-session yoga of many deities. On the twentieth of the tenth month, he made an extensive offering to Heruka and that night meditated on the Adamantine Recitation, a special tantric breathing exercise. Very early on the morning of the twenty-fifth, sitting in full lotus posture, he meditated on emptiness then at dawn made a series of inner offerings, although no one present could understand why.

His breathing ceased and his body regained the vibrance of a sixteen year old, taken on the generally depicted appearance of the youthful Mañjushri. Many disciples present witnessed the emission of variegated light rays from his body which substantiates the belief that Tsongkhapa entered the intermediate state as an Enlightened Being.

For the following forty-nine days, an offering of one hundred thousand butter lamps and many other offerings were made at Ganden and Drepung. Many saw a rain of flowers descend from the sky. A high Lama of the Kargyu tradition, Kargyu Panchen, came to Ganden fifteen days after the passing away and composed *The Eighty (Main Deeds) of Tsongkhapa,* which is regarded as the standard biography and which contains elaborate details of his life.

The disciples consulted oracles—those who, in a state of trance, become the accessory of certain Doctrine Protectors, in order to divine the most appropriate treatment for the body. The oracles' prophesy was that it should be enshrined in a stupa. A special hall was built to accommodate a silver platform on top of which was a solid gold stupa that became very-well-known and was visited by many Tibetans and Mongolians. Another famous stupa associated with Tsongkhapa is the one containing the tree which grew from his afterbirth. It appeared in the middle of his parent's house in Amdo, now the site of Kumbum Monastery and this stupa still exists. The other stupa was descrated during the Cultural Revolution of the mid-sixties when the whole of Ganden was demolished. However, some of Tsongkhapa's hair was recovered and there are a number of statues containing clippings in Tibetans in homes in India. What is extraordinary is that the mummified body of Je Tsongkhapa was still intact in the middle of this century.

Gyaltsab Dharma Rinchen was requested by the other disciples to ascend the throne of Ganden, signifying that he was to be head of the monastery. His incumbency lasted for twelve years until his own demise. Gyaltsab Je was a prolific writer and his work are contained in eight volumes. Khaydrub Rinpoche then succeeded to his office until he passed away at the age of fifty-four. These two are always depicted flanking Je Tsongkhapa in Scroll paintings of the *Hundred Gods of Tushita.*[6]

Khaydrup Je received five visions of Tsongkhapa after his Master's decease. The first occured when Khaydrup Je had grown disheartened at being unable to give clear teachings on emptiness. Tsongkhapa appeared and advised him concerning the correct view. Later Khaydrup Je was again downhearted at his failure to fathom a difficult tantric text written by Tsongkhapa and since he was the best scholar of the time, he could not refer to anyone. Tsongkhapa appeared on an elephant and answered many questions. Again, while reading the *Great Exposition on the Stages of the Path*, he was struck by the brilliance of Tsongkhapa as a master and, at that moment, his teacher appeared.

Je Tsongkhapa, who was only sixty-two when he passed away, taught and achieved so much. This is especially true considering the much longer life-spans of Asanga and Nagarjuna which were one hundred and fifty years and six hundred years respectively.

On another occasion, Tsongkhapa appeared and fortified Khaydrub Je when he became discouraged after musing on the decline of the Buddha's doctrine. Khaydrub Je, who often thought of joining his master in the Tushita Pure Land, received the final vision when he wished to ascertain whether Tsongkhapa had been born in Tushita as had been predicted. Tsongkhapa appeared on a tiger, holding a sword and a skull-cup and this time, Khaydrub Je asked for Tsongkhapa's approval of his decision to enter parinirvana, which was given. Khaydrub Je prepared to leave this life but was urged by Six-Handed Mahakala, in a vision, to remain for the benefit of sentient beings. However, Khaydrub Je felt that he had done everything possible and so went to the Land of Dakinis.

His body was placed inside another stupa beside that of Tsongkhapa and the same was done with Gyaltsab Je's remains. However, the lineage of the throne holder of Ganden, who is also the head of the Gelug sect which Tsongkhapa founded, did not cease. The present incumbent and ninety-seventh successor to Tsongkhapa is the Senior Tutor to His Holiness the Fourteenth Dalai Lama, Kyabje Ling Dorje Chang.

Many of Tsongkhapa's disciples benefitted sentient beings through the foundation of religious institutions, such as the great monasteries of Drepung, Sera and Ganden. Furthermore, the First Dalai Lama founded Tashi Lhunpo Monastery at Shigatse, about half-way between Lhasa and the Nepalese border to the South. The two Tantric colleges in Lhasa were also inaugurated.

After Tsongkhapa's passing away several biographies were written by lamas from the different traditions. They all agreed that he was a teacher without parallel. The ninth Karmapa praised Tsongkhapa as one "who swept away wrong views with the correct and perfect ones".

It is generally accepted that the three greatest contributors in the annals of Tibet were Guru Padmasambhava, Atisha and Tsongkhapa, all of whom appeared when a great teacher was needed. It was the thirty-seventh Tibetan King, Trisong Detsen, who first invited the Bodhisattva Shantarakshita to Tibet. At that time, there were many evil forces in Tibet strongly resenting the appearance of the Buddha's doctrine there, thus hindrances and calamities occurred. Shantarakshita advised the king to invite Padmasambhava, who came and subdued these malignant forces, and then instigated the construction of the first monastery at Samye, south of Lhasa. After the repression of the Doctrine by King Lang Darma, there was a period in Tibet when a very degenerate form of religion was practiced. During this time, no one could find compatibility between the systems of sutra and tantra, which were considered to be an irreconcilable dichotomy. It was Atisha who dispelled such views and started the Kadam tradition. Later, when people could not see how learning and yogic practice were to be united, Tsongkhapa came and revealed the correct path.

Today we should strive to emulate Tsongkhapa's peerless progress along the path. To hear as many teachings as possible and never to be satisfied with less than ultimate knowledge as the most important lessons that can be applied in life. It is imperative to appreciate and work towards the peerless goal of wishing to achieve enlightenment in order to help every other sentient being do exactly the same. Je Rinpoche's example of scriptural learning and meditative application taken as a unified path show the essence of Buddha's intent and the truly quick method of achieving enlightenment.

Bibliography

Books mentioned in *A Short Biography*

The numbers beginning with a "P" refer to the Suzuki Edition of
the Peking Kagyur and Tengyur.

Bodhisattva Levels   P5538 vol 110 (T)
Yogacaryā Bhūmalu Bodhisattvabhūmi
rNal 'byor spyod pa'i sa las byang chub sems dpa'i sa
by Asaṅga

Commentary on the Compendium of   P5709 vol 130 (T)
Valid Cognition
Pramāṇavarttika Kārikā
Tshad ma rnam 'grel gyi tshig le'ur byas pa
by Dharmakīrti

Compendium of Knowledge   P5550 vol 112 (T)
Abhidharma Samuccaya
Chos mngon pa kun las btus pa
by Asaṅga

Compendium of Training   P5336 vol 102 (T)
Śikṣa Samuccaya
bSlab pa kun las btus pa
by Shāntideva

Discourses on the Three Heaps of the Doctrine   P950 vol 38 (K)
Ārya Triskandhaka Nāma Mahāyāna Sūtra

*'Phags pa phung po gsum pa zhes bye ba theg
pa chen po'i mdo*

Entrance to the Bodhisattva's Way of Life   P5272 vol 99 (T)
Bodhisattva Cāryāvatāra
Byang chub sems dpa'i spyod pa la 'jug pa
by Shāntideva

Entrance to the Middle Way   P5261 vol 98 (T)
Madhyamakāvatāra Kārikā Nāmā
dBu ma la 'jug pa zhes bya ba'i tshig le'ur byas pa
by Chandrakīrti

Essence of the Eloquent, An Analysis of
Interpretive and Definitive Teachings   P6142 vol 153
Drang nges legs bshad snying po
by Tsongkhapa

Expression of the Names of Mañjushri   P3383 vol 75 (T)
Mañjuśrī Nāma Saṃgīti Kuśalamūla
Pariṇāma
*'Jam dpal gyi mtshan yang dag par brjod pa'i
dge ba'i rtsa ba bsngo ba*
by Mañjushrīmitra

Fifty Stanzas on the Master   P4544 vol 81 (T)
Guru Pañcāśikā
Bla ma lnga bcu pa
by Ashvagoṣa

Five Works of Maitreya, The
(1) Ornament of the Mahayana Sutras   P5521 vol 108 (T)
Mahāyāna Suātrālaṃkāra Kārikā
*Theg pa then po'i mdo sde rgyan gyi tshig
le'ur byas pa*

(2) Distinguishing Between a Middle Way and
Extremes   P5522 vol 108 (T)
Madhyanta Vibhaṅga
dBus dang mtha' rnam par 'byed pa

(3) Ornament for the Realisations,   P5525 vol 108 (T)
Abhisamayālaṃkāra
mNgon par rtogs pa'i rgyan

(4) Verses on Distinguishing Between Phenomena
and their True Nature   P5524 vol 108 (T)
Dharma Dharmatā Vibhaṅga Kārikā
*Chos dang chos nyid rnam par 'byed pa'i tshig
le'ur byas pa*

The Eternal Buddha nature   P5525 vol 108 (T)
Mahāyāna Uttaratantra Śāstra
Theg pa chen po'i rgyud bla ma'i bstan bcos

Four Hundred Stanzas   P5246 vol 95 (T)
Catuḥśataka Śāstra Kārikā Nāma
bsTan bcos bzhi brgya pa zhes bya'i tshig le'ur byas pa
by Aryadeva

The Golden Rosary of Eloquent Teaching   P6150 vol 154
Legs bshad gser 'phreng
by Tsongkhapa

Great Exposition of the Secret Mantra   P6210 vol 161
sNgags rim chen mo
by Tsongkhapa

Great Exposition on the Stages of the Path   P6001 vol 152
Lam rim chen mo
by Tsongkhapa

Hearer Levels   P5537 vol 110 (T)
Yogacaryā Bhūmalu Śrāvaka Bhūmi
rNal 'byor spyod pa'i sa las nyan thos kyi sa
by Asaṅga

Light on the Path to Enlightenment   P5378 vol 103 (T)
Bodhipathapradīpa
Byang chub lam gyi sgron ma
by Atīsha (Dīpaṅkara Shrījñāna)

Ordered Stages of the Means of
Achieving Guhyasamaja   P2675 vol 62 (T)
Śrī Guhyasamāja Maṇḍalopāyikā Viṃśati
Vidhi Nāma
dPal gsang ba 'dus pa'i dkyil 'kor gyi cho ga
nyi shu pa zhes bya ba
by Nagabodhi (plus related works P2674 7)

Ornament for the Realisations (See Five Works of Maitreya, The)

Perfection of Wisdom Sutras   P730 vol 12 to
Prajñāpāramitā   P759 vol 21 (K)
Shes rab kyi pha rol to phyin pa
The name includes many individual sutras.

Root Tantra of Hevajra   P10 vol 1 (K)
Hevajra Tantra Rāja Nāma
Kye'i rdo rje zhes bya ba rgyud kyi rgyal po

Root Text of the Guhyasamaja Tantra   P81 vol 3 (K)
Sarva Tathāgata Kāya Vāk Citta Rahasya
Guhyasamāja Nāma Mahā Kalpa Rāja
De bzhin gshegs pa thams cad kyi sku gsung
thugs kyi gsang chen gsang ba 'dus pa zhes
bya ba brtag pa'i rgyal po chen po

Six Works on Reason by Nagarjuna
(1) Fundamental Treatise on the Middle Way   P5224 vol 95 (T)
Prajñā Nāma Mūla Madhyamaka Kārikā
dBu ma rtsa ba tshig le'ur byas pa shes rab
ces bya ba

(2) Seventy Stanzas on Reason   P5225 vol 95 (T)
Yuktiṣaṣṭikā Kārikā Nāma
Rigs pa drug cu pa'i tshig le'ur byas pa zhes
bya ba

(3) A Thorough Investigation   P5226 vol 95 (T)
Vaidalya Sūtra Nāma
Slob mo rnam par 'thag pa zhes bya ba'i mdo

(4) Seventy Stanzas on Emptiness   P5227 vol 95 (T)
Śūnyatāsaptati Kārikā Nāma
sTong pa nyid bdun cu pa'i tshig le'ur byas pa zhes bya ba

(5) Refutation of the Objections   P5228 vol 95 (T)
Vigraha Vyāvartanī Kārikā Nāma
rTsod pa bzlog pa'i tshig le'ur byas pa zhes bya ba

6) The Precious Garland   P5658 vol 129 (T)
Rāja Parikathā Ratnāvali
rGyal po la gtam bya ba rin po che'i phreng ba

Sutra Of Discipline   P5619 vol 123 (T)
Vinaya Sūtra
'Dul ba'i mdo
by Guṇaprabha

Treasure of Knowledge   P5590 vol 115 (T)
Abhidharma Koṣa Kārikā
Chos mngon pa'i mdzod kyi tshig le'ur byas pa
by Vasubhandu

Destiny Fulfilled

rTogs brjod mdun legs ma

Tsongkhapa's Education as a Song of Realization

OM! May all be happy and well!

I bow to the feet of the kind Guru,
Root of all good fortune,
And of the Holy Wisdom Treasure, Mañjushri,
Who are the eye to see the liberation of enlightenment
And even all ascendance in the world,
And who are the place of recuperation
From the weary wandering in the roads of life!

When one's efforts still are slight,
It is said to be best to congratulate others' virtues
In order to gather the momentous stores (of merit and
  wisdom).
And one feels an even greater joy, especially,
When free of claims to one's own past virtues,
Thinking "increase past virtues ever more,"
In order to live up to the impact of the Victor's teaching,
Also seeing many other dire necessities—
It is excellent, O my mind, when you feel such joy!

First, I sought out often extensive learning,
Then all teachings dawned as trainings,

Finally, I practiced all day and all night,
Completely dedicated to spread the Teaching!

Thinking this over, how well my destiny saw fulfilled!
Thank you so very much, O Holy Wisdom Treasure![7]

I. *Quest of Extensive Learning*

If the darkness that hides the basis of right and wrong
Is not illuminated by the lamp of true learning,
You cannot know even the path; not to speak of
Entrance into the supreme city of liberation!
Therefore, not satisfied with partiality and rough ideas,
I trained carefully in all the treatises of the Invincible Lord
    of Dharma,
And of those (great sages) widely renowned in India
As the "Six Ornaments" and the "Two Superiors."[8]

Thinking this over, how well my destiny was fulfilled!
Thank you so much, O Holy Wisdom Treasure!

Especially for an egocentric person, the sole door
For determining the precise reality of things
Is the treatise on valid reasoning; so with many efforts
I studied its crucial points again and again.

Thinking this over, how well my destiny was fulfilled!
Thank you so very much, O Holy Wisdom Treasure!

Though I had worked hard on the treatises of Sutra and
    Tantra,
And I was practicing and teaching the impact of the
    profound,
I saw that my view had not advanced far beyond
The view that has learned nothing and nothing knows.
So then I studied thoroughly all the essential keys
That bring out the authentic view, which I found
On the path of subtle philosophy that examines the
    profound,

Especially in the scientific treatises of Nagārjuna;
And I resolved all my doubts completely!

Thinking this over, how well my destiny was fulfilled!
Thank you so very much, O Holy Wisdom Treasure!

It is said that "there are two vehicles
For the journey to perfect enlightenment,
The Transcendence Vehicle and the deep Vajra Vehicle;
And the Secret Tantras are very much superior
To the Vehicle of the Transcendences!"
This is as well known as sun and moon.
Yet there are those, weighty with pretended wisdom,

Who while verbally asserting the truth of that saying,
Make no inquiry into that vehicle of the profound!
If such as they are supposed to be intelligent,
How could anyone else ever be thought dumb?
Alas! It is amazing that any should repudiate
Such an unexcelled path, so hard to come across!
Therefore, I entered that deep treasury of twin
    accomplishments,
The supreme vehicle of the Victors, the Vajra Vehicle,
More rare even than the Buddhas;
And I worked hard at it, and studied it long.

Thinking this over, how well my destiny was fulfilled!
Thank you so very much, O Holy Wisdom Treasure!

Seeing clearly that if I did not understand
The methods of the paths of the three lower Tantras,
My decision that the Unexcelled Yoga Tantra is best of all,
Would be no more than an unsupported assertion,
So I inquired deeply into the general and specific
Three types of Action Tantra, such as *Sāmānya
    Vidhirāmguhyatantra
Susidhi*, the *Subāhuparipṛccha*, and the *Dhyānottara*.[9]

When I think it over, how well my destiny was fulfilled!
Thank you so very much, O Holy Wisdom Treasure!

Among the second class, Practice Tantras,
I studied the main Tantra, *Vairocanābhisambodhi*,
And I ascertained thoroughly the precise orientation
Of all the Practice Tantras.
Among the third class, Yoga Tantras,
I studied the main Tantra, the glorious *Tattvasaṃgraha*
And its explanatory Tantras such as *Vajrashekharal*,
And I enjoyed the banquet of the Yoga Tantras!

When I think it over, how well my destiny was fulfilled!
Thank you so very much, O Holy Wisdom Treasure!

Among the fourth class, Unexcelled Yoga Tantras.
I studied the Root Tantras and Explanatory Tantras
Of the Father Tantras *Shrī Guhyasamājā*,
Renowned as sun and moon among the Indian sages;
And of the Yogini Tantras such as *Saṃvara* and *Hevajra*,
And the *Kālachakra*, Tantra of the Champions,
Whose method differs from other Sutras and Tantras,
Along with its commentary, the *Vimalaprabha*.

When I think this over, how well my destiny was fulfilled!
Thank you so very much, O Holy Wisdom Treasure!

II. *All Teachings Dawn as Training*

With a firm, intense, and enduring faith in Mañjushri,
Best at banishing the darkness from the disciple's mind,
I prayed that all the teachings might dawn as training,
And I applied myself to all the requisite conditions.

When I think this over, how well my destiny was fulfilled!
Thank you so very much, O Holy Wisdom Treasure!

Working in that way, I found a special certainty
In the stages of the path of enlightenment,
The tradition descended from Nagarjuna and Asanga,
And the *Transcendent Wisdom*, best book on the profound,
Dawned as a practical training.

When I think this over, how well my destiny was fulfilled!
Thank you so very much, O Holy Wisdom Treasure!

In this northern land, many speak out in unison,
Whether they have studied the logical texts or not,
"There is no stage of practice of the path to enlightenment
In the *Pramānasamuccaya* and the *Seven Branch Treatises.*"
But one should take as authoritative the direct revelation
Granted by Mañjushri to Dignaga, saying explicitly that
"This book will in the future become the eye for all beings!"
Thus seeing that (the above view) was absolutely wrong,
And especially investigating deeply the procedure therein,

And I developed a deep-seated conviction
About the import of the dedication of *Pramānasamuccaya;*
That the Lord, as the personification of reason,
Is authoritative for the seeker of liberation,
Because of (his unerring description) of evolution and
    cessation,
And that therefore His Teaching is the only haven
For those who would be free. And I found a special joy
In getting clear all keys of the paths of both vehicles,
By studying them in combination on the path of reasoning.

When I think this over, how well my destiny was fulfilled!
Thank you so very much, O Holy Wisdom Treasure!

Then through the hard, methodical work of interconnecting
The *Bodhisattvabhūmi* and the *Mahāyānasūtralamkāra,*
All the treatises of the Invincible Dharma Lord,
And those following them, arose as practical training.

When I think this over, how well my destiny was fulfilled!
Thank you so very much, O Holy Wisdom Treasure!

Especially, depending on the *Shikshāsamuccaya,*
Which grants certainty about all the essentials of the path
By arranging the profound and magnificent scriptures in
    stages,

I saw clearly as stages of practice the many meanings
Of the best treatises of Nagarjuna such as *Sūtrasamuccaya.*

When I think this over, how well my destiny was fulfilled!
Thank you so very much, O Holy Wisdom Treasure!

Then, relying on Buddhaguhya's lucid practical instructions
On the *Dhyānottara,* and the *Vairocanābhisambodhi*
All the keys of the path dawned well as training.

When I think this over, how well my destiny was fulfilled!
Thank you so very much, O Holy Wisdom Treasure!

Seeing how the essentials of the path of the *Shrī
Tattvasaṃgraha*
Are contained in the three samadhis, and realizing
How hard to fathom is the way of meditation on that
profound import,
I relied on the great Pandit Buddhaguhya's correct
explanation
Integrating the *Root, Explanatory,* and *Combined Yoga
Tantras,*
And on the *Stages of Meditation's* proper explanations
Of the profound practices of the three Tantra classes;
And the confusion in my mind was dispelled!

When I think this over, how well my destiny was fulfilled!
Thank you so very much, O Holy Wisdom Treasure!

The ultimate of all eloquent teachings of the Sage
Is the glorious Unexcelled Yoga Tantra,
And among them the most unutterably profound
Is the king of Tantras, the Glorious *Guhyasamāja.*
The supreme philosopher Nagarjuna said about it
That "the essentials of the path of the *Root Tantra*
Are sealed therein by the six limits and the four ways,[10]
And thus they must be understood following the Guru's
instructions
In accordance with the *Explanatory Tantras.*
Holding that fact as essential, I inquired deeply

Into all the subtleties of the Holy tradition of the *Samāja*,
The ultimate private instructions contained in the *Five
    Stages,*
The Lamp of Concentrated Practice, and the *Stages of
    Arrangements* etc.
Relying on their lamp-like illumination of the *Root Tantra,*
Combining the five great Explanatory, *Tantras*
I practiced with enormous efforts.
With practice I discovered all the essentials
Of the *Samāja's* two stages in general,
And especially the essentials of the perfection stage.

When I think this over, how well my destiny was fulfilled!
Thank you so very much, O Holy Wisdom Treasure!

By the power of that, the essential imports of many Tantras,
Such as, *Saṃvara, Hevajra,* and *Kālachakra*
Dawned in my mind as practical trainings.
I have explained these fully elsewhere,
This just opens the door for the discerning.

When I think this over, how well my destiny was fulfilled!
Thank you so very much, O Holy Wisdom Treasure!

III. *Constant Practice and Total Dedication*

Thus having become filled with the treasure of instructions,
I practiced by combining the two Mahayana paths,
The ordinary path (of the Transcendences),
And the two stages of the extraordinary path,
Into a complete path of concentrated essentials.

When I think this over, how well my destiny was fulfilled!
Thank you so very much, O Holy Wisdom Treasure!

"All the Ganges Rivers of the vows of the Bodhisattvas
Are contained within the vow to uphold the Holy Dharma,"
Thus whatever base of virtue I accumulated,
All was dedicated to the spread of Buddha's Teaching

When I think this over, how well my destiny was fulfilled!
Thank you so very much, O Holy Wisdom Treasure!

In order to extend enormously my own virtue
And to show the entrance without error in a way appropriate
To the many fortunate persons of clear discernment,
I wrote this record of my education.
By the mass of virtues thus attained,
May all beings, through this same procedure,
Maintain the unexcelled discipline of the Buddha,
And enter the path that pleases all the Victors!

Written by the Eastern Bhikshu Tsongkhapa Losang Drakpae pal, at the Triumph of Virtue Monastery on Nomad Mountain, with Kabshipa Rinchen Pal as scribe.

Song of the Mystic Experiences of Lama Je Rinpoche

rJe rin po chei gsang bai rnam thar

by Jamyang Choeje Tashi Palden (1379-1449)

O sun-like Prince of the Conqueror,
Whose wisdom, vast as the heavens,
Has the brilliance of knowledge
That sees what ultimately is
And what merely seems to be;[11]
O Venerable Lord of Dharma, Most Perfect Guru,
The dust of your feet I place on the crown of my head.

Even the Buddhas and Bodhisattvas,
Who fill the ten directions,
Cannot describe the excellence
Of your body, speech and mind;
Yet out of passionate inspiration
I shall sing of them; pray,
Listen for but a few moments.

As a blossoming garland of flowers
To adorn the necks of the clear minded,
And as a precious jewel
To enhance the force of conviction,
This song in praise of your oceans of splendour
To delight all sages, I have composed.

Like a cloud, the merit of your superb deeds
Releases a torrent of rain that swells
The virtue of those to be trained,
And proclaims with a dragon's thundering roar
The sweetness of the vast and profound;[12]
O glorious, powerful, billowing Lama.

Foremost of tantric adepts, the mighty yogi
Who mastered the many millions of samadhis,
Composed faultless expositions,
And made true effort in practice,
Most resplendent of Lamas,
You tower over the heads of all.

At Vajrasana[13] in a former birth,
To the Victorious One you offered
A rosary of one hundred crystal beads.
Thus you acquired the fortune
Later to attain the perfect view;[14]
O Illustrious Lama, at your feet I pay homage.

At the age of seven you directly perceived
Dipamkara Atisha, the great Path Clearer,
And Vajrapani, Lord of the Secret.
The exhortations of both the sutras
And tantras dawned upon you;
O Illustrious Lama, at your feet I pay homage.

O Jetsun, Lord of phenomenal existence,
You directly perceived Mañjushri,
Bodhisattva of the wisdom of emptiness,
Seated in a radiant aura as blue
As the colour of a perfect sapphire;
O Illustrious Lama, at your feet I pay homage.

From this time onward, O High One,
Whenever desired, you could invoke
Mañjushri, Treasure of Stainless Wisdom,
And constantly listen to the teachings

Of both Sutrayana's *Transcendent Wisdom*
And Tantrayana's *Secret Assembly*;[15]
O Illustrious Lama, at your feet I pay homage.

When practising the seven-limbed ritual
Of the thirty-five Purification Buddhas,
Continually and clearly you beheld them,
And all their forms, mudras and symbols;
O Illustrious Lama, at your feet I pay homage.

Seated in the auspicious posture,
Hands in the Dharma-teaching mudra,
Buddha Maitreya prophesied that,
Just as the Sugatas who possess the ten powers,
You will one day perform the twelve acts
Of a supreme, universal teacher;
O Illustrious Lama, at your feet I pay homage.[16]

Victorious Master of both life and death,
Truth visions you received
Of Amitabha Buddha, the Medicine Buddhas,
And that teacher of men and gods,
Shakyamuni, Prince of the Shakya Throne,
Each with a retinue vast as the oceans;
O Illustrious Lama, at your feet I pay homage.

Saintly Tara, source of all siddhis,
Ushnisha Vijaya, the one exalted and radiant,
Ushnisha Sitatapatra, dispeller of obstacles,
And other such mystic female Buddhas
Again and again you directly perceived;
O Illustrious Lama at your feet I pay homage,

Bodhisattva Nagarjuna, Aryadeva, Holy Buddhapalita,
Magnificent Chandrakirti and the mighty yogi Nagabodhi[17]
Appeared, then constantly cared for you.
O Illustrious Lama, at your feet I pay homage.

Exalted Asanga, who delights the three worlds,
The Brother, Vasubandhu, a Second Buddha,

And Dignaga[18], child of Mañjushri,
Appeared, then constantly cared for you;
O Illustrious Lama, at your feet I pay homage.

Dharmakirti, a moon amongst teachers,
As well as Gunaprabha, Shakyaprabha,
Shantideva and the glorious Abhaya,
Appeared, then constantly cared for you;
O Illustrious Lama, at your feet I pay homage.

All the mahasiddhas of India and Tibet,
Such as Indrabudhi, Saraha, Luipa,
Krisnacharin, Tilbupa, Tilopa and Naropa[19]
Appeared, then constantly cared for you;
O Illustrious Lama, at your feet I pay homage.

Clearly Mañjushri prophesied
That, relying upon these lineages,
You would produce colossal spiritual boons
For yourself and for all sentient beings.
Great Bold One who spontaneously
Fulfills the wishes of the world;
O Illustrious Lama, at your feet I pay homage.

When the samadhi of the yoga combining
Mental tranquility with cognition of emptiness
Increased like the waxing moon,
You beheld the form of the Destroyer
Yamantaka, "Opponent of the Lord of Death",[20]
Complete with all mudras and expressions.
O Illustrious Lama, at your feet I pay homage.

Having touched your heart
To the wisdom sword of Mañjushri,
A stream of undefiled ambrosia
Flowed into the depth of your being,
Spontaneously arousing the propitious
Absorption of highest joy.
O Illustrious Lama, at your feet I pay homage.

Prayer for Rebirth in the Land of Bliss
And *An Eulogy of the Perfect Intent*
Of the Dauntless Protector Maitreya Buddha[21],
As well as their graduated levels of meaning
Mañjushri lucidly conveyed to you,
Who recorded and skillfully presented them;
O Illustrious Lama, at your feet I pay homage.

Whenever you consecrated a religious image,
The Wisdom Beings actually entered
Into the Symbolic Beings.
This host of deities that you summoned
Still generates fields of merit within beings;
O Illustrious Lama, at your feet I pay homage.

One night you dreamed of Nagarjuna
And his five spiritual sons
Amongst themselves discussing
The fabric of dependent origination.
From their midst came Buddhapalita,
Who touched you with a scripture.
The very next day within you
Rose the mind of a High One;[22]
O Illustrious Lama, at your feet I pay homage.

By focussing on the pith of the six branches
Of Kalachakra, "The Wheel of Time",
You directly perceived his Buddha-form.
He foretold that soon you
Would equal even King Suchandra;[23]
O Illustrious Lama, at your feet I pay homage.

When for the first time you led
The Great Prayer Festival of Lhasa,
A hundred magical omens appeared.
At your making this joyous offering,
The Buddhas and their sons in the ten directions
Were filled with supreme delight.[24]
O Illustrious Lama, at your feet I pay homage.

Generating the form of a great bliss deity
Through the yoga of the non-duality
Of profound luminosity and illusory appearances,
You attained the vajrayoga body;
O Illustrious Lama, at your feet I pay homage.

By practising the mantric science of inhaling
And exhaling OM AH HUM on the lotus heart,
The vital energies entered the central nadi,
Rested as breathing stopped, and then dissolved.
Thus you experienced the clear light, Mahamudra, the great
    seal,
Attaining the vajrayoga speech;
O Illustrious Lama, at your feet I pay homage.

Raising the navel chakra's mystic heat
Which rests at the base of the central channel,
The letter HAM at the crown of your head
Melted and fell to your heart
As simultaneously the experience
Of the blisses dawned upon you.
Thus you attained the vajrayoga mind;
O Illustrious Lama, at your feet I pay homage.

Having been invoked as witnesses
To your pure and perfect aspirations,
All Buddhas and Bodhisattvas came forth.
Only when you had summoned each of them
Into his respective position
Did you honour them with offerings;
O Illustrious Lama, at your feet I pay homage.

While contemplating the principal mandala
Of Mañjushrivajra, Guhyasamaja,
You dreamed that Maitreya and Mañjushri,
Who were speaking of Dharma, passed down to you
A jewelled vase brimming with water,
Portending that you would master all teachings.
O Illustrious Lama, at your feet I pay homage.

On a throne adorned with precious gems
Sat the omniscient Kargyu Lama Buton Rinchen Trub.
A text of the Guhyasamaja Root Tantra
He gave to you, exhorting
You to be its keeper;
O Illustrious Lama, at your feet I pay homage.

Accepting this responsibility,
With mudras and mantras thrice
You touched the text to your head.
By its blessings it became obvious
That the tantra *Separating and Mixing,*
Obtained by Marpa of the Southern Hills,
Is the true oral tradition of Exalted Nagarjuna;
O Illustrious Lama, at your feet I pay homage.

Your mind absorbed in the mystic circle of Heruka—
Chakra Saṃvara, the Wheel of Perfect Bliss—myriads
Of dakinis of the outer, inner and secret places
Made you offerings of vajra songs,
Transporting you in ecstasy;
O Illustrious Lama, at your feet I pay homage.

In meditation destroying the forces of darkness,
You beheld the radiant Buddha, Mighty Demon Tamer,
Having an aura as pure as burnished gold,
More brilliant than a million suns.
O Illustrious Lama, at your feet I pay homage.

Your being having become indivisible from
The body, speech and mind of all Buddhas,
The might of the power of evil was subdued.
As the Dharma protectors crushed the demon families,
Shrieks of the defeated satanic forces
Resounded across the universe.
O Illustrious Lama, at your feet I pay homage.

These multitudes of Dharma protectors,
That you brought under control,

In a previous aeon had been subjected
By Buddha Vajradhara to guard your doctrine.
With profound reverence they work this still;
O Illustrious Lama, at your feet I pay homage.

That you would, after entering parinirvana,
Sit in the presence of Dauntless Maitreya
In Tushita, Pure Land of Joy,
And would be known as Wisdom Essence[25]
Was, O Lord of Life, rightly prophesied
By both Mañjushri and Vajrapani.
O Illustrious Lama, at your feet I pay homage.

By the strength of this eulogy
Sung from the depths of pure love,
May the afflictions of beings
Limitless as the sky be extinguished.
In this and all future lives
May all be nurtured by true teachers
And embraced by the sacred Dharma.

May the innate wisdom of great bliss
Rain throughout the world;
May the stains of erroneously grasping
Mind and its objects be uprooted;
And may all be inspired quickly to become
Like you, a Jetsun Lama.

May the wisdoms of learning, contemplation
And meditation overtake the earth;
May the arts of deliberation,
Debate and composition flourish;
May the ordinary and supreme siddhis
Come to each and every practitioner;
And may all be inspired quickly to become
Like you, a Jetsun Lama.

By the limitless oceans of merit
Of having presented, like Samantabhadra,

Clouds of offerings spanning the skies,
Of having bared every negative imprint
And downfall accumulated since infinity,
Of having rejoiced in the spirituality
Of those on the paths to enlightenment,
And of having beseeched the Lamas
To turn the Wheel of Dharma
And not to enter parinirvana.

May all beings experience peerless samadhi;
May goodness swell like the waxing moon;
And may the doctrine of Omniscient Tsongkhapa
Thrive until time's end.

The colophon: Written at Drepung Choekyi Dechen at the request of the two meritorious Drungtrapa Palzangpo brothers, by Lama Tashi Palden, a Buddhist monk and teacher who had searched many hundreds of thousands of scriptures with the lights of his wisdom.

PART II

The Stages of the Path to Enlightenment

This part contains the essence of the "Path-to-Enlightenment" *(Lamrim)* type of teaching; a comprehensive arrangement of the stages of practice from the beginning in attainment of human life up to the end in perfect enlightenment of Buddhahood.

The first chapter, *The Three Principles of the Path*, stems from a revelation granted by Mañjushri to Tsongkhapa on the roof of the Lhasa Cathedral, at the time when Tsongkhapa was bidding farewell to Lama Umapa. It is thought of as the 'seed' of the whole 'Path-to-Enlightenment' teaching. The Venerable Geshe Wangyal first published its translation in his *Door of Liberation,* I being among the translators who worked on it then. I am sure I still do not understand it as well as the Venerable Geshe, but my English translation varies a bit nowadays, still trying to get nearer to the crystal clarity of the original Tibetan.

The second chapter, *Lines of Experience,* present the shortest form of path teaching written by Tsongkhapa, the first stage of expansion of the *Three Principles.* Its style is expressive and communicative rather than literal, and so it is quite helpful to make the practices clear to the beginner.

The third chapter is yet a further expansion of the complete path, here including both sutra and tantra practices, written in a letter form to Konchok Tsultrim, a colleague of Tsongkhapa. The section is concluded with a short prayer for conducive circumstances throughout practice of the path. These last three selections have been translated by Sherpa Tulku and Alexander Berzin based on oral explanations by Geshe Ngawang Dhargye.

The Three Principles of the Paths

Lam gtso rnam gsum

Reverence to the Holy Gurus!

I will explain as best I can
The essential import of all the Victor's Teachings,
The path praised by all the holy Bodhisattvas.
Best entrance for those fortunates who seek freedom.

Listen with clear minds, you lucky people,
Who aspire to the path that pleases Buddhas,
Who work to give meaning to leisure and opportunity,
Who are not addicted to the pleasures of cyclic life.[1]
Lust for existence chains all corporeal beings—
Addiction to the pleasures of the life-cycle
Is only cured by transcendent renunciation.[2]
So seek transcendence first of all!

Leisure and opportunity are hard to get,
And there is no time to life; keep thinking on this,
And you will turn off your interest in this life!
Contemplate the inexorability of evolutionary effects[3]
And the sufferings of life—over and over again—
And you will turn off interest in future lives!
By constant meditation, your mind will not entertain
A moment's wish even for the successes of life,
And you will aim for freedom all day and night—

Then you experience transcendent renunciation!
Transcendence without the spirit of enlightenment[4]
Cannot generate the supreme bliss
Of unexcelled enlightenment—therefore,
The Bodhisattva conceives the supreme spirit of
    enlightenment.

Carried away on the currents of four mighty streams,
Tightly bound by the near-inescapable chains of evolution,
Trapped and imprisoned in the iron cage of self-concern,
Totally wrapped in the darkness of misknowledge,
Born and born again and again in endless life-cycles,
Uninterruptedly tormented by the three miseries—
Such is the state of all beings, all just your mothers—
From your natural feelings, conceive the highest spirit!

Even though you experience transcendent renunciation
And cultivate the spirit of enlightenment,
Without the wisdom from the realization of emptiness,
You cannot cut off the root of the life-cycle—
So, you should strive to understand relativity.[5]

Who sees the inexorable causality of all things
Both of cyclic life and liberation
And destroys any sort of conviction of objectivity—
Thereby enters the path pleasing to Victors.

Appearance as inevitably relative,
And emptiness as free of all assertions—
As long as these are understood apart,
The Victor's intent is not yet known.
But, when they are simultaneous without alternation,
The mere sight of inevitable relativity
Becomes sure knowledge rid of objective habit-patterns,
And the investigation of authentic view is complete.

Further, while appearance eliminates absolutism,
Emptiness eliminates nihilism,
And you know emptiness manifest as cause and effect—
Then, you will not be deprived by extremist views.

When you realize the essentials
Of the three principles of the path,
Rely on solitude and powerful efforts,
And swiftly achieve the eternal goal, my son!

Lines of Experience

Lam rim nyams mgur

Popularly known as "The Abbreviated Points of the Graded Path
(Lam rim bsdus don)

(1)

I prostrate before you, (Buddha) Head of the Shakya Clan. Your enlightened body is borne out of tens of millions of positive virtues and the perfect accomplishments.[1] Your enlightened speech grants the wishes of limitless beings. Your enlightened mind sees all knowables as they are.

(2)

I prostrate before you, Maitreya and Mañjushri, supreme spiritual sons of this peerless teacher. Assuming responsibility (to further) all Buddha's enlightened deeds, you sport emanations to countless worlds.

(3)

I prostrate before your feet, Nagarjuna and Asanga, embellishments of our Southern Continent. Highly famed throughout the Three Realms,[2] you have commented on the most difficult to fathom "Mother of the Buddhas"[3] according to exactly what was intended.

(4)

I bow to Dipamkara (Atisha), holder of a treasure of instructions (as seen in your "Lamp for the Pathway to Enlightenment").[4] All the complete, unmistaken points concerning the paths of profound view and widespread action, transmitted intact from these two great forerunners, can be included within it.

(5)

Respectfully, I prostrate before my own (two) spiritual masters.[5] You are the eyes allowing (disciples) to behold all of the infinite scriptural pronouncements, the best ford for those of good fortune to cross to Liberation. You make everything clear through your skilful deeds which are moved by intense loving concern.

(6)

The stages of the path to Enlightenment have been transmitted intact by those who have followed in order both from Nagarjuna and Asanga, those crowning jewels of all erudite masters of our Southern Continent, and the banner of whose fame stands out above the masses. As (following these stages) can fulfil every desirable aim[6] of all nine kinds of beings,[7] They are a power-granting king[8] of precious instruction. Because they collect the streams of thousands of excellent classics, they are indeed an ocean of illustrious, correct explanation.

(7)

(Atisha's text) makes it (easy) to understand how there is nothing incompatible in all (Buddha's) teachings, and makes every scriptural pronouncement, without exception, dawn on your mind as a personal guideline. It makes it easy to discover what Buddha intended[9] and protects you as well from the abyss of "the great mistake".[10] Because of these (four benefits), what discriminating person among the erudite masters of India and Tibet will not have his or her mind be completely taken by these stages of the path (arranged) according to three levels of motivation,[11] the supreme instructions to which many fortunate ones have devoted themselves.

(8)

Although (there is much merit to be gained from) listening to or reciting even once this brief manner (of Atisha's text) in which can be included the essential points of all the scriptural pronouncements, yet it is certain that you will amass even greater waves of beneficial collections from actually teaching and studying the sacred Dharma (contained within). Therefore you should consider the points (for doing this properly).

(9)

Then after (having taken refuge), you should see that the root cause excellently propitious for as great a mass of good fortune as possible for this and future lives is proper, zealous devotion in thoughts and actions to your sacred Guru who shows you the path (to Enlightenment). Thus you should please him by offering your practice of exactly what he says, which you would not forsake even at the cost of your life. I, the yogi,[12] have practised just that. If you would also seek Liberation, please cultivate yourself in the same way.

(10)

This working basis (of a human form endowed) with liberties[13] is superior to a wish-granting gem. Moreover, such is only obtained this very one time. Difficult to acquire and easily lost, (it passes in a flash) like lightning in the sky. Considering how (easily this can happen at any time) and realising that all worldly activities are as (immaterial as) chaff, you must try to take advantage of its essential significance at all times, day and night. I, the yogi, have practised in the same way.

(11)

After death, there is no assurance that you will not be reborn in one of
the three unfortunate states.[14] Nevertheless, it is certain that the Three
Jewels of Refuge[15] have the power to protect you from their terrors.
For this reason, your taking of refuge should be extremely solid and
you should follow its advice without ever letting (your commitments)
weaken. Moreover, (your success in) so doing depends on your
considering thoroughly which are the black or the white karmic actions
together with their results, and then living according to the guides of
what is to be adopted or rejected. I, the yogi, have practised just that.
If you would also seek Liberation, please cultivate yourself in the
same way.

(12)

The fullest strides (of progress) in actualising the supreme paths will
not come about unless you have attained a working basis (of an ideal
human body) that is complete with (all eight ripened favourable)
qualities.[16] Therefore you must train in the causal (virtuous actions)
that will preclude (your attainment of such a form) from being
incomplete. (Furthermore) as it is extremely essential to cleanse away
the stains of black karmic debts and downfalls (from broken vows)
tarnishing the three gateways (of your body, speech and mind), and
especially (to remove) your karmic obstacles (which would prevent
such a rebirth), you should cherish continually devoting yourself to
(applying) the complete set of four opponent powers[17] (which can
purge you of them). I, the yogi, have practised just that. If you would
also seek Liberation, please cultivate yourself in the same way.

(13)

If you do not make an effort to think about true sufferings and their
drawbacks, you will not properly develop a keen interest to work for
Liberation. If you do not consider the stages whereby (true) origins of
all suffering place and keep you in cyclic existence, you will not know

the means for cutting the root of this vicious circle. Therefore you should cherish exuding total disgust and renunciation of such existence, while knowing which factors bind you to its wheel. I, the yogi, have practised just that. If you would also seek Liberation, please cultivate yourself in the same way.

(14)

Ever enhancing your Enlightened Motive of Bodhichitta is the mainstay for the Supreme Vehicle's path. It is the basis and foundation for great waves of (altruistic) conduct (to bring you to Enlightenment). Like a gold-making elixir, (it turns) everything (you do) into the two collections,[18] (building up) a treasure of merit gathered from infinitely collected virtues. Knowing this, the Bodhisattvas have held this supreme precious mind as their innermost mental bond. I, the yogi, have practised just that. If you would also seek Liberation, please cultivate yourself in the same way.

(15)

Generosity is the wish-granting gem by which you can fulfil the hopes of sentient beings. It is the best weapon for cutting the knot of miserliness. It is the (altruistic) conduct which enhances your self-confidence and undaunted courage (to help everyone towards Enlightenment). It is the basis for your good reputation to be proclaimed in the ten directions. Knowing this, the wise have devoted themselves to the excellent path of completely giving away their body, possessions and merit. I, the yogi, have practised just that. If you would also seek Liberation, please cultivate yourself in the same way.

(16)

Moral discipline is the water to wash away the stains of faulty actions. It is the ray of moonlight to cool the scorching heat of the delusions. (It makes you) radiant like a Mount Meru in the midst of the nine kinds of beings. By its power, you are able to bend all beings (to your good influence) without (recourse to) mesmerising glares. Knowing this, the holy ones have safeguarded, as they would their eyes, the rules they have accepted (to keep) purely. I, the yogi, have practised just that. If you would also seek Liberation, please cultivate yourself in the same way.

(17)

Patience is the best adornment (to wear) for those with power and the perfect ascetic practice for those tormented by delusions. It is the high-soaring eagle as the enemy of the snake of anger, and the thickest armour against the weapons of abusive language. Knowing this, (the wise) have accustomed themselves in various ways and forms to the armour of supreme patience. I, the yogi, have practised just that. If you would also seek Liberation, please cultivate yourself in the same way.

(18)

Once you wear the armour of resolute and irreversible enthusiastic perseverance, your expertise in the scriptures and insights will increase like the waxing moon. You will make all your actions meaningful (for attaining Enlightenment) and will bring whatever you undertake to its intended conclusion. Knowing this, the Bodhisattvas have exerted great waves of joyous effort, washing away all laziness. I, the yogi, have practised just that. If you would also seek Liberation, please cultivate yourself in the same way.

(19)

Meditative concentration is the king wielding power over the mind. If you fix it (on one point), it remains there immovable like a mighty Mount Meru. If you project it, it can permeate any virtuous object (at will). It leads to the great exhilarating bliss of having your body and mind be applicable (to any virtuous task). Knowing this, the yogis of (mental) control have devoted themselves continuously to single-minded concentration which overcomes the enemies of mental wandering (and dullness). I, the yogi, have practised just that. If you would also seek Liberation, please cultivate yourself in the same way.

(20)

Discriminating awareness is the eye with which to behold profound Voidness and the path by which to uproot (ignorance) the source of cyclic existence. It is the treasure of genius praised in all the scriptural pronouncements and is renowned as the supreme lamp that eliminates the darkness of closed-mindedness. Knowing this, the wise who have wished Liberation have advanced themselves along this path with every effort. I, the yogi, have practised just that. If you would also seek Liberation, please cultivate yourself in the same way.

(21)

In (a state of) merely single-pointed meditative concentration, you do not have the insight (which gives you) the ability to cut the root of cyclic existence. Moreover, devoid of a path of mental quiescence, discriminating awareness (by itself) cannot turn back the delusions, no matter how much you analyse them. Therefore, on the horse of unwavering mental quiescence, (the masters) have mounted the discriminating awareness that is totally decisive about how things exist. Then with the sharp weapon of the Middle Path logic, devoid of extremes, they have used wide-ranging discriminating awareness to analyse properly and destroy all underlying supports for their (cognitions) aimed at grasping for extremes. In this way they have expanded their intelligence which has realised Voidness. I, the yogi, have practised just that. If you would also seek Liberation, please cultivate yourself in the same way.

(22)

Once you have achieved single-minded concentration through accustoming yourself to single-pointedness of mind your examination then of individual phenomena with a proper analysis should itself enhance your single-minded concentration settled extremely firmly, without any wavering, on the actual way in which all things exist. Seeing this the zealous have marvelled at the attainment of a union of mental quiescence and penetrative insight. Is there need to mention that you should pray (to attain one as well)? I, the yogi, have practised just that. If you would also seek Liberation, please cultivate yourself in the same way.

(23)

(Having achieved such a union) you should meditate both on space-like Voidness while completely absorbed (in your meditation sessions) and on illusion-like Voidness when you subsequently arise. By doing this you will, through your union of methods and awareness, become praised as someone perfecting the Bodhisattvas' Conduct. Realising this, those with the good fortune (to have attained Enlightenment) have made it their custom never to be content with merely partial paths. I, the yogi, have practised just that. If you would also seek Liberation, please cultivate yourself in the same way.

(24)

(Renunciation, an Enlightened Motive and a correct view of Voidness) are necessary in common for (achieving) supreme paths through either of the two Mahayana Vehicles of (practising) causes (for Enlightenment)[19] or (simulating now) the results (you will achieve).[20] Therefore once you have properly developed these (three principal) paths, you should rely on the skilful captain (of a fully qualified Tantric Master) as your protector and set out (on this latter, speedier vehicle) across the vast ocean of the (four) classes of tantra. Those who have (done so and) devoted themselves to his or her guideline instructions have made their attainment of (a human body with all) liberties and endowments have its full meaning (by achieving Enlightenment in their very lives). I, the yogi, have practised just that. If you would also seek Liberation, please cultivate yourself in the same way.

(25)

In order to accustom this to my own mind and also to benefit others as well who have the good fortune (to meet with a true Guru and be able to practise what he or she teaches), I have explained here in easily understandable words the complete path pleasing to the Buddhas. I pray that the merit from this may cause all sentient beings never to be parted from these pure and excellent paths. I, the yogi, have offered prayers for just that. If you would also seek Liberation, please offer prayers in the same way.

This concludes *The Abbreviated Points of the Graded Path* to Enlightenment, compiled in brief so that they may not be forgotten. It has been written at Ganden Nampar Gyelwai Monastery on Drog Riwochey Mountain, Tibet, by the Buddhist monk, Losang Drakpa, a meditator who has heard many teachings.

A Letter of Practical Advice on
Sutra and Tantra

*A Brief Indication of the Graded Stages of the Path
(Lam gyi rim-pa mdo tsam du bstan pa)*

Homage to Guru Mañjughosha.

May I always be cared for by you, the foremost of the peerless (Dharma) expounders. Your flawless wisdom is unimpeded even concerning the subtlest points. This is due to your acquaintance with the ways of the widespread (altruistic actions) and the profound (insight of Voidness which you developed) over a long time with many magnificent skilful means.

O my excellent spiritual mentor and friend, first you strove to hear and study many scriptural pronouncements. Then you spread the teachings with your good explanations. In the end, it was over a long period that you made such great effort to realise their practice. May your feet be firm throughout a long life!

I have received the perfectly delightful tree of your letter together with its tasteful fruit of your presents which you have sent, my undying dear friend, out of your affectionate thoughts for me. Not being quenched by the well-explained accounts (already available) as an ocean (cannot be satisfied) by a great cloudful of rain, you have requested that I write and send you in a letter further (practical advice on) how to apply yourself to the two stages (of the highest class of tantra, anuttarayoga. A mind of) little intelligence can easily be filled by hearing (merely a few teachings), as a small pond (can readily be plenished) by a babbling brook. Thus it is awe inspiring that minds of superior intelligence (such as your own) are so vast they cannot be satisfied by these wonderful accounts.

However, granted that this may be so, it is quite preposterous for them to be any call for someone like myself to appease the mind of a great man like you. I have heard and studied few (teachings). My intelligence is low; my Dharma actions are meagre. Although I may have a few words (in my mind), I have been very lax in living up to their meaning. Nevertheless, dandelion seeds, animated by the wind, can soar to compete with the eagles though they lack the power to do so on their own. Similarly uplifted by your ennobling words, I shall try to offer you something in brief.

Well then, (as for lowly people like myself) we have in fact found the excellent working basis (of a human rebirth complete) with all the liberties (for Dharma study and practice). We have in fact met with the precious teachings of the Victorious (Buddhas), and have in fact been cared for by superb Gurus. With such an opportunity and when we do have the power of mind to discriminate between what should be adopted and rejected, we must strive definitely to take advantage of such an excellent working basis. This, of course, depends solely on our becoming involved in the Buddhas' teachings. But to do so merely by having kind thoughts is not enough. Either we ourselves must know, without any disorder, the (proper) stages for entering the teachings, or we must definitely rely for guidance on someone who does.

Moreover (not any teacher will do). He or she must be a skilful one who knows the nature of the paths, the definite count (or their details), as well as their graded order and the disciples' level of understanding. He must be like this because if he mistakes wrong paths for right ones, or right for wrong ones, then even if we were to realise and achieve such (mistaken) paths as he has taught us, we will not accomplish any of our aims. Similar to having been wrongly prescribed some medicine, (in the end) we will have received no benefit and nothing but harm.

But even if he knows the nature of the paths well, it will still be ineffective if he (adds) extra unnecessary (stages) or leaves them incomplete. Thus if he does not know the definite count (of the detailed points of the stages), then even while on the course of these (paths) we will be unable to progress in the most direct fashion. This is, because we will proceed while having omitted certain recognised essentials and will sidetrack onto the superfluous practice of what is unnecessary.

But then even if he does know the nature and the definite count (of the specific details of the paths), still if he does not know which (points) to apply at each stage of our mental development as he leads us from the beginning to the middle to the end (he will be acting as in the following example). Suppose (a doctor) thought here is a medicine and, since it is the best of all medicines, it is proper to prescribe it to (any) patient for (any) disease. If, thinking, (like this) he were actually to give it (to someone it did not suit), then because it was such a powerful drug, not only might it not help (this patient), it might actually cause him the great harm of taking his life. Likewise, suppose he thought here is a sacred Dharma teaching and, since it is the most profound Dharma, what wrong could there possibly be in teaching it? If, thinking like this, he were actually to lead us by means of it, then if he accords it with our level of understanding (and follows the graded order from there) it will bring only benefit. But if he does not accord it with our level, then not only will he not benefit us, he might actually cause us (by our own confusion) to kill our opportunity to attain a fortunate rebirth or Liberation. Therefore it is especially important for him to know the graded order (of the stages of the teachings and the disciples' level of understanding).

Furthermore, even though he may be skilled in these important practical points like this, nevertheless he must also be someone whose certainty gained about the complete stages of the path has come from his own (experience of) having been set straight himself and led by a holy being through not a cursory, nor sporadic, but a thorough (study) of the great classics themselves, as composed by the standard, valid authors. (For you see) the abbreviated guideline instructions for how to lead (disciples) through these (paths) are in fact only what have been condensed from these great classics. Actually, the very meaning of a guideline instruction is that it is something to give us certainty more easily into the classics, which themselves are very extensive, the meanings of which are extremely difficult to comprehend and which, for necessary (reasons), scramble the graded order of understanding (and practice) in their showing of the teachings. Because these (guidelines) have been compiled (with this purpose in mind), then to take the great classics as Dharma for lecturing and the brief guideline instructions as Dharma for practising, and thereby to hold these two as disharmonious, is not to understand the point of the teachings at all. This is so because Buddha's scriptural pronouncements as well as their (Indian) commentaries are in fact—like we recite, "hearing, debating and eagerly practising"[1]—only for eager practice and aimed at such practice.

This being so (how should we begin our practice? As Nagarjuna) has said in *The Friendly Letter*, "O you who are free from fears, it is not necessary (for me) to tell you much. But this is an essential and beneficial piece of advice, 'Tame your mind!' As Buddha has said, 'The mind is the root of Dharma (practice).' "[2]

Also as (Aryadeva) has said in *The Four Hundred (Stanzas)*, "Because we cannot see (any action) such as going and so forth (becoming) meritorious and so on except through the thought (that immediately motivates it), the mind therefore is said to be first (before) all karmic actions."[3]

Thus as these Noble Ones, father and spiritual son, have said, the root of everything right or wrong is but the mind. This is because it is definite that the channels for acting wrongly or engaging in what is right are in fact (only) three and (of these) the body and speech themselves are controlled by the mind.

Therefore first of all (before any Dharma practice) it is extremely important for our motivating thought to be one which we have (properly) worked ourselves up to and not one that has (simply) come from mere words. Although the stages for working ourselves up (to a proper motivation) have been explained in many (different ways), the most commonly helpful scheme for minds of superior, middling and all (scopes of capacity is as follows).

First (on an initial level) we should make ourselves continually mindful of our (forthcoming) death and not staying long in this world. We should also familiarise ourselves a great deal with the two ways in which we can go to our next life (either up to a fortunate rebirth or down to an unfortunate one), together with their causes (our virtuous or non-virtuous acts). In this way we should turn our mind from working with keen interest for this life (alone) and thereby develop as much as possible the attitude to work with keen interest for the happiness of future lives beyond.

Then (on an intermediate level) we should exert much effort in thinking about the faults of all the various (rebirth states) of cyclic existence and the advantages of the peaceful (attainment of Liberation). In this way we should turn our mind from working with keen interest for the (so-called) good things of cyclic existence and thereby develop the strong and continuing attitude to work with keen interest for Liberation.

Then (progressing to an advanced level motivation) we should see that just as we ourselves are benefitted from being happy and harmed by suffering, so too are all sentient beings. Thereby we should thoroughly familiarise ourselves with love, compassion and an Enlightened Motive of Bodhichitta. If we do this, we will turn our motivating intentions completely away from eagerly endeavouring for only our own aims, not caring at all about bringing happiness to sentient beings and eliminating their suffering. Thereby we will see the aims of others as actually the (only) aims we strongly wish (to work for). By doing this and also by being certain that the supreme method for accomplishing these (aims) is in fact only if we become a Buddha ourselves and that alone, we will then develop the very firm motivating intention of wishing to attain (the state of) a Buddha because of these reasons. (These then are the actual stages for working ourselves up to having such an Enlightened Motive of Bodhichitta for our Dharma practice.)

But suppose we were to take as the foundation (for our practice) the self-deception of having only a partial, merely intellectual understanding of the verbal formulations of these (stages for building up our motivation) and then were to engage ourselves in hearing, thinking and meditating (on a certain Dharma practice). We might then say with many sweet-sounding words that "I am doing these for the sake of my future lives" or "I am doing these for liberation" or "I am doing these for the benefit of sentient beings". But despite (such noble claims), I think the way our mind probably has been working will have in fact been nothing other than one in which it has been aiming for the sake of either (benefits in) this lifetime, or for certain pleasurable fruits of cyclic existence to which we have given the name "Liberation", or for a partial (ultimate) aim for ourselves (and not Enlightenment at all). Therefore to develop these motivating thoughts non-artificially, it is not sufficient to have merely an intellectual understanding (of them). We must meditate (in order to build them up as a natural, instinctive habit).

As for how to meditate, we need to actualise and achieve (these motivations) by acquainting ourselves over and again with the examination meditation with which we meditate by examining, in many aspects, (the situations that are) the causes pertinent for (developing) each of these kinds (of motivations) like this. (For instance, by examining many aspects of others' suffering, we can develop compassion.)

In regard to this, even though cultivating (repeatedly meditating with the proper) aspects and focal objects for these (motivations) is the main cause (for actually developing them, such as focussing on others' suffering with the wish that they be parted from it as the way to develop compassion), just (to do) this much is not enough. In between sessions we should make (our understanding of how to develop them) firm and certain by looking at the stainless expositions (of Buddha), the (Indian) treatises and also the guideline instructions that have been composed around (the themes of) these (motivations). Thus we should read, for example, the accounts of how Buddha developed renunciation, compassion and Bodhichitta in his previous lives.) In addition we must reach the heart (of our problems preventing us from developing them) by doing a great deal of collecting (of merit) and cleansing (of obstacles) in order to eliminate the contrary factors (such as our selfishness) and bring about conducive conditions (such as a kind heart) for (developing) these motivating thoughts (like compassion). This to eliminate our black karmic debts we should openly admit our past wrongs and apply the four opponent powers of regretting them, promising never to commit them again, invoking the Three Jewels of Refuge and a Bodhichitta motivation as our basis and amassing as much counteracting virtue as we can. This might include the accumulation of a hundred thousand prostrations, mandala offerings, recitations of the hundred-syllable Vajrasattva mantra and of our Guru's name mantra and so forth.)

Like this, then, we need to make the causal factors (for developing these motivations) be never partial, but complete and thus fully effective. In addition, we need also to meditate and examine well with discriminating awareness and in detail (to differentiate) for each individual (type of motivating thought) what is detrimental (such as self-cherishing which would hinder developing compassion) and what is beneficial (for it, such as an attitude of cherishing others). When we have (done both of these), we will then understand deeply (how to assure that if we meditate over and again) by having such and such a focal object, such and such an aspect and such and such a manner in which we work ourselves up (to having this feeling), we will develop on our mind-stream such and such an uncommon imprint as a result. In doing this we will thereby come to gain confidence in (our ability to actualise) even the subtlest points of these practices.

At such a time we should also be aware of the special functions of each (of these motivations) to bring about what is beneficial and end what is detrimental, for in fact we must be certain of what is to be abandoned and adopted for any and all (of the paths. Thus, for instance, compassion makes us cherish others, which brings about happiness, and also blocks our self-cherishing which has been causing us our unhappiness.) By (knowing this) and also by thinking that (developing) just (some of) these (motivating thoughts) is not enough (for in fact we must generate the entire progression), then for certain it will come about that we will never abandon any of the sacred Dharma (stages for building up our motivation).

(Although) we must indeed generate these motivating thoughts before (any actual session of meditation of puja), yet just to develop them is not sufficient. (We must maintain them) steadily and continuously (throughout). Not only that, we must try to increase them as much as possible. Therefore (it is a mistake) to think that since they are preliminary practices, it is unnecessary to have continual familiarity with them (throughout our session) or that it is not necessary to work at all times for them not to degenerate (because) it is enough just to send (these motivations) ahead once (at the start of our session. Or it is also a mistake) to think, on the other hand, that as these are yogas that are like crusts or chaff. It is all right to leave them (aside) and, not taking them into consideration, to think to familiarise ourselves (only) with the actual practices. (To think in any of these mistaken ways) is not to understand the essential point of the paths at all. This is because meditations in which we have acted out Dharma practices but devoid of these previously explained motivating thoughts, and especially (if devoid of) Bodhichitta in the manner explained above, turn out in fact to be just seemingly Dharma (practices which do not bring about their intended result). And furthermore, even if we meditate perfectly with single-minded concentration on Voidness, it is not at all fit (to be considered) a Mahayana (practice if we lack a Bodhichitta, motivation) and this has been said not once.

Meditating on Bodhichitta at the beginning of a session and directing (the merit towards our Enlightenment) with great waves of prayer at the session's end are in fact great skilful means for causing the merit cultivated during the main part of the session to hit the mark (of our intended aim) and become inexhaustible. Therefore as this is the case, we must be certain to integrate them with our mind, never allowing ourselves sometimes to act (negligently) in just any fashion.

If we cherish enhancing in this way motivating thoughts like these, holding them without ever letting them degenerate, and we would then, on top of this as our foundation, practise the two stages of the secret tantra path (we should do so as follows). In general, when we enter the doorway of whatever (Buddhist) Vehicle it may be, we must set as the basis (for our practice) our own specific moral discipline (of whatever set of lay or ordination vows we hold). And especially when we enter the Tantra (Vehicle) it is very important to have (as our basis) a stable (development of an Enlightened Motive). This is because Bodhichitta, as explained before, is the ultimate essential point of all the Mahayana paths. In addition, there are the (tantra) vows and close bonds (to the Buddha families) which we will have received when we have taken a pure empowerment (into any of the higher deity systems) from a fully qualified Guru. It will be best if we then (also) have (as our foundation these in a state of) their never having been forsaken by giving them up and never having been degenerated by violating them. Otherwise (if we have forsaken or caused them to weaken, then to continue to have a firm basis for practice) we need to have restored or revitalised them, having taken (another) empowerment, and purified and cleansed ourselves of these former faulty actions and downfalls. And further, having recognised well and with certainty the faulty actions (which violate) our root and branch (vows), we need to restrain ourselves definitely to stop (ever breaking them) again. Thus we should make a strong effort never to be stained by the downfall (of transgressing any) of our root (vows). And further, if we happen to commit any faulty actions (of breaking some) of the rest (of our branch vows), we must, having recognised this, carefully expiate (the consequences by applying the appropriate antidotes).

Thus as I see it (the facts of the matter are these). We must enter into the meditations of the two (anuttarayoga tantra) stages with these (tantra vows and close bonds) indispensably (set) as our foundation. Furthermore, even if we do not meditate on the two stages, still if we have received an empowerment we are required to keep them by all means. As these are the case, we must therefore strive to develop great certainty in this (matter concerning vows). This is because (of two points Buddha has made). He has said that having received an empowerment, if we keep our close bonds and vows purely, then even if we have not meditated on the two stages during this lifetime, we can still reach the supreme attainment (of Buddhahood) in seven or sixteen lifetimes and so on (of consecutively keeping them). And also he has said that if, treating them lightly, we give up the close bonds and vows we have promised to keep, then even having done seemingly meditation on the two stages, we will fall to an unfortunate rebirth and thereby not attain (Enlightenment).

(Another point can be seen from two more of Buddha's statements.) He has said that if our working basis for practising tantra is as a householder, we must practise while continually maintaining the five (vows of lay) discipline or, if as ordained, then while maintaining either the two or three sets (of novice or full vows). Further he has said that for upholding (and practising) tantra it is best to be fully ordained, next best a novice and at minimum someone with lay vows. Therefore it follows (from these statements) that (Buddha's) presentation (of this ranking) is by means of the number of vows that are (actually safeguarded and not merely by the (number that are) promised to be kept. This is why (Kamalashila) has said in his *Beholding Reality* that if someone maintaining both individual liberation and Bodhisattva vows practises tantra, he or she will actualise results more quickly.[4] (In stating this) he is asserting that the actualisations gained by having taken the tantra vows while already safeguarding Bodhisattva and ordination vows are (gained) much more quickly than those from having safeguarded only the tantra vows themselves.

It is similar also in the case of actualising paths on the (non-tantric Mahayana Vehicle of the Perfections. The actualisations gained by having taken Bodhisattva vows while having already been ordained (on one of the levels) according to the Vinaya (rule) are best (compared) to those gained by having maintained only Bodhisattva vows alone. This is what (Buddha) meant when he said in many sutras that if there were two Bodhisattvas equal in all respect, (except that) one was a lay person (with no vows of individual liberation) and the other ordained, the latter would be more praiseworthy. (Buddha has clearly set forth all these points) in his presentation of these (vows). But despite this, although people frequently appear who can explain them by expounding forth merely their verbal formulations, and partial ones at that, yet when it comes time to apply these to personal practice, those who do so appear ever so rarely. This falls in the category of something very difficult to understand.

Be that as it may, (Nagarjuna) has said (in *The Five Stages*), "Those who wish for the completing stage should (first) abide well on the generating stage, for the method to complete Buddhahood is said to be like (climbing) rungs of a ladder."[5] (This means) that just as we must depend on climbing the lower rungs of a ladder in order to proceed to the higher ones, (likewise) we must travel (the path to Enlightenment) by meditating on the generating and completing stages in their (proper) order. It will not do to (practise them) in just any order of understanding or to leave out the generating stage. As (this is what Nagarjuna) has said, we must meditate on the generating stage.

Even though there is no certainty that (while on its stage) its (practice) will smooth away the undesirable occurrences that occasionally befall us (such as sicknesses) or bring us the subtle actual attainments we desire (such as clairvoyance), yet it is a fact that the generating stage can bring us to the attainment of peerless Enlightenment. This point has been established clearly from the tantric texts of scriptural authority and well-attested to by learned masters who themselves are valid sources. Therefore we must please practise (this generating stage) in the circle of a mandala.

Also on this stage we must perform the actions for accumulating the collections (of merit and insight, such as the yogas for eating, sleeping and waking), and in between sessions be mindful of (viewing everything in a) pure (form, such as ourselves and all others as meditational deities, our surroundings as a mandala palace and so forth, we must first meditate forth. Likewise we must) recite the (pertinent) mantras, make offerings and perform the rituals of the torma offering cake. Since we must build up (the impressions of) all these, in fact, on our mindstream at their appropriate occasions while remaining ever mindful of the meanings of this (point) and that, without letting ourselves just merely recite the words (of the ritual texts and mantras mindlessly), why shouldn't we please take pleasure (in so doing)?

Then, as it is very important to know how to meditate with singleminded concentration on (ourselves as) the meditational deities during the actual main body (of our sessions), let me say a little about how to do this. It will be easier to develop certainty about how to meditate on this, in fact, if we know (beforehand) what the single-minded concentration is like that we need to have developed when we have finished accustoming ourselves to meditating on the generating stage. Therefore if we ask what do we need to have developed (it is like this). By meditating now on (ourselves as having) the bodily colours, hand implements, jewellery and garb (of all the deity figures of the supported as well as of the supporting (mandala of the palace and its surroundings), in short on (our having all) the aspects of their colours and shapes, then at the conclusion (of our training) we need to have actualised being able to visualise ourselves appearing clearly as all of these, in toto and simultaneously, in one state of single-minded concentration. We should meditate (aspiring for this scope of attainment).

Therefore we must train by focussing first on one focal object (out of this entire visualisation). If we train by focussing (first), for instance, on (visualising ourselves as) the main central figure (of the mandala) and ask how we should train (it is like this).

Actually, two traditions for doing this appear (in the literature). One is to train from fine details upwards by focussing (first) on one of the finest details of the body, thereby actualising its clear appearance (and then building up from there by progressively adding more and more details). The second is to train from the rough stage downwards (by visualising) the entire body (roughly from the start and then progressively filling in the details one by one. Of these) the former is fit for only a few special individuals, while the more commonly beneficial (method) is in fact the latter, because it is easier to develop.

Therefore, for instance, of the two aspects of the main figure, namely the rough whole and its fine details, we should (first) visualise (ourselves) as the complete (deity), from the head to the feet, in merely the roughest form. When this appears clearly, we must hold (our attention) on just this without letting our mind wander. If the general form of the body is clear, we should hold this, and if the general is unclear but a few of its parts are lucid, we should hold (our attention) on whatever is clear. If these fade as well, we should visualise the (entire) general (rough form once more) and hold that. If some aspect arises that is totally extraneous to what we should be meditating on, we should hold our mind (only) on the main focal object without following out (any spurious ones).

For beginners in these (visualisation practices), it has been said that if the meditation sessions are too long, we will not at all progress in the most direct fashion. This has also appeared to be so (from experience as well). Therefore, if we meditate holding as many extremely short sessions as possible, our development of single-minded concentration will proceed without fault.

Furthermore, in the beginning we must also keep our faculty of discernment alert and hold on to it tightly. This is because if we do not meditate while carefully checking whether or not we have come under the power of mental dullness or agitation, we might meditate passing a great deal of time in a muddled state, holding ourselves to our meditation with (only) the roughest discernment. In so doing we will never develop in our entire lifetime any single-minded concentration as we had wished. Therefore we must keep a careful check (with discernment for any meditational faults).

(In this way) we will come to gain a single-minded concentration having four defining characteristics and (focussed) on the general form of, for instance, the main figure. (These four are) we must be able to have (the visualisation) appear (clearly) whether it takes a strong or an easy amount of effort. Further, we must be able to extend (this concentration on the visualisation) throughout our session. During it, we must never come under the power of either mental dullness or agitation and (lastly) we must come in contact with an exhilarating joy and bliss of both body and mind. (Such a concentration, then) is a similar equivalent (for what is developed by training) in the direction of mental quiescence meditation.

Once we have (gained concentration with these four characteristics) and our mind has both maintained (its attention) firmly on this (rough, general form of ourselves as the main figure of the mandala), as well as held (the clarity of) its fine details, we must then extend our focus to (include visualising ourselves as) the other deities (around the mandala as well). But when we do so, we must expand our focus on top of (the foundation of) still maintaining it on the deity on which we had been previously focussing and not forsake this. If we hold our attention focussed on these latter (deities around the mandala) while having given up (our focus on the main, central figure), how will it ever come about that we can (visualise) ourselves appearing as all these deities simultaneously?

Therefore since the generating stage (as explained) like this is in fact an indispensable (part) of the subject matter of the precious tantric texts and is both very important and widely praised as one of the essentials of the tantric paths, it is extremely crucial for us to do its meditations.

The completing stage was known to the earlier (masters) in terms of having two (parts): the non-profound and the profound completing stages. The first of these appears (in their literature) to be constituted of meditations on the energy-channels, winds and vital drops, and are to be sought in their individual guideline instructions. The latter appears as consisting of meditations on Voidness. Whether or not these two form (distinct categories for a valid division scheme) for the completing stage (and whether or not they are exclusive to that stage) need to be investigated. But no matter which way it turns out to be, they (both) are similar to what is practised on the completing stage.

Concerning this, (Buddha) has spoken in fact about the view of Voidness in exactly the same fashion (and as having the same significance) in both the Tantra and the Perfection (Vehicles). The learned masters have also spelt this out (explicitly). Because of this, then even though differences do exist, such as in the Perfection (Vehicle) the methods for generating single-pointed concentration on (Voidness) are less well-known while they are more abundant and easier in the Tantra Vehicle. Still there is in fact nothing better than the Perfection (Vehicle's teachings) for methods for initially seeking an understanding of it. Since quotations and lines of reasoning (for establishing Voidness) are clearer on the side of the sutras, we must come to have a decisive understanding (of its correct view) by hearing, studying and thinking about (teachings) that accord with what derives from (Buddha's) scriptural pronouncements of the Perfection (Vehicle) as well as from their commentaries. (More specifically) the foundation for this upon which we should base our hearing, studying and thinking should be in fact (Buddha's) scriptural pronouncements about the profound meaning of Voidness and such (Indian) treatises of sound reasoning as the (six) logical works (of Nagarjuna)[6] and so forth. (Such texts as these latter) can dispel all our doubts concerning extreme (positions) extraneous (to what Buddha intended) and which would lead us to some meaning of (Voidness) other than (the correct one). Thereby in not allowing us to be misled to any aspects (of understanding) other than (the truth), they can bring us certainty (about Voidness) in accordance with reality.

There do exist some special persons who have trained themselves thoroughly (by studying and thinking) like this in past (lifetimes). As a result, then even though they may not train for long in this life, they gain a deep understanding of the meaning of profound (Voidness because of their instincts). But even so, such cases as these are extremely difficult (to come by). Therefore, for all of us who are other than that, we should seek (our understanding) through (studying and thinking about) such lines of reasoning as "neither one nor many". (This is the line that a person, for instance, is void of existing inherently as something findable from his own side because he does not exist so as either one or many with his basis for imputation.) Even though we might claim something else as the gateway for entering into a quick and easy (realisation of Voidness) by ascribing this name to (a method which) cuts off fantasies in general (without such reliance on sound lines of reasoning), we will not be able to please the intelligent (masters with such a claim).

When we seek (our understanding of Voidness) by training like this in (studying and thinking about) scriptural quotations and lines of reasoning, there are two ways in which such an understanding can be generated—a deviant and a non-deviant one. Of these, the first might be (as follows). Suppose we had analysed from the viewpoint of many lines of reasoning the arisal, cessation and so forth of phenomena. When (we had done so), the entire presentation of conventional things had fallen apart (for us) and thereby we could not find (any way of) taking anything as being conventionally "this". (Thus we felt there was nothing conventionally true or real.) Because (of that), we might come (to the wrong conclusion) that all bondages and liberations (from cyclic existence) are in fact like only so many bondages and liberations of children of barren women. Then we would go on (to wrongly imagine) that the occurrence of happiness and suffering from virtuous and non-virtuous actions was in fact no different than the arisal of horns from a rabbit's head. Thereby we would come to a (completely false) understanding of all conventional objects as being distorted conventional phenomena and all conceptual cognitions as being distorted cognitions deceived with respect to the objects about which they conceptualise.

If we see the meaning of the Madhyamaka Middle Path in this (mistaken manner), there are two (further wrong conclusions we could draw). Of these, the first (would be as follows). If this were the case (that if all things lacked inherent, findable existence, then all conventional phenomena would be distorted), then since the entire presentation (of conventional reality) would be improper, (we would feel that) the view of all phenomena as lacking inherent existence was in fact a view of nihilism and therefore not Buddha's intention. In so thinking, we would be abandoning (the teachings of) the Perfection of Wisdom (by denying that the lack of inherent existence was what Buddha meant by Voidness). Even karmic obstacles that are completely uneradicable by other (means) can be purified away by relying on a (correct) view of Voidness. But even though (that is the case), with this (incorrect view) we become like what (Buddha) said, "He who abandons (Voidness) and thereby comes to lack any refuge, goes in fact to the (Avichi Hell of) Uninterrupted Pain." In other words, since there are no other refuges nor anything else to rely upon (once we have rejected the true meaning of Voidness), we must remain in the Hell of Uninterrupted Pain for a very long time. This was said (by Buddha) in the chapter on hell beings (from the *Sutra on the Great Close Contemplations).*[7]

The other (wrong conclusion from this misunderstanding would be like this). We might accept the position of Voidness with the highest (meaning as the lack of inherent, findable existence). And (we might also accept that) all mental trainings on the side of widespread actions, such as going for refuge, training to have an Enlightened Motive, meditating on the generating stage and so on, as well as all actions of hearing and thinking (about teachings) are (only) what can be imputed by conceptual thoughts. But by (incorrectly) regarding all conceptual thoughts as (distorted and thus) functioning to bind us in cyclic existence, we would repudiate, ignore and cast away all (such) excellent (and virtuous) karmic actions (as these). In so doing, we would only be opening the door for (us to fall to) an unfortunate rebirth.

These two (mistaken positions) are similar in that both are deep misunderstandings of Voidness (bringing) nothing but the false pride (of inflatedly feeling we have understood something when in reality we have not). But (there is one big difference). With the former (by totally denying that Voidness means the lack of inherent existence) we are in fact divorced from any causes for having fervent regard for (the true meaning of) Voidness (and thus incentive to study it further and correct our view). With the latter (on the other hard) we have actually still retained the causes for such fervent regard (by at least accepting Voidness as the lack of inherent existence, although misunderstanding its implications).

If, by taking Voidness mistakenly (as not meaning the lack of inherent existence) like this (while still accepting it but with another, more limited meaning), our fervent regard (for correcting our understanding) is burnt away, then what need to mention those who, in taking the totally distorted position (of denying any type of Voidness whatsoever), are thereby hostile (to this view)? This is (the point Nagarjuna was making when he) said in *The Precious Garland*, "(Consider) someone who has faith (in something but misunderstands it) by his misconception and another who despises (that same thing and totally rejects it) out of (closed-minded) hostility. If it has been explained that even someone with faith can burn away (his incentive to search for a correct understanding of what in theory he accepts), what need be said about someone with his back turned in hostility?"[8]

(Nagarjuna) has also said (in this same work), "This doctrine (of Voidness) when wrongly understood can cause the unlearned to become ruined in fact, for by their (misunderstanding) like this they sink into a mire of nihilism (denying everything). Moreover, because of their having taken (Voidness) incorrectly, these fools with the pride of (thinking they are) clever go headfirst to the Hell of Uninterrupted Pain as they have a nature unfit (now for Buddhahood) because of their rejection (of the correct view of Voidness)."[9]

As for the way to develop an unmistaken understanding, (Nagarjuna has said in *A Commentary on the Enlightened Motive of Bodhicitta*), "Anyone who, from understanding this Voidness of phenomena, can thereby adhere to (the conventional existence of) karmic actions and their effects is more amazing than amazing and more wondrous than wondrous."[10]

Also (Matrcheta/Ashvaghosha) has said in *Praises Extolling the Praiseworthy*, "You do not act while ignoring Voidness (as irrelevant), but harmonise it in fact with the conventional (world)."[11]

Thus as has been said (in these two quotations), we must see that no matter what (conventionally existent object) we take as the focal aim for our grasping for truly (findable) existence, what is conceptualised (by that mind, namely the appearance of this object as being truly findable) has not even an atom (existing as inherently findable). Then, taking the fact of this Voidness as a (causal) condition, we must thereby find the deepest conviction that (conventionally) "this comes about from that" with respect to everything such as bondage and Liberation, karmic actions and their effects, and so on. When we have taken to be on the side of what is reasonable the first part (of this realisation, namely the fact of the ultimate unfindability of everything), we need not (make excuses) about the latter (concerning the functioning of conventional appearances), feeling uncomfortable with it in our own system and therefore ascribing it (to be true only) to the face of others or on the face of deception. When it comes about that we can see how both (parts of this realisation) are reasonable to our own (Madhyamika Prasangika) system, then something truly amazing and wondrous has occurred. This is because we will have achieved the skilful means of understanding deeply how what appears as contradictory to ordinary persons is (in fact) non-contradictory.

Therefore, with a (correct) understanding of Voidness we must come to (the conclusion) that the presentations of cyclic existence and the (Nirvana) State Beyond Sorrow are reasonable (and function). But suppose, while not understanding what this (Voidness of inherent, findable existence actually means), we came to (the conclusion) that if we were to understand it as being reasonable, then these presentations would not function. If (we were to reason falsely like that), then with (our position) no different from the way of understanding of those who assert truly existent phenomena, we would be formulating lines of reasoning (about Voidness) without understanding at all what Voidness meant. (Thus we would be asserting absurd consequences that follow only from our own mistaken notion of Voidness and not from Voidness as correctly understood.)

(An example would be, for instance, what Nagarjuna) has said in *(Stanzas of) the Middle Wall, (called) the Root (of Discriminating Awareness),* "(You might argue with us debating that) if all these things were void, then the absurd conclusion would follow for you that arisings would be (totally) non-existent, disintegrations would not exist (at all) and there would be no such thing as the Four Noble Truths."[12] This (verse) presents the charge (based on the misconstruction that the Prasangika view of Voidness is tantamount to nihilism) that if everything were void of inherent, findable existence, then the presentations of cyclic existence and the (Nirvana) State Beyond Sorrow would be improper. In answer to this (Nagarjuna) has said (it is just the opposite), "If all these things were not void, then the absurd conclusion would follow for you that arisings would be (totally) non-existent, disintegrations would not exist (at all) and there would be no such thing as the Four Noble Truths."[13] In other words, with such lines (Nagarjuna) has said that these things are improper in terms of non-Voidness (namely, if phenomena either inherently existed as ultimately findable or totally did not exist at all, then they could never arise or fall), but in terms of the (correct) position of Voidness, these are completely reasonable. He has said this even more clearly in the same work through a statement of an implication and its converse, "Everything becomes proper for those to whom Voidness is proper and every thing becomes improper for those to whom Voidness is improper."[14]

Therefore if the finding of a (correct) view of Voidness were to entail merely developing the understanding that if phenomena were divested of their spatial and temporal contexts there would be no way for them to be apprehended as anything, then it would be pointless (for the masters to have said that the understanding of Voidness) is difficult (to gain). This is because even extremely dull-witted persons who have not trained (their minds) at all can understand (this point that nothing can exist independent of its context). Thus merely this much (insight) is not enough. It will only be sufficient when for ultimate truth we have the total stillness (or absence) of any underlying support (for any cognition's being) aimed (at the inherent existence of anything, in other words we understand for ultimate truth the Voidness of inherent findable existence) and for conventional truth which is like an illusion we accept the entire presentation of cyclic existence and the (Nirvana) State Beyond Sorrow. What makes the understanding of Voidness so difficult, then, is that it is difficult to hold (the realisation of) these two (truths) jointly (without feeling there is any contradiction).

Since it is necessary to have both, it has been said that if we do not know the classification scheme of the two levels of truth, we do not know Voidness as taught (by Buddha), while if we do know it, we are not muddled about what Buddha intended. And also, by accumulating the two collections (of insight and merit) in reliance of the ultimate and conventional (levels of truth) we can go to (a state of Buddhahood which is) the total completion of what is supreme. (These are the points made in the following two quotations. Nagarjuna) has said in *The Root (of Discriminating Awareness)*, "Those who do not understand the division scheme of the two aspects of truth do not understand the profound fact (of Voidness found) in Buddha's teachings."[15] And (Jñana garbha) has said in *(The Division Scheme of) the Two Truths*, "Those who understand the division scheme of the two truths are not muddled about the words of the Sage (Buddha).

By accumulating the complete collections (of merit and insight), they travel to the far shore of perfection."[16]

It is said that this was difficult to understand even for the circle (of Buddha's direct disciples) at the time when the Blessed Buddha was alive. This has been stated in *The Compendium of Precious Good Qualities,* "This teaching (on Voidness) of the Guiding (Buddhas) is profound and difficult to see. No one has understood it and no one has attained (its realisation without the help of a Guru and extensive study, meditation and a vast accumulation of merit). Therefore after (Shakyamuni Buddha), who always had the loving compassion to benefit others, attained his Enlightenment, he taxed his mind to think who among the masses of sentient beings could come to know it.[17]

Concerning how it is impossible for our mind to penetrate into Voidness quickly and easily, together with an example for this, as well as concerning the meaning of the (quotation from the above) sutra, (Nagarjuna) has said in *The Precious Garland,* "The uncleanliness of our body for its own part is something gross, an abject (knowable) by bare perception and in fact can be seen all the time. Yet when it is the case that this does not stay in our mind, then how can this sacred teaching of non-inherent abiding (in other words, the Voidness of phenomena) quickly and easily penetrate our mind when it is so subtle, non-obvious to bare perception and profound? Therefore, realising that this teaching, because it is so profound, is difficult for ordinary people to comprehend, the Sage Buddha turned away (at first) from showing this teaching."

Therefore, since in general a (fully qualified) teacher and student of this (Voidness), and in particular (such) a teacher and student of the techniques for developing on our mind-stream single-minded concentration on this (Voidness), are extremely difficult to find, I think that (these accomplishments) will not come about if we have approached them in just any haphazard manner. ('We must study and train in them properly.)[18]

An actual finding (of a realisation) of the perfect view of Voidness, through faultless hearing, studying and thinking like this, is of course completely necessary and indispensable for developing perfect single minded concentration on Voidness. Otherwise, if we have not deeply understood the Voidness of all phenomena, then on what shall we focus in order to develop (such concentration on Voidness)? Not only that, but we must also definitely seek either an actual state of mental quiescence realised through the unmistaken methods for achieving one or a state of single-minded concentration having the four characteristics as previously explained and which would be a similar equivalent for mental quiescence. Once we have provided ourselves with these two, we must then actualise the single-minded concentration of a joint mental quiescence and penetrative insight settled single-pointedly on the meaning (of Voidness) devoid of all mentally fabricated (modes of existence).

In other words, if we lack a (correct) view (of Voidness) as explained above, then even if we have achieved a single-pointed settling (of our mind), it will not be settled on the meaning (of Voidness) devoid of all mental fabrications (or fantasies). Because of that, then except for its being a state of mental quiescence, (our achievement) will not be what penetrative insight means. Likewise, even if we have found an understanding of the unmistaken view, yet lack a stable state of mental quiescence, our mind will waver a great deal about its object. Then no matter how much we might analyse with individualising discernment, we will be unable to conjoin mental quiescence with penetrative insight. Therefore this is the point (being made) when most standard classics discuss the necessity for having both.

If I were to have written only in brief about the way to cut off all mistaken deviations and thereby develop an unmistaken view (of Voidness), it seemed I would not satisfy your wishes. Yet if I were to have been very extensive, it seemed that this would have become extremely overburdening with words. Therefore today I have tried not to write (in either of these ways) in this letter.

In general, even if I were to present the (sutra and tantra) paths like this (in a letter form), it did not seem as though it would be of much benefit. Therefore whether those who have requested me to do so have been lofty or humble, I have never in the past consented (to write such a letter). But you, my holy (teacher), are not like the other. Since you have requested me so earnestly to discuss (this topic) and since other pressing reasons appeared as well from your noble letter, I have offered you these brief (words), having dispensed with much correlation with scriptural quotations and elaborate arguments to cut off extreme positions with logical reasoning. After examining over and again (what I have written), if it seems to accord with reason, I humbly request you please to implement this with your lofty practice.

(In a previous life) when you were the Master Translator Loden Sherab, you travelled with countless difficulties to the Noble Land (of India) and served there many learned spiritual masters. By so doing, you found an exact (realisation) of the total and complete points of the Victorious Buddha's teachings. Because of this, whatever marvellous (works and translations) you prepared brought clarity to this land (Tibet) of the darkness of ignorance. The banner of your fame still waves on among all beings, including the gods, for, as this Eye of the World who had a heart of compassionately cherishing others more than himself, you attained the enlightened state of a successor to the Victorious Buddhas.

(Now you have taken birth as) Konchog Tsultrim, someone who keeps vows strictly, is learned, vastly intelligent and who (as your name indicates) has respect for the Supreme Jewels of Refuge and excellent moral discipline. In order to fulfil your wishes, I, Losang Drakpa, a follower of learned masters who have exactly realised all the points they have heard and studied from many faultless scriptural classics and who am (now) a renunciate meditator favouring quiet places, have exhausted (my meagre knowledge and insight in trying to satisfy you) in this way. By the good force of the virtue obtained from this (humble attempt), may all beings understand the classics exactly as (Buddha) the Guru of the Three Realms has well explained and thereby spread a festive array of realisations perfect to the rule.

You with a virtuous and confident mind and I are like (Buddha's disciples, the close friends) Maudgalyayana and Shariputra. I pray that whichever of us receives the nectar (of Buddhahood) first will be able to share it with the other.

Ah, isn't it wonderful to have had the excellent fortune of obtaining (a human rebirth with full) liberty (to study and practise the Dharma) and to have met with the teachings of the Victorious (Buddhas)! Now the (only thing) reasonable is to work day and night to make our body, with which we can accomplish great purposes, have its full meaning. This is because (Buddha) has said that those who make a marginal (effort) gain marginal results, while those who make a complete (effort) gain a complete result. And what sensible person would be satisfied with something partial?

(In the past) there has never been any living being who has escaped being gobbled up by the cannibal of impermanence. As this is still only the case, mind, how can you sit and relax? Therefore we must give up meaningless activities which, even though we might exert ourselves in, we will have to discard anyway (when we die). Instead we should always think in fact about our two kinds of karmic actions (virtuous or non-virtuous, the effects of) which will follow us no matter where we go. Having thought like this, then with a sense of shame and decency and also consideration, as well as with mindfulness, alertness and conscientious care, we will in fact be able to tame our mind well, which is so difficult to subdue. May this thereby spread joy to our mind at the time of our death.

May the (Buddhas') teachings, the basis of all happiness and excellence, abide (forever). May no harm come to those who practise the sacred Dharma. May all beings' hopes be fulfilled in accordance with the Dharma and may they never be parted from a heart of loving one another.

This "Brief Indication of the Graded Stages of the Path" has been in response to a letter of request from the holy personage of Konchog Tshultrim, a great renunciate meditator who has exactly realised all the points he has heard and studied so extensively and thus become a sacred close friend of the precious teachings and a guide for many beings. It has been composed by the Buddhist monk Losang Drakpa in the (Tibetan) district of E at the Teura Monastery."[19]

❖

The Prayer of the Virtuous Beginning, Middle and End

Thog ma dang bar dang tha mar dge ba'i smon lam

(1)

May the boundless prayers I have offered with a pure, extraordinary wish to be able to free countless beings from cyclic existence be fulfilled as true words by the might of the non-deceptive Three Jewels of Refuge and the powerful sagely masters.

(2)

In all my lives, one after the next, may I never be born in any rebirth state in which I have reverted to being a miserable creature in an unfortunate realm. But rather, may I (always) attain a human body with complete liberty and endowments (for Dharma study and practice).

(3)

From the moment I am born, may I never be attached to worldly pleasures. But rather, in order to attain Liberation, may I, by my thoughts of renunciation, involve myself with unrelenting joyous effort in seeking to live a pure moral life.

(4)

In order that I might take robes, may none of my circle or possessions cause me any interference. But rather, may all favourable conditions come about as I have wished.

(5)

Once I am ordained, then as long as I live, may I never be stained by the fault of (committing any) proscribed or naturally unspeakable negative actions just as I promised before the eyes of my Abbot and Spiritual Master.

(6)

By relying on pure moral conduct, may I, for the sake of all my mothers, be able to actualise over countless eons, with the myriad difficulties (involved), every profound and vast Mahayana teaching that exists.

(7)

May I be continually cared for by a holy Spiritual Master whose mind-stream abounds with good qualities of scriptural knowledge and insight, whose senses are calmed, who has self-control, a heart of loving-compassion and the courage of mind to accomplish undauntedly the purposes of others.

(8)

Just as Sadaprarudita devoted himself to Dharmodgata,[1] may also totally please my holy Spiritual Master unpretentiously with my body, life and all my possessions, thereby never causing him displeasure for even a moment.

(9)

May the meaning of Perfected) Discriminating Awareness in all its profundity, stilled (of extremes) and devoid of mentally fabricated (modes of existence), be shown to me always as it was taught to Sadaprarudita, unpolluted by the fouling waters of distorted conceptions.

(10)

May I never fall under the influence of misleading friends or wrong-minded Gurus who are teachers of either nihilist or eternalist views which transgress the meaning of what Sage (Buddha) intended.

(11)

By securing myself to the boat of listening (to teachings), thinking about and meditating upon them, and by flying the mainsail of a pure, extraordinary wish, being propelled by the wind of unrelenting joyous effort, may I free all beings from the ocean of cyclic existence.

(12)

However much I might improve my mind by listening (to teachings), being especially generous, keeping pure moral discipline and developing analytical discriminating awareness, may I be free to the same extent from all consequent feelings of haughty conceit.

(13)

Without being quenched, may I hear endless (teachings on Buddha's) scriptural pronouncements close at the side of a learned master who opens up the exact meaning of these texts by relying on nothing but the force of pure logic.

(14)

Having analysed fully and correctly with the four types of reasoning,[2] day and night, the meaning of (the teachings) I have heard, may I cut off all doubts with the critical awareness I have gained from having thought about the points to be contemplated.

(15)

When, through an awareness that has come from having thought about the extremely profound ways of the teachings, I have found certain conviction (in what they actually mean), may I devote myself to solitude with the joyous effort that severs all entanglements with this life and thereby actualise (the insights) with proper (meditation).

(16)

When, by having listened (to the teachings), thought about and meditated upon them, I have developed on my mind-stream (the insights of) the essential points of the Victorious (Buddha's) intentions, may I never have any attitudes arise of longing for my own happiness or for the appearances of this lifetime which would just cause me attachment to worldly existence.

(17)

When, with an attitude of detachment from all objects of wealth, I have overcome miserliness, may I first gather beings into my circle by material generosity and then satisfy them completely by teaching the Dharma.

(18)

Having thought well about renunciation, may I always uphold the victory banner of Liberation for which I would never forsake until my attainment of Enlightenment even the most minor (moral) training I have assumed, though my life be at stake.

(19)

Whenever I see, hear or recall any beings who would beat, tease or humiliate me, may I be free of anger and in response address myself to their good qualities and thus meditate on patience.

(20)

Having completely abandoned the three types of laziness[3] that prevent me from gaining virtues not yet attained and from improving further upon those that I have, I exert joyous effort (in virtuous practices).

(21)

Having forsaken the mental quiescent states that would practically propel me into cyclic rebirth by their missing the power of penetrative insight to deflate the extreme of worldly existence and their lacking the moisture of compassion to soften away the extreme of tranquil passivity, may I meditate instead on a joint achievement (of all three).

(22)

Having fully abandoned the endless variety of wrong, distorted views which take as supreme a partial idea of Voidness which the mind has made up from having become frightened at the true meaning of the profound nature of reality, may I gain the insight that all phenomena are primordially void (of inherent, findable existence).

(23)

May I yoke to the flawless rules of discipline those (monks) who with an inconsiderate attitude discard the pure moral trainings, never fearing the actions despised by the holy and who, in breaking their precepts, are in fact trainees in virtue in outward appearance alone.

(24)

May I quickly and easily lead to the path praised by the Victorious (Buddhas) anyone who has missed the right path and is on a distorted, wrong trail, having come under the influence of a wrong-minded Guru or a misleading friend.

(25)

When I have captivated the bold masses of foxes of misinformed speech with my lion-like roar of (correct) explanation, debate and written exposition, may I then care for them with whatever means might be skilled for their taming and thus uphold the victory banner of the underlined teachings.

(26)

Each time I am born and can drink of the nectar of the Sage (Buddha's) words, may I be endowed with a good family, body, wealth, power and wisdom, a long life, no sickness and great happiness (so that I might be best equipped to help others).

(27)

Towards those who continually harbour thoughts of harming my body, life or possessions and also towards those who speak unpleasantly to me, may I especially develop love as if I were their mother.

(28)

By developing on my mind-stream a pure, extraordinary wish and an Enlightened Motive of Bodhichitta through meditating on cherishing others more than myself, may I thereby confer on those (who would harm me) the peerless attainment of Enlightenment without any delay.

(29)

May everyone who sees, hears or recalls these prayers be undaunted in realising (the aim of) all the great waves of the Bodhisattvas' prayers (that they become enlightened).

(30)

By the force of offering these extensive prayers which have come into being by the power of my pure, extraordinary wish, may I fully complete the perfection of prayer and thereby fulfil the hopes of all living beings.

This "Prayer of the Virtuous Beginning, Middle and End" has been composed at the holy Drikhung thil Monastery in the Zhotaw District by the itinerant (monk) Losang Drakpa who has heard many teachings.

❖

PART III

Middle Way Critical Philosophy: Insight Meditation

When Je Rinpoche Tsongkhapa was forty, he was already famous throughout Central Tibet as a scholar and a teacher of exceptional greatness. He himself, however, was still dissatisfied with his own inner realization of the ultimate reality of emptiness, and so he felt he needed still more intensive study and meditation on the profound teachings of the Middle Way. So, in 1397, he withdrew from his active teaching program in the Nyal area, to spend a year at the Ol Kha hermitage known as O'de Gungyal. He threw himself into intensive studies of the Middle Way, particularly rereading those sections of Chandrakirti's *Clear Words,* Buddhapalita's *Middle Way Commentary,* and Bhavaviveka's *Flames of Reason* that concern the utmost subtleties of the differences between the Dialectical Madhyamikas and the Dogmatic Madhyamikas.[1] After many months of study and meditation he still could not generate a complete certitude free of all anxiety concerning the ultimate. He then dreamed one night that he was present at a discussion of these points among Nagarjuna himself and his spiritual sons, Aryadeva, Buddhapalita, Bhavaviveka, Chandrakirti, Nagabodhi, and so on, and Buddhapalita rose from the assembly and blessed Tsongkhapa with a copy of his own commentary. He awoke feeling great bliss, and, characteristically, turned to that very commentary to reread a section in the 18th chapter.

While he was reading the words, "the self is not the same as the aggregates, nor is it anything other than the aggregates..." he effortlessly experienced the ultimate realization of absolute reality, along with perfect understanding of all the Dialectical Madhyamika subtleties concerning the authentic view. On that very morning of his triumphal joy at clearly and non-conceptually experiencing the actual nature of absolute reality, he overflowed with faith in the Buddha Shakyamuni, since after all, it was he who first had understood the absolute relativity of all things, mundane and transcendental, and had flawlessly taught this reality to his disciples then and in future generations. This poem so directly born of Tsongkhapa's own enlightenment experience is what we have translated here as the first chapter in this part, the *Praise for Relativity.* The translation is my own, although it is totally indebted to the teaching I originally received from the Venerable Geshe Ngawang Wangyal. My wording and interpretation differ somewhat from the version that appeared in the *Door of Liberation,* translated under his supervision.

After his enlightenment experience of that morning, Je Rinpoche went on to write five main works on Middle Way philosophy; the *Greater Transcendent Insight,* (the last section of his *Stages of the Path to Enlightenment),* the larger *Essence of the Eloquent,* the *Ocean of Reason,* the *Brilliant Elucidation of the Intention,* and finally, the herein presented *Middle Length Transcendent Insight,* the final section of his medium *Path to Enlightenment.* All of these works are extremely difficult for the depth of their thought and the subtlety and precision of their expression. They conclusively disprove the popular misconception that Buddhism has no philosophy, no refined conceptual thinking, since its goal is non-conceptual realization. The fact is that truly insightful conceptual thought brings the philosophical meditator to the ultimate confrontation with reality where even conceptuality is transcended. In the present translation, I have restrained myself from elaborating scholarly detail in footnotes, as the argument refers to a very vast philosophical literature produced by a tradition almost two thousand years old by Je Rinpoche's time. However, in keeping with the spirit of this anthology, the translation is for the philosophical yogi, who seeks to follow the thought and realize the gist, temporarily bracketing information such as names, dates, places, and so on. It is to be read as a formulation of a 'simulated transcendent insight practice,' in that the pattern of critical analysis contained here is a systematic warm-up for the actual practice of transcendent insight, which ensues when it is combined with one-pointed mental quiescence.

A final point is that actual transcendent insight must occur in integration with actual mental quiescence. It would therefore have been better to present this chapter together with the preceding section of the original work on mental quiescence. It is hoped that this will be possible in a later edition, until when we beg the readers' indulgence for our present inability. The chapter begins with a short section from the quiescence and insight section of the Path work, then skips the quiescence section, and translates the entire insight section.

Praise of Buddha Shakyamuni for his Teaching of Relativity

Reverence to the Guru, Mañjughosha!

Homage to that perfect Buddha,
The supreme Philosopher,
Who taught us relativity
Free of destruction and creation,
Without annihilation and permanence,
With no coming and no going,
Neither unity nor plurality;
The quieting of fabrications,
The ultimate beatitude!

Homage to Him whose vision and speech
Made Him unexcelled as Sage and Teacher,
The Victor, who saw the relativity[2] (himself)
And then taught it (to us all)!

Misknowledge[3] is the very root
Of all the troubles in the world;
Who saw that and got rid of it
Proclaimed universal relativity.

Thereupon, how could it be possible
That the Geniuses[4] would not understand
The path of relativity
As the very pith of Your Teaching?

This being so, whoever could find
Anything even more wonderful,
To praise You with, O Protector,
Than the proclamation of relativity?

"Whatever depends on conditions,
That is empty of intrinsic reality!"[5]
What method of good instruction is there,
More marvellous then this discovery"

Of course the naive can seize upon it
As just confirming their extremist chains,
But the wise find that very (relativity)
The way to cut the whole net of fabrications.

This Teaching is not seen elsewhere,
So You alone may be entitled "Teacher,"
Merely a word of flattery for Fundamentalists,[6]
As when you call a fox "a lion".

Marvellous Teacher! Marvellous Refuge!
Marvellous Philosopher Supreme!
Marvellous Protector!
I pay full homage to that Teacher
Who proclaimed universal relativity!

O Benefactor, to heal living beings
You proclaimed (this relativity),
The peerless reason to ascertain
Emptiness, the essence of the Teaching!

How can such a one who sees
The process of relativity
As contradictory, or unestablished,
Ever understand Your method?

Your position is that when one sees
Emptiness as the import of relativity,
Emptiness of intrinsic reality does not rule out
The viability of purposeful activity;

Whereas when you see the opposite,
Activity becomes impossible in emptiness,
Emptiness cannot be during activity,
And one falls into the abyss of anxiety!

Therefore, the experience of relativity
Is highly recommended in Your Teaching,
And not as utter non-existence,
Nor as existence through intrinsic reality.

The non-relative is like a sky-flower,
So there is nothing non-dependent.
And things' existence with objective status
Precludes dependence on cause and condition.

Therefore You proclaimed that just because
Nothing at all exists outside of relativity,
So nothing at all exists outside of
Emptiness of intrinsic reality.

And you proclaimed that if it were so
That things each had some intrinsic reality,
Since that intrinsic reality could never disappear,
Nirvana would become impossible,
Since fabrications could not disappear.

Thus You dauntlessly proclaimed
Again and again in the assemblies of the wise,
The lion's roar, "Freedom from identity!"
Who is there able to rival this feat ?

All systems are completely viable
When the two facts are not contradictory,
Absence of intrinsic reality, and relativity,
What need to mention their complementarity?

"By the reason of relativistic origination,
Extremist views lack confirmation!"
This excellent statement is the reason You, Protector,
Are the unexcelled Philosopher!

All this is objectively empty,
And this effect occurs from this cause;
These two certainties are mutually non-obstructive,
They actually complement each other.

What is there more marvellous than this?
What is there more miraculous than this?
If you are braised for this method,
It serves as praise, and otherwise not.

Those held in the thrall of delusions
React angrily to challenge you;
Is it any wonder they should find unbearable
Your word on lack of intrinsic identity?

But those who formally accept relativity,
The precious treasury of Your speech,
When they cannot bear the roar of emptiness,
That really does amaze me!

The unexcelled relativity,
Doorway to identitylessness,
They hold it as a nominal identity,
How they fool themselves!

These should be led by whatever method
Into that good path which pleases You,
The matchless haven well-frequented
By all the supreme Holy Ones.

Instrinsic reality is uncreated and non-relative,
Relativities are created and relational;
How can these two facts come together
In a single instance without contradiction?

Thus, what is relatively occurrent
Has aver been Tree of intrinsic reality,
Yet it still appears to have such: (reality);
So You, said all this is like illusion!

From this very fact, one deeply understands
(Nagarjuna's) statement that the way You taught
Those who would challenge Your Teaching
Rationally can find no weakness there.

Why? Because Your exposition of relativity
Makes extremely remote any tendencies
Of reification and repudiation[7]
Concerning visible tend invisibly things.

This very path of relativity,
The proof that Your speech is matchless,
Also generates complete certitude
Of the validity of Your other statements.

You speak well from experience of reality,
And those who train themselves under You
Go far beyond every kind of trouble,
Having abandoned the root of all evil.

But those who turn their backs on 'Your Teaching,
Though they have struggled for a long time,
Decry many faults once outside again,
Because of a firm conviction about the self.

O wonder! The wise one understands the difference
Between following and not following Your Teaching.
Then how could he fail to feel most deeply
Great respect for You (and Your Teaching)?

What need is them to mention Your many Teachings?
To find even a rough, general certainty
About the precise meaning of every a small part
Confers, even that the supreme Happiness!

Alas as, my mind is conquered by delusions,
Though came from far to refuge
In Your mass of such good qualities,
And I found not even a fraction of such excellence.

Yet when I confront the Lord of Death,
And the stream of life has not quite ceased,
I will consider myself most highly fortunate
To have even the slightest faith in You!

Among teachers, the Teacher of relativity,
Among wisdoms, the wisdom of relativity;
These are like Imperial Victors in the world,
Making You World Champion of Wisdom, over all.

Whatever You ever taught
Is penetrated through relativity,
And since that leads unto Nirvana,
No deed of Yours does not bring peace.

Yea! Whoever hears Your Doctrine
Everything becomes peaceful for them;
So who is there who does not respect
The upholders of Your Doctrine?

My enthusiasm ever grows for this system,
Which overcomes all sorts of opposition,
Is free from any internal contradictions,
And brings fulfilment of humanity's two goals.

For the sake of this, You gave away
Again and again during innumerable aeons,
Sometimes body, other times life,
Loved ones, and great wealth of possessions.

When 1 see such excellence of Yours,
I see that Your great heart brings forth the Teaching,
Just like the fishhook drags out the fish;
What a sorry fate not to hear it from You!

But even with the force of that sorrow,
I will not let my mind waver (from the Teaching),

As the mind of the mother
Always goes after her beloved child.

And even when I think upon Your speech,
Thinking "That Teacher, surrounded completely
With nets of light-rays, blazing with the glory
Of the auspicious signs and marks,

Spoke in this way with his Brahma-voice!"
Then the image of great Shakyamuni
Just dawning in mind, heals me well,
As moon rays heal the pains of fever.

Though that good system is thus marvellous,
Inexpert persons get totally confused
In every respect, as if they were
Tangled up in jungle grasses.

Seeing this method, I myself
Followed after the sages
With repeated efforts,
Seeking Your intent again and again.

And I studied numerous treatises
Both Buddhist and non-Buddhist,
But, still outside, my mind
Agonized in the trap of doubts.

So I went to the night-lily garden
Of the treatises of Nagarjuna,
Prophesied to elucidate correctly
The method of Your Unexcelled Vehicle,
Free of the extremes of being and nothingness.

And there I saw, by the kindness of the Guru,
Everything illumined by the garland of white light
Of the eloquent explanation of the glorious Moon
   (Chandrakirti),
Whose expanding orb of taintless wisdom
Courses unobstructed in the sky of Scripture,

Dispelling the darkness of the extremist heart,
Eclipsing the constellations of false teachings;
And then and there,
My mind attained relief at last![8]

Of all deeds, speech is supreme.
And for this very reason, experts
Commemorate the Buddhas
For this (highest Teaching).

I renounced the world on the example of that Teacher,
My study of the Victor's speech is not inferior,
I am a Buddhist monk, energetic in yoga-practice;
And such is my respect for that great Seer!

By the Guru's kindness, I was able thus to meet
The Teaching of the Unexcelled Teacher.
And I dedicate this virtue as a cause of all beings'
Being looked after by the holy spiritual teachers.

May the Teaching of that Benefactor, till world's end,
Be undisturbed by the winds of wrong prejudices,
And, finding faith in the Teacher by understanding
The natural way of the Teaching, may it ever increase!

May I uphold the good system of the Muni
That illumines the real fact of relativity
Through all my lives, though I give up body and even life!
And may I never let go of it even for an instant!

May I spend all day and night reflecting
On the methods to propagate this (Teaching),
Achieved by that best Leader through boundless hardships,
By making strenuous efforts the essence (of His lives!)

As I strive in this way with pure high resolve,
May Brahma, Indra, and the World-protectors,

And Mahakala and the other Dharma-protectors,
Always befriend me without fail!

*This "Essence of Eloquent Teaching", a praise of the Unexcelled Teacher
Lord Buddha, the unsolicited best friend of all peoples, from the perspective
of his teaching of profound relativity, was composed by the learned monk,
Losang Drakpae Pal, at the royal mountain retreat of Tibet, the heavenly
retreat of O'de Gungyal, otherwise known as Victory Monastery. The
scribe was Namkha Pal.*

The Middle Length Transcendent Insight

From Je Tsongkhapa's
Middle[9] Stages of the Path of Enlightenment

Benefits of Meditating on Quiescence and Insight

The Buddha stated in the *Elucidation of Intent*[10] that all mundane and transcendent excellences of Individual and Universal Vehicles[11], are the effects of mental quiescence and transcendent insight.

One might object that, "well, aren't quiescence and insight themselves excellences of the character of one who has already attained the fruits of meditation? In that case, how is it correct for all those excellences to be the effects of those two?"

Since actual quiescence and insight, as will be explained, are indeed excellences of the character of one accomplished in the fruits of meditation, it is granted that all excellences of Individual and Universal Vehicles are not their effects. However, there is no contradiction, since all samadhis beyond one-pointedness towards virtuous objectives are classified under the heading of 'quiescence,' and all virtuous wisdoms that analytically discriminate phenomenal and neomenal objects are classified under the heading of 'insight.' With this in mind, the Lord said that all excellences of the three vehicles are the effects of quiescence and insight.

He further states in the *Elucidation of the Intent*; "If a person practices quiescence and insight, he will become liberated from bad-conditioning—and signifying— bondages." Ratnakarashanti explains in the *Instruction in Transcendent Wisdom*[12] that this means that "bad conditioning" (bondages), which are the instincts lying in the mental processes capable of generating ever-increasing distorted subjectivities, and "signifying" (bondages), which create those instincts in the form of prior and posterior attachment to distorted objects, are abandoned by insight and quiescence, respectively. Now those are the benefits of what are designated as "quiescence" and "insight," and the meaning is the same even if you do not so designate them, as when you designate them the benefits of "meditation" and "wisdom." They still are to be known as the benefits of these two, quiescence and, insight.

How the Two Contain All Samadhis

The Buddha also stated in the *Elucidation* that all samadhis of Individual and Universal Vehicles that he ever mentioned are included in quiescence and insight. Therefore, since those eager for samadhi cannot possibly explore all separate categories of samadhis, they should explore thoroughly the method of cultivation of quiescence and insight, which provide a general framework for all samadhis.

The Identification of Mental Quiescence

Buddha states in the *Elucidation*; "One sits alone in isolation, one absorbs oneself within, one impresses in the mind the well-considered teachings, and one goes on impressing this within the mind continuously, the very mind which is doing the impressing. Entering in this way and repeatedly abiding therein, when physical and mental adeptness emerge, it is called "mental quiescence." This means that when the mind no longer vacillates but works continuously, naturally abiding with its chosen object, and when the joyous ease of mental and physical adeptness is produced, then that samadhi becomes (actual) mental quiescence. This is produced just from holding the mind within without wavering from its chosen object, and does not require any realization of the thatness of things.

The Identification of Transcendent Insight

The Buddha said in the *Elucidation,* "Then, after attaining the physical and mental adeptness, one abandons the mode of keeping the mind focused on one thing, and one individually investigates the well-considered things arising as internal images in the realm of the samadhi; one confronts each one of them. Thus, with regard to those objects of knowledge which arise as images in the objective sphere of samadhi, their discernment, investigation, examination, thorough analysis, tolerance, acceptance, differentiation, viewing, and discrimination; all these are called "transcendent insight." And in this way, the Bodhisattva becomes expert in transcendent insight."

Here, "discernment" refers to differentiation of the phenomenological content of reality and "investigation" to penetrating its ontological condition. "Examination" refers to a crude consideration, and "thorough analysis" refers to a fine analysis.

Buddha also states in the *Jewel-Cloud Sutra,*[13] "Quiescence is one-pointed mind. Insight is individual consideration." And Maitreya states both "This concentration of all named teachings should be recognized as the path of quiescence. And the path of insight should be recognized as the analysis of those imports;" and also, "Quiescence and insight are so called because, respectively, the one is a focus of mind in mind based on authentic stability, and the other is the analytic discrimination of phenomena."[14] Thus quiescence is said to be the focus of the mind based on authentic samadhi, and insight is said to be the wisdom that analytically discerns all things. Asanga agrees with this in *Bodhisattva Stages,*[15] while Kamalashila adds from the second *Meditation Stages,*[16] "It is called "quiescent stability" because all distractions of external objects are quieted, and then one stabilizes the mind itself, endowed with joy in continuous focus on the inner object, as well as special adeptness. And "insight" is the analysis of ultimate reality while staying in that very quiescence." Ratnakarashanti explains in the same way in his *Instruction in Transcendent Wisdom.*

So according to Ratnakarashanti and Asanga, quiescence and insight are not differentiated according to their chosen objects, since each of them can take either ultimate or relative as their object. There is such a thing as a quiescence that realizes emptiness, and there is such a thing as an insight that does not realize emptiness.

Therefore, one is called "quiescent stability" because it is a quieting of the mind's attraction towards external objects and a stabilizing of the mind on the inner object. And the other is called "transcendent insight" because there is an "excessive" or "distinctive" experience.

Now there are some who assert that quiescence is the lack of the sharp clarity of the intellect through keeping the mind thought-free, and insight is the presence of such sharp clarity. But they are mistaken, since such contradicts all the above explanations, and since that difference is merely the difference between samadhi afflicted by depression and samadhi without depression. All quiescence samadhis must definitely be cleared of depression, and all samadhis free of depression definitely arrive at sharp clarity of mind. Therefore, we must recognize whether a samadhi or wisdom is or is not oriented toward emptiness by whether or not the intellect involved understands either of the two selflessnesses or not, since there are innumerable samadhis which have bliss, clarity, and thoughtfulness, without having any interest in the objective ultimate reality. It is established by experience that it is enough (to generate quiescence) to hold the mind completely free of thought, without discovering the view that understands the real situation. Failure to understand emptiness in no way precludes the generation of non-discursive samadhi. By the power of holding the mind (thought-free) for a long time, one produces fitness of neural wind-energies.[17] This production is marked as the arisal of joy and bliss in body and mind, so (lack of realization of emptiness) does not preclude the generation of bliss. Once that has been generated, by the power of the vividness of feeling of bliss, clarity dawns in the mind. Therefore, one cannot represent all blissful, clear, thought-free samadhis as realizing Thatness. Thus, while it does happen that non-discursive bliss and clarity occur in samadhi realizing emptiness, it also often happens in samadhis not at all oriented toward emptiness. So it is necessary to distinguish the difference between the two.

Reason for the Necessity to Meditate on Both

Why is it not sufficient to meditate on quiescence and insight one by one, but rather both must be meditated upon?

For example, if one is in a temple at night and wishes to view the wall-paintings and so lights a lamp, one can see the painted deities quite clearly if one has both a bright lamp and it is undisturbed by the wind. If the lamp is not bright, or if its brightness is too agitated by the breeze, one cannot see them clearly. Similarly, to view the impact of the profound, one can see Thatness clearly if one has both the wisdom which ascertains unerringly the import of Thatness and also the unwavering concentration that stays focused on its chosen object. Even though you might have the non-discursive Samadhi which stays put without being distracted elsewhere, if you do not have the wisdom to be aware of the real situation, however much you may cultivate that samadhi, it will be impossible for you to realize the real situation. And, even if you have the view that understands selflessness, if you do not have the stable samadhi where the mind stays put on one point, it will be impossible for you to see clearly the impact of the real situation. Therefore, both quiescence and insight are necessary.

Kamalashila supports this from the second *Stages of Meditation*, "Practicing insight exclusively apart from quiescence, the yogi's mind will be distracted soon by external objects, and will not achieve stability, like a lamp caught in the wind. And then the clear illumination of intuition will not occur. Thus, both must be equally practiced." And further, he states, "By the strength of quiescence the mind will not be disturbed by the winds of discursive thought, like a lamp protected from the wind. Then insight can abandon the whole network of wrong views, which cannot be opened up by anything else. As the Buddha stated in the *Moon Lamp Sutra*,[18] "One becomes unmoved on the strength of quiescence. Through insight, one becomes like a mountain.""

Thus intending that one can come to understand the import of reality by investigating with wisdom combined with the equipoise of quiescence wherein the mind is not imbalanced through excitement or depression, it is stated in the *Dharma Encyclopedia,*[19] "When the mind is equipoised, you will correctly understand reality." And Kamalashila adds in, the first *Stages of Meditation,* "Since the mind moves just like so much water, it cannot stay put without the ground of quiescence. And the unbalanced mind cannot understand reality correctly. The Lord proclaimed that "Through equipoise, reality is correctly understood!"

If you achieve quiescent stability, not only will you get rid of the faults of distraction of wisdom that correctly analyzes selflessness, but all meditation practices using individually discriminating wisdom, such as cultivations of impermanence, effects of evolution,[20] the evils of the life-cycle,[21] love, compassion, and the spirit of enlightenment;[22] all these will eliminate the fault of distraction from their objects, and will engage their objects without wandering away to anything else. Then all your virtuous actions will become very powerful. Before attaining quiescence, all virtuous practices are weak in impact because usually you become distracted to other objects. As Shantideva says in the *Entrance to the Bodhisattva Career,*[23] "The person of wavering mind is caught between the fangs of passions;" and "The Reality-Knower said that if your mind still gets distracted, even if you practice for a long time reciting mantras, austerities, etc., it is all to no avail."

Determination of their Proper Order

According to Shantideva, in his *Entrance,* "it is acknowledged that the transcendent insight combined with firm quiescence conquers the passions. So first seek quiescent stability." Thus, you should first achieve quiescence and then practice insight on that basis.

Here one may wonder, "why should I first seek quiescence and only then practice insight? Kamalashila says in his first *Stages* that there is no fixed object, that the object of quiescence is not determined. Further it was already explained that the object of quiescence has both objectivity and character.[24] So, if I first understand the impact of selflessness and then meditate taking that as my object, then the quiescence without mental wavering to other objects and the insight oriented toward emptiness would be generated simultaneously, so that would seem to be perfectly alright."

Now, as for the way in which quiescence must precede insight, it is not that quiescence must precede the generation of understanding of the view that realizes selflessness, since it does happen that some generate the view without having quiescence. It is also not that quiescence must precede the generation of transformative experience regarding the view, since the lack of quiescence does not preclude the arisal of spiritual transformation through the repeated practice of critical analysis by means of individually discriminative wisdom. If it did preclude such transformation, then the absurd consequence would follow that spiritual transformation through the practice of impermanence, revulsion from the life cycle, and spirit of enlightenment and so forth would depend also on quiescence; for the reasons are the same (in all these cases).

Then what is the way in which quiescence must precede insight?

Here, the generation of insight is in the context of the common individual who has not previously generated meditative realization and must newly do so. In that context, except for the exceptional way to be explained below, in which a distinctive subjectivity for the realization of emptiness meditates on selflessness,[25] in the (usual) context of the Transcendence Vehicle and the three lower Tantra divisions, analytic meditation is necessary, since without practicing analytical meditation which cultivates the discriminating wisdom's analysis of the import of selflessness, meditative realization will not emerge. Now in that case, before one has achieved quiescence, one seeks the understanding of selflessness repeatedly analyzing its meaning. Now, if quiescence has not been achieved already, it is impossible to achieve it based on that (sort of analytic meditation). And while quiescence is achieved by the practice of focusing meditation apart from analysis, there is no method of practice of insight apart from the method of practice of quiescence. Therefore, insight must be sought subsequently. And therefore ultimately, you cannot get around the order that quiescence is first sought, and then insight is meditated based on the achieved quiescence.

Therefore, on this interpretation, if the process of generating insight is not understood as being the generation of adeptness by means of discriminating analytic meditation, there is no genuine reason why the meditation of insight must be based on the prior quest of quiescence.[26] And it is extremely wrong not to meditate according to that order.

The Buddha said in the *Elucidation* that one meditates insight relying on the attainment of quiescence, as mentioned already. And the order of the "meditation" and "wisdom" in the six transcendences, as well as the order of the generation of the exceptional wisdom training based on the exceptional samadhi training, namely that "the latter is generated based on the former;" these are the very same as the order of meditating insight after already having meditated quiescence. Asanga affirms in the *Bodhisattva Stages* and in the *Disciple Stages*[27] that insight is meditated based on quiescence. And Bhavaviveka, in his *Madhyamika Essence,*[28] Shantideva, in his *Entrance,* Kamalashila in all three *Stages of Meditation,* Jñana kirti,[29] and Ratnakarashanti, all of them affirm that first you seek quiescence and then you meditate transcendent insight. Therefore, just because some Indian masters prescribe that you should not seek quiescence separately, but should generate insight by analyzing with discriminating wisdom from the beginning, intelligent persons should net rely on that, since it contradicts the treatises of the Great Champions.[30]

Of course, this order of quiescence and insight is in terms of their initial generation. Once attained, there is no fixed order, since sometimes one will first meditate insight and later quiescence.

Here one objects, "Well, what about Asanga's statement in the *Compendium of Abhidharma,*[31] that "Some achieve insight, and do not achieve quiescence, so they should strive to achieve quiescence dying on their insight?"

This statement does not refer to a failure to attain the quiescence included in the threshold state of the first realm of meditative trance, but only to the failure to attain the quiescences from the actual state of the first realm of meditative trance on up. And in that case, one achieves the quiescences from the actual first realm of meditative trance on up by relying on one's direct realization of the four holy truths. As Asanga says in the *Actuality of the Stages*,[32] "Further, while one understands thoroughly and correctly from the truth of suffering to the truth of the path, one has not attained the first meditative trance and beyond. Immediately, one should focus the mind, and refrain from investigating the mind. Then, depending on that very same exceptional wisdom one applies oneself to the exceptional mind."

In general, in loose usage of the terms, there are statements wherein the nine stations of the mind are referred to as "quiescence," and the four mental functions "discernment," "investigation," "appraisal," and "thorough examination," are referred to as "insight." Nevertheless, actual quiescent stability and transcendent insight can only be presented beyond the generation of the special (mental and physical) adeptness, as will be explained below.

Skipping from Tashi Lhunpo, pha, 137b2 to 164b5

Conditions Necessary for Transcendent Insight

General Set-Up of Conditions (APS)

(Kamalashila), in his *Second Stages of Meditation*, states the three conditions for transcendent insight to be reliance on a holy person, eagerness to hear the teachings from him, and suitable reflection upon them. More (explicitly), the reliance on an expert who knows unerringly the essentials of the (Buddha's) Scriptures, the study of the flawless scientific treatises, and the generation of the view of awareness of reality by the wisdoms of learning and reflection—these constitute the indispensable preconditions for transcendent insight. If there is no penetrating certainty about the import of actual reality, it is impossible to generate that realization which is the transcendent insight into the nature of reality.

One must seek such a view by relying on (teachings) of definitive meaning, and not on (those of) interpretable meaning. And one comes to understand the impact of the definitive discourses by knowing the difference between interpretable and definitive (discourses). Further, if one does not rely on the philosophical treatises which elucidate the (Buddha's) inner thought, written by one of the great champions who personified living reason itself, one is like a blind person wandering in a dangerous wilderness without any guide. Thus, one should rely upon the flawless scientific treatises.

On what sort of person should one rely?

The Holy Nagarjuna was renowned throughout the three realms and was very clearly predicted by the Lord himself in many Sutras and Tantras as the elucidator of the essence of the Doctrine, the profound import free of all extremes of being and nothingness. So, one should seek the view which realizes emptiness by relying on his treatises. Aryadeva also was taken as equal in authority to the Master by the great Madhyamikas such as Masters Buddhapalita, Bhavaviveka, Chandrakirti, and Shantarakshita.[33] Hence, since both Father (Nagarjuna) and Son (Aryadeva) were the sources for the other Madhyamikas, the old-time scholars called these two the "Grandmother-Treatise-Madhyamikas" and the others, the "Partisan Madhyamikas."[34]

A certain old-time Geshe maintained that there are two types of Madhyamikas, when designated according to their presentation of Conventional reality; namely, the Traditionist-Madhyamikas,[35] who assert the conventional existence of external objects, and the Idealist-Madhyamikas,[36] who assert the conventional lack of external objects. (He) also (maintained that) there are two types, when designated according to their acceptance of ultimate reality; namely, the Illusionists,[37] who assert that ultimate reality is the coincidence of truthless appearance and things such as sprouts, and the Dissolusionists,[38] who assert that ultimate reality is that isolated by the exclusion of all fabrications regarding appearance. He maintained that Masters Shantarakshita and Kamalashila were exemplars of the former class. (He was supported by the fact that) certain Indian scholars also accept the names "Illusionist" and "Dissolutionist." However, the great Translator (Ngog Lo)[39] said that the twofold classification according to position on the ultimate is foolish, an astonishing idea.

Concerning this, Master Jñana sena[40] said that the Holy Father and Son were not explicit in their Middle Way treatises about the existence and non-existence of external things, but subsequently Master Bhavaviveka refuted the Idealistic school and founded the school that held external things to be conventionally existent. Later, Master Shantarakshita founded still another distinctive Middle Way methodology, teaching the conventional nonexistence of external things and the ultimate realitylessness of the mind. Thus, two kinds of Madhyamikas arose, the former called Traditionist Madhyamika and the latter, Idealist Madhyamika. Thus, (Jñana sena) was quite clear about the historical sequence in which the great treatises elucidated (the profound meaning).

Which one of these Masters should one follow to seek the ultimate intention of the Holy Father and Son?

The eminent former Gurus in the line of (my) oral tradition followed the practice of the Great Lord (Atisha)[41] in holding the system of Chandrakirti as the supreme one. Master Chandrakirti perceived that, among the commentators on the *Wisdom*,[42] it was Master Budhdhapalita who most completely elucidated the intention of the Holy Ones. He took the latter's system as his basis, and while he used many of the good statements, he refuted points that seemed slightly incorrect in the work of Master Bhavaviveka, when he worked out his own elucidation of the holy intention. Therefore, since I see the explanations of these two Masters. (Buddhapalita and Chandrakirti), as extremely superior in explaining the treatises of the holy Father and Son, I will follow them here in determining the intention of the holy Father and Son.

Now, while Master Chandrakirti asserts the conventional existence of external objects, his system does not agree with any other philosophers, it not being proper to call him a Traditionist and incorrect to assert him to agree with the Analysts.[43] (Thus), the expert of the later dissemination in the Land of Snows used the appellations "Dialectical" and "Dogmatic" for the Madhyamikas, following the *Clear Words*. Thus, while there are two kinds of Madhyamikas according to their position on the conventional existence of external objects (namely, Traditionist and Idealist), it is also certain that there are two kinds if one classifies them according to their respective methods of generating in awareness the view definite about emptiness, namely the Dialectical and the Dogmatic.

The Method of Determining the View: Identification of Afflictional Misknowledge

Misknowledge is the basis of all ills and faults since all the Victor's teachings against other afflictions such as attachment are only partial medicine and only His teaching against misknowledge is a comprehensive medicine. As Chandrakirti says in the *Clear Words:* "Buddhas are renowned in this world as regulating the activities of people, by their nine modes of teaching such as *Sutras,* based on the two realities. Therein, teachings dispelling lust will not bring hatred to an end. Teachings dispelling hatred will not bring lust to an end. Teachings dispelling pride etc. will not conquer the other taints. Thus, those teachings are not all-pervasive and do not bear the great import. But teachings dispelling delusion conquer all afflictions—for Victors declare that all afflictions truly depend on delusion."

That being so, the meditation on Suchness is necessary as the medicine for misknowledge and since one does not know how to cultivate the medicine without identifying the misknowledge itself, it is very important to identify misknowledge.

Misknowledge is the opposite of knowledge, and knowledge here should not be taken as whatever type (of common knowledge), but as the wisdom of the knowledge of the Suchness of selflessness. The opposite of that, again, is not properly (understood) as the mere absence of that wisdom or as merely something else than that, but as its very antithesis. That is (precisely) the reification of a self, and, as there are two reifications of selves, of things and of persons, the personal self-habit and the phenomenal self-habit together constitute misknowledge. As for the manner of that reification, it is the habitual sense that things have intrinsically objective, intrinsically identifiable, or intrinsically real status.[44]

(The Buddha) states that things are established by force of mental construction, in the *Question of Upali,*[45] "The varied delights of blossoming flowers, the pleasure of the glitter of a golden palace—these (things) have no (intrinsic) function, but are there on the strength of our constructs; the whole cosmos is constructed by force of thought . . . ."

(Nagarjuna) states in his *Philosophical Sixty*,[46] "The perfect Buddhas do declare misknowledge is the condition for the world; so why should it be wrong to say, 'This world is a mental construct'?" And (Chandrakirti) comments that this means that the worlds are not objectively established, but are merely constructed by conceptual thought.

(Again, Aryadeva) states in his *Four Hundred*,[47] "Since there is nothing existent in desires etc. without mental constructs, what intelligent person adheres to 'true objects' and 'constructs'?" (Chandrakirti) comments in explanation that desires etc. are like a snake imagined in a rope insofar as they are mentally constructed while not existing objectively, as existence itself goes only with mental construction, and not without it, hence it is doubtless sure that there is no objective status (in things) just like a snake imagined in a striped rope; he does not mean that (rope-snake) and desires etc. have the same conventional existential status.

These reasons (bring out) the mode of the habitual sense of truth-status, the negates,[48] which is the habitual notion that it is not merely imposed by force of beginningless mental construction, but is established upon objects as their own objectivity. The presumed conceptual object of that (habit-pattern) is called "self" or "intrinsic reality." Its absence in the designated "person" is called "personal selflessness," and its absence in things such as eyes, ears, etc. is called "selflessness of things" (or "phenomenal selflessness"). It is thus understandable by implication that the habitual notions of the existence of that intrinsic reality in persons and things are the two "self-habits." As (Chandrakirti says) in his *Four Hundred Commentary*: "The 'self' is the 'intrinsic reality' which is that objectivity in things independent of anything else. Its absence is selflessness. It is understood as twofold by division into persons and things, called 'personal selflessness' and 'phenomenal selflessness'."

As for the objective condition of personal self-habits, (Chandra) explains in the *Introduction to the Middle Way*[49] that certain Sammitiyas assert all five aggregates, and certain others only the mind, to be the objective condition or support of self-convictions. As for that mind, the Idealists[50] and certain Idealistic Madhyamikas assert it to be the fundamental consciousness; other Dogmatic Madhyamikas such as Bhavaviveka and the majority of the Individual Vehicle scholars do not accept that; but assert it to be the mental consciousness. In regard to the systems of all of these schools, it is both necessary to know that the referent for the designation "person" is merely the "I," and necessary to be familiar with the methods of positing a substantive basis for that "I" such as the fundamental consciousness etc.

With regard to the innate egoistic view[51] which is the self-habit, in the *Introduction* (Chandra) refutes (the position) that its object is the aggregates and comments that its object is the dependently designated self. He also states that the conventional self is not the mere conglomerate of the aggregates. Thus, as its object is neither the conglomerate of the aggregates at any one time nor the congolomerate of the temporal continuum of the aggregates, one must take the mere "person" and the mere "I" as the objective basis of the mere thought "I". Thus one should not put either the separate or the conglomerate aggregates as the substance of that "I". This is the unexcelled distinctive specialty of this Dialectical system, and has been explained extensively elsewhere.[52]

In regard to the objective basis of innate egoistic views, it must generate internally the cognition that thinks "I" and therefore the innate habit that holds other persons to be intrinsically identifiable is innate personal self-habit but is not the innate egoistic view of that (same person).

The object of the innate egoistic view which is the property-habit[53] is the actual "mine," object of the innate cognition that thinks "mine," and is not held to be objects such as one's eye, etc. The mode (of this habit) is the habitual holding of the objects perceived as "mine" as if they were intrinsically identifiably so.

As for the innate phenomenal self-habit, its objects are the form aggregate etc., the eyes, ears, etc. of both self and others, and the impersonal inanimate objects etc.; and its mode is as explained above.

In the *Introduction Commentary*, (Chandra) affirms that "delusion is misknowledge, which functions as the reification of the intrinsic objectivity of non-objectively existent things. It is superficial, with a nature of obscuration—seeing intrinsic realities in things." He states further that ". . .thus, by the force of the afflictive misknowledge[54] included in the 'existence' member . . ." He thus accepts that misknowledge which is the truth-habit[55] about objects is the same as afflictive misknowledge. Thus, while there are two systems of classification of phenomenal self-habits either as afflictive or as cognitive obscurations,[56] this system chooses the former way.

This is also the statement of the Holy Father and Son, as in the *Emptiness Seventy*,[57] "Reification of the reality in things born of conditions—the Teacher called it 'misknowledge'; therefrom twelve members arise. Seeing truly and knowing well the emptiness of phenomena, misknowledge does not occur, is ceased; thereby the twelve members cease." Here, "reification of the reality in things" indicates the habitual perception of "truth" or "reality-status" in those things.

In the *Jewel Rosary*, (Nagarjuna) also states in the same vein, that "as long as there is the aggregate habit, so long will there be the "I"-habit ..." That is, that egoistic views will not be reversed as long as the truth-habit about the aggregates is not.

In the *Four Hundred*, (Aryadeva) states, "Just as the body-sense is to the body so delusion adheres to everything—and thus, when delusion is conquered, all afflictions will be conquered. Seeing relativistic origination delusion will not occur. Thus, here, with all one's efforts, one should teach just that message."

The context here is the identification of that "delusion" which is one of the three poisons and hence equivalent to afflictive misknowledge. To get rid of that misknowledge, he declares it necessary to understand the import of the profound relativity, which happens when the import of emptiness arises as the import of relativity. Therefore, one must interpret afflictive delusion according to (Chandra's) explanation in the *Four Hundred Commentary* as the reification of reality in things.

This system was lucidly proclaimed by Chandrapada, following Buddhapalita's elucidation of the intention of the Holy Ones.

Now that just explained misknowledge which is thus habituated to the two selves is not a holding of persons and things hypothesized by the distinctive beliefs of Buddhist and non-Buddhist philosophers, such as unique, permanent, and independent person; objects which are external yet are the aggregates of indivisible atoms without east etc. directional facets; subjects which are internal cognitions yet which are consciousness-continua composed of indivisible instantaneous consciousnesses without any temporal prior and posterior components; and such as a true nondual apperception[58] devoid of any such subjects and objects. It rather consists of the two unconscious self-habits, which exist commonly both for those affected by theories and for those unaffected by theories and which has persisted from time immemorial without having dependend on any theoretical seduction of the intellect. Therefore, it is that very (unconscious self-habit) that is here held as the root of the samsaric life-cycle.

Chandrakirti states in the *Introduction* that "...those who fall into bestial existence for many aeons do not see this thus unproduced, permanent (self) and yet the "I"-habit is seen to function in them." This reason (reveals) that all living beings are bound in the life cycle by the unconscious misknowledge. Further, since the intellectual misknowledge only exists for those philosophers, it is not properly considered to be the root of the samsaric life-cycle.

It is extremely important to come to an exceptional certitude about this point. If one does not know this, at the time of determining the view, one will not know how to hold as principal the determination of the non-existence of the hypothetical object held by unconscious misknowledge, while keeping the refuting of the intellectually held objects subordinate. And if one refutes the two selves and neglects the negation of the habit-pattern of unconscious misknowledge, then one will have determined a selflessness which is merely a rejection of those "selves" hypothesized by the philosophers, as explained above. And even at the time of meditation, one's meditation will only be the same, since the "determination of the view" means also meditation. Thus, even in meditation only the manifest habits will be involved in the final analysis, and one will experience (only) the absence of two selves which are merely those hypothesized by the intellectual habits. To think this will eliminate the unconscious afflictions is a great exaggeration.

(Chandrakirti) states in the *Introductions,* that "When selflessness is understood, the 'permanent self' is eliminated, but this is not acceptable, even as the support of the 'I'-habit. Therefore, to say 'by knowing selflessness the self-conviction is totally wiped out'—this is extremely amazing."

In the commentary, he adds, "... in order to illustrate this point of mutual unconnectedness with an example, it is like when one sees a snake-hole in the wall of one's house and one removes one's worry by saying. 'There is no elephant here!' and if this were to remove the fear of the snake, alas, how ridiculous it would seem to others!"

This was stated in connection with personal selflessness, but is similarly applied to phenomenal selflessness. Again, he states in the *Introduction.* "When one understands selflessness, and abandons the intellectual self, this is not accepted as even the support of misknowledge. Thus, it is very strange to say that knowing selflessness will totally wipe out misknowledge."

Some may object that there is a contradiction in the fact that (Nagarjuna) states, in the *Jewel Rosary,* that the phenomenal self-habit, the truth habit about the aggregates, is the root of the life-cycle: "As long as there is the aggregate-habit so long will there be the "I"-habit; when there is the "I"-habit, there is action, and from actions there is birth;" while (Chandrakirti) states in the *Introduction* that the egoistic views are the root of the life-cycle: "The intelligent see absolutely all of the faults of the afflictions as coming from the egoistic views;" because it is incorrect for there to be two different roots of the samsaric life-cycle.

There is no problem here. According to this Dialectical system, the two self-habits are differentiated according to their objects, and not according to any different aspects of their habit-patterns; because both of them have the mode of adhering to intrinsic identifiability, and because for there to be two contradictory roots of the life-cycle, these roots of cyclic existence would have to be taken as two different habit-patterns applied to objects. Thus, when phenomenal selflessness is shown to be the cause of the egoistic views, these two different categories of misknowledge are shown to be cause and effect, and when both are shown to be the root of afflictions, they are shown to be the root of all other afflictions that have different habit-patterns from them. Since such a process exists in both of them, there is no contradiction between them, just as there is no contradiction in former and later instants of homogeneous misknowledge being equally roots of the Samsaric life-cycle.

Although Chandrapada did not explicitly explain the egoistic views as misknowledge, without distinguishing between person and phenomenon, he declared in general that the truth-habit about things is afflictive misknowledge, and he asserted that the personal self-habit is the adherence to the intrinsic identifiability of the person. Thus, since he often states that the innate egoistic views are the root of the life-cycle, if he thought them to be something other than the misknowledge of the truth-habits, he would be contradicting himself by setting up two different habit-patterns as the root of the life-cycle. (Since this is not the case) one must construe both as misknowledge.

Since it is upon the very object projected by the above-explained unconscious misknowledge that all the other innate and intellectual afflictions function, each holding that object in its own special way, it is like the eye etc. and the other faculties depending on the body faculty, and not adhering independently to any objects. So, all other afflictions function depending on innate misknowledge, and hence it is stated that delusion is the principal affliction, (as here by Aryadeva): "Just as the body-sense adheres to the body, so delusion adheres to everything..." And (Chandrakirti) comments in the *Four Hundred Commentary*: "Desires etc. function through projecting qualities such as beauty and ugliness upon precisely the objective nature constructed in things by delusion; hence they cannot function apart from delusion, and become dependent upon it, since delusion is the principal (affliction)."

Therefore, once delusion holds on to intrinsic identifiability in objects, if the held object is agreeable to the mind, it is perceived with desire, and if it is disagreeable to the mind, then aversion arises toward it. And if it appears neither agreeable nor disagreeable, and ordinary indifference remains in regard to it, then it is perceived without other afflictions but with a homogeneous continuation of delusion. As (Nagarjuna) states in the *Philosophical Sixty*, "Why should not the great poison of affliction arise for those whose minds have room for it? Even those who remain at ease (temporarily) will eventually be seized by the snake of afflictions." And the commentary here explains as above.

It also seems necessary, from the *Jewel Rosary* statement, that the egoistic views (be considered to) arise from the truth-habit about the aggregates. As for the mode of arisal of the other afflictions, this should be understood by extrapolation from the explanations given in the context of the mediocre person.[59]

One should also understand according to the statement (of Dharmakirti) in the *Commentary on Validating Cognition*:[60] "Who sees a self always reifies an "I" there; supposing, he identifies with that; identifying, he becomes obscured with faults. Seeing qualities, he desires them, he grasps their attainment as "mine." Thus, as long as one is attached to the self, so long will he revolve in the life-cycle."

Although the system explained above and this system (Dharmakirti) are different in interpretation, they both can be understood using this sequence in the process of arisal of afflictions.

First, once one holds to intrinsic identifiability in the objective basis of the thought "I," attachment to the self arises. Therefrom, craving for the happiness of the self arises. Then, since the self's happiness cannot arise without dependence on one's property, craving arises for property (the "mine"). Then being obscured by such faults, one begins to see the qualities in those things. Then, one grasps onto the property (the "mines") as the means of accomplishing the happiness of the self. Through the afflictions thus produced, conceptually motivated action occurs, and from such action, the life cycle itself is constantly held together. As (Nagarjuna says) in the *Emptiness Seventy*, "Action has its cause in afflictions: construction's nature is from afflictions; the body has its cause in actions; and all three are empty of intrinsic reality." By such a method, one must practice finding certainty in the sequence involved in the evolution of the Samsaric life cycle.

Reason for the Need to Seek the View that Understands Selflessness, Wishing to Abandon such Misknowledge

It appears extremely necessary to will to abandon utterly the above misknowledge, the twofold self habit, so one should intensely cultivate such a will. Even so, having such a desire, not to strive to understand how self-habits become the root of the life cycle, and, having seen a part of that, not to strive to generate in mind a pure view of selflessness, having properly negated the objects held by self-habits with the help of the definitive scriptures and reasoning; such a person has to have extremely dull faculties, since he thinks nothing at all of completely losing the life of the path leading to liberation and omniscience. Therefore, the glorious Dharmakirti said, "Without rejecting this object one cannot abandon that (habit). For to abandon attraction and aversion according to (an object's) good points and faults is done by not seeing the object (itself) and not by external methods."

That is, one does not abandon abandonees in the inner mind in the way that one extracts external things such as thorns by using a needle and digging them out, without having to abandon one's way of perceiving that object, but rather one must abandon such as self-habits by seeing the non-existence of the objects they purport to hold.

As glorious Chandra said, seeing that afflictions such as desire and faults such as birth and old age all arise from self-habits, the yogi feels a desire to cease and abandon them, and he negates rationally the personal self, the object presupposed by the personal self-habit. He clearly states in the *Introduction*, "....when he logically sees that afflictions and faults entirely arise from the egoistic views—and he understands the self as the object of his habit, the yogi accomplishes the negation of the self." Here he calls "yogi" the meditator on suchnesss.

This method is the holy inner thought of the Protector Nagarjuna, as in *Philosophical Sixty*: "That is the cause of all views, without that, afflictions do not arise. Therefore, when that is truly understood, views and afflictions are completely ceased. Whereby is that understood? From the fact that dependent birth is non-birth, as the supreme Knower of Suchness says."

Thus, he teaches that the truth-habit positing things is the cause of all afflictive views. And all other afflictions are abandoned by the realization of the real condition of things as not intrinsically really produced, by reason of their relativity. For the vision of their intrinsic realitylessness will not arise without negation of the object held as the intrinsically real status of things. Although we have already quoted Aryadeva in agreement with that, further, from the *Four Hundred,* he says, "When you see selflessness in objects, the seeds of existence will be ceased."

That is, by seeing the selflessness of the object perceived as object of the self-habits, misknowledge, the root of cyclic life is cut. Reverend Shantideva also states, "Thus, personal emptiness is extremely established. Therefore, by cutting the root, all afflictions will not arise. As stated in the *Holy Secret of the Transcendent One*[61]: 'Shantamati, it is like this: for example, when a tree is cut from the root, boughs, leaves and new shoots will all wither away. Shantamati, likewise, when egoistic views are eliminated, primary and subsidiary afflictions will all be removed.' "

That is, he states that by cultivating the understanding of emptiness, as emptiness of the intrinsically real status of things, the egoistic views are eliminated, and by eliminating them all other afflictions are eliminated; since it is impossible to understand selflessness without negating the object of the personal self-habit. That scriptural reference shows the egoistic views as the root of all other afflictions; and they should be understood to constitute misknowledge, since otherwise if they were something different, there would be two different roots of cyclic life.

In short, the many supreme experts in elucidating the meaning of the profound discourses investigate with many references and reasonings when they determine the import of Suchness. And, seeing that selflessness and emptiness cannot be understood without seeing that the self, as held by the false habits, is not existent and is empty, they spoke thus (as above); because it is crucially important to find certitude about this.

If one does not meditate on the import of this negating of the Object of the error fundamental to cyclic bondage, even if one meditates on any other would-be profound import, it will not disturb the self-habits at all; because it is impossible to eliminate self-habits without applying the intelligence to the Suchness of selflessness and emptiness; and because, eventhough without negating the object of self-habits one can at least withdraw the mental gravitation toward that object, that is not acceptable as applying (the mind) to selflessness.

The reason for this is that, when the mind is applied to an object, there are three habits: one holding that object in truth, one holding it as truthless, and one holding it without either qualification. So, just as the non-holding of truthlessness is not necessarily the truth-habit, so the disconnection from the two selves is not necessarily the application to the two selflessnesses; because there are limitless states of mind included in the third option.[62]

The two self-habits, further, function through perceiving things chiefly as persons and phenomena, and therefore it is necessary to determine right on the very basis of error the non-existence of that thereon so held; otherwise, it is like searching for footprints in the house of a thief already gone into the forest.

Therefore, since errors will be terminated by meditating on the import thus determined, such an emptiness is the supreme import of Suchness. And if some other false import of Suchness is determined, it is no more than wishful thinking, and you should consider it outside the meaning of the Scriptures.

Thus, the misknowledge of truth-habits about fabrications of persons such as males and females and phenomena such as forms and sensations is eliminated by finding and meditating upon the view that understands the emptiness which is selflessness. When it is eliminated, the conceptual thoughts which are improper attitudes which reify the signs of beauty and ugliness etc. by perceiving the objects of truth-habits are eliminated. When they are eliminated, all other afflictions, desire, etc., which have egoistic views as their root are eliminated. When they are eliminated, actions motivated by them are eliminated. When they are eliminated, involuntary birth in cyclic life as propelled by actions is eliminated.

(Considering this process) the firm determination "I will attain liberation!" is generated, and thence one seeks the utterly incisive view of Suchness. As Nagarjuna said in the *Wisdom*: "Liberation comes from terminating actions and afflictions; actions and afflictions come from imaginations. From their fabricating come fabrications, which will be ceased by emptiness."

Thus understanding the sequence of origin and cessation of cyclic life, one must actively cherish the understanding of the import of Suchness; and this will not happen by making oneself dizzy (in meditation) without a clear discernment of the objective.

Methods to Generate the View Realizing Selflessness: Sequence of Generating the Two Views of Selflessness

In regard to the sequence of generation of the two self-habits, it is the phenomenal self-habit that generates the personal self-habit. Nevertheless, in entering the truth of selflessness, it is by first generating the view of personal selflessness that one must later generate the view of phenomenal selflessness. As (Nagarjana states) in the *Jewel Rosary*: "A creature is not earth, water, fire, wind, space, or consciousness—if it is none of these things, what else might a creature be? Since the creature as collocation of elements is not real in itself, so each element, itself a collocation, is not really real either." Thus, he first declares the nonreality of the person and then the nonreality of its designative bases, the elements earth etc.

(Chandrakirti) in the *Clear Words* and (Buddhapalita) in his *Middle Way Commentary* explain that the first entrance into reality of Suchness is through personal selflessness, and Shantideva also agrees. As for the reason why one must understand it that way, while there is no variation of degree of subtlety in the selflessness to be ascertained in the basic person or in the basic phenomenon, because of the essentiality of the subject of concern, it is easier, to ascertain (selflessness) in the poison and harder to ascertain it in the phenomenon. For example, it is difficult to ascertain phenomenal selflessness in the eye, ear, etc., but easy to ascertain it in things such as images, etc., and this can be used as an example of the varying ease of determining selflessness with regard to the former objects.

It was with this in mind that (the Buddha said) in the *King of Samadhi,*[63] "Use your intellect to apply to all else your understanding of the self-concept—all things have an utterly pure nature just like the sky. By a single (insight), all things are known—by one (vision), all things are seen." 'That is, if one knows well the real condition of the "I" which anchors the concept of self which thinks "I", and one applies the reasoning about it to internal things such as eye and nose and external things such as vases etc., one should come to understand them in just the same way. Then, knowing the nature and seeing the reality of one thing, one can be able to know and see the natures of all other things.

The Actual Generation of the Two Views in Order
Determination of Personal Selflessness
Identification of the Person

The "person" is (a term used in contexts such as) the six species of persons such as gods, or the types of persons such as individual persons or holy persons, and also in referring to the accumulator of evil and good action, the experiencer of their effects, the traveller in cyclic life, the practicer of the path for the sake of liberation, and the attainer of liberation. (Chandrakirti) in his *Introduction Commentary* quotes a standard Scripture: "You come to adopt a view of the demon-mind 'self'. This heap of emotions is empty, therein no sentient being. Just as one says 'chariot' depending on its aggregate of components, so depending on the aggregates, one says 'superficial sentient being.'"

The first verse teaches the personal selflessness which is the ultimate absence of "person." The first phrase calls the personal self-habit the "demon-mind"; the second phrase shows the holder of that habit to be the victim of evil views; and the third and fourth state that the aggregates are devoid of any personal self. The second verse teaches the conventional existence of the self, the first two phrases giving the example and the last two applying it to the meaning. It teaches that the "person" is a mere designation based on the aggregates; because this Scripture states the aggregate-conglomerate to be the designative base of the person, and the designative base cannot properly be the designation itself. The aggregate-conglomerate must be understood as either the simultaneous conglomerate of aggregates or their sequential conglomerate. Thus, neither the (spatial) conglomerate nor the temporal continuum of the aggregates can be posited as the "person." When the conglomerate is put as designative base that conglomerated is also put as a designative base so it is illogical for either to be the "person" (itself).

As Chandra says in the *Introduction*, "In the Scripture, he said it depends on the aggregates; thus the self is not the mere aggregate collection...If you assert that the aggregates are the self because the Teacher said 'The aggregate is the "self" ' (you are wrong). In fact, He (merely) refutes the self's being other than the aggregates since in other Scriptures, He says 'Form is not self' etc." Thus, as when Buddha says, "Any ascetic or priest is viewing just these five aggregates, when he holds the views of "I" and 'mine' ", he is refuting with the word "just" that any self other than the aggregates exists as the object of the innate "I"-habit. Such refutation (by itself) does not indicate that the aggregates are (themselves) the object of the "I"-habit. Otherwise it would contradict the statements in other Scriptures that refute the self's being the five aggregates, since if, among the object and aspect of the "I"-habit, the aggregates were the objective object, then they would have to be put as the self.

Therefore; the meaning of the statement in the Scripture about looking to the aggregates must be explained as urging the attempt to apprehend the self that is designated upon the aggregates. Therefore, one must differentiate between statements about the conventionally existent self, intending the mere "I", and about the intrinsically real person, not existent even conventionally, and one should not maintain that this system accepts the conventional existence of the personal self. Such an identification of the person is the unexcelled distinctive speciality of this system, and the thorough ascertainment of this is the excellent method to realize the extraordinary personal selflessness.

Determination of Nonreality of that (Personal Self) Determination of Nonreality of "I"

Here, (one uses) the first of the four keys, analyzing one's own mental process in order to identify one's own mode of habitual adherence to a personal self. This has been previously explained.[64]

The second key (is as follows): if that person has intrinsically real status, it must be established as actually the same or actually different from the aggregates, and thus one decides that there is no way for it to be established in any other way. In general, in regard to such things as pots and pillars, if one determines them on one side as matching, one excludes them on the other side from differing, or such a thing as a pot, if determined here as differing, is excluded on the other side from matching—as this is established by experience, there is no third option other than sameness or difference. Therefore, one must become certain that it is impossible (for a self to exist and) to be neither the same nor different (from the aggregates). The third (key is to) see the faults in (the hypothesis that the person and the aggregates are intrinsically really the same. The fourth (key is to) see well the faults in (the hypothesis that) the person and the aggregates are really different. Thus, when these four keys are complete, then the pure view realizing the Suchness of personal selflessness is generated.

Thus, if self and aggregates were a single entity with intrinsically real status, three faults would accrue. The first is that there would be no point in asserting a self, since if the two were intrinsically really established as a single entity they would never be at all differentiable, since the two being absolutely established as a single entity could necessarily never appear as different to a cognition that perceived them. The reason for this is that, while there is no contradiction for a false, superficial thing's appearance being different from its real mode of existence, such a difference does preclude any truth-status in that thing, since a true thing must really exist in just the way it appears to any cognition.

Thus, the postulation of an intrinsically objective self is (only) for the sake of establishing an agent for the appropriation and discarding of the aggregates, and this is not plausible when the self and the aggregates have become the same. As (Nagarjuna) states in the *Wisdom*, "When it is asserted that there is no self but for appropriation, and then that the appropriation itself is the self, then that self of yours is nonexistent."

The second fault is that the self would become a plurality. If the self and the aggregates were really the same, then just as one person has many aggregates, so he would come to have many selves. Or else, just as the self would become many, so (if self and aggregates were the same) the aggregates would become one; as (Chandrakirti) says in the *Introduction*, "If the aggregates were the self, as they are, many so the self would become many."

The third fault is that the self would become endowed with production and destruction. As (Nagarjuna) says in the *Wisdom*: "If the aggregates were the self, then it would become endowed with production and destruction." That is, just as the aggregates are endowed with production and destruction, so the self would become endowed with production and destruction, since the two are a single entity.

Now, if one thinks this is merely an acceptance of the momentary production and destruction of the self or the person each instant, while it is admitted that there is no fault in accepting this merely conventionally, the opposition here asserts the intrinsic identifiability of the person, and so must assert the intrinsically objective production and destruction of that person, which assertion has three faults.

(Chandrakirti) states the first of these faults in the *Introduction* and its *Commentary*: "It is incorrect for that which is intrinsically identifiably different to be included in a single continuum". Thus it is illogical for things which are objectively established as different, in being former and later, to relate with the later depending on the former; because the former and later things are self-sufficiently and independently established and cannot properly relate to one another.

Thus, since it is incorrect to include them in one continuum, the "I" cannot rightly remember its former life "At that time I was like that," just as two different persons such as Devadatta and Yajna cannot remember each other's lives. In our system, although things are destroyed in every instant, there is no contradiction for former and later instants to be included in a single continuum (conventionally), so it is possible for former lives to be remembered. Those who do not understand this point generate the first wrong view of the four wrong views mentioned in Scripture as relating to a former limit. When the Buddha often says, "I was this former person," they think that the person at the time of Buddhahood and the person of this former life are the same, or that, since created things are instantaneously destroyed, they cannot be the same, so both of them must be permanent, and so forth. In order not to fall into such (views), one must understand properly the way, at the time of remembering former lives, in which the general "I" is remembered without specifically qualifying it as to country, tune, and nature.

The second fault is the fault of the evolutionary effect of action being lost. For, (if they are identifiably different) it is impossible to bring the agent of the action and the experiencer of the evolutionary effect together on a single basis, the mere "I".

The (third) fault is that of receiving the evolutionary effect of actions not performed, and it is an absurd consequence that a single personal continuum would experience all evolutionary effects of all actions performed and accumulated by other different personal continua. These two faults, as explained above in the *Introduction*, accrue through the key point that if the person has objectively (real) status, it is impossible for his former and later instants to be included in a single continuum. As (Nagarjuna) says in the *Wisdom*, "If the god and the man are different, they cannot logically belong to one continuum."

Here one may object, "What is the fault if one asserts the intrinsically real difference of person and aggregates, (this not being a problem of two different persons)?" Nagarjuna gives the fault in the *Wisdom*, "if it were different from the aggregates, it would become devoid of the nature of the aggregates." If the self were objectively different from the aggregates, it would become devoid of the created nature of the aggregates and would have no production, duration, and destruction, just as a horse does not have the nature of an ox, being established as a different thing. But the objector here thinks, "Well, isn't that how it is after all?" But then it would not be logical for the innate mental habit to perceive (such an absolutely different isolated and permanent self) as the object that is the basis of conventional designation of "self"; because it is not a created thing (i.e., not subject to ordinary relations), just like a skyflower or Nirvana. Furthermore, if it were really different from the nature of the aggregates etc. which is "formful" etc., it would have to be perceived as such, just as matter and mind are perceived as different. But since it is not perceived in any such manner, the self is not a thing different (from the aggregates). As Nagarjuna says in the *Wisdom*, "It is not correct for the self to be something different from appropriation; if it were different, it should be perceived apart from appropriation, logically, but it is not so perceived." And Chandrakirti in the *Introduction* says, "Thus the self does not exist apart from the aggregates since its perception beyond them is not established."

By means of such reasonings, one should cultivate a firm certainty that sees the faults of the self being objectively different from the aggregates. If you do not derive a correct certainty about the faults of these two positions of sameness and difference, your decision that the person is intrinsically realityless will merely be a premise, and you will not discover the authentic view.

Determination of the Nonreality of "Mine"

Thus having inquired rationally into the existence or absence of intrinsically real status in the self, when you negate its intrinsic reality by not finding (any self) either the same or different (from the aggregates), that same rationality analytic of Thatness will not discover any intrinsic reality in one's property. If you cannot perceive the son of a barren woman, his property such as eyes etc. will also not be perceived. Nagarjuna says in the *Wisdom,* "If the self itself does not exist, how can its property exist?" And Chandrakirti says in the *Introduction,* "When there is no agent, there is no action, and thus without the self there is no property. That yogi who sees the emptiness of self and property will reach liberation." Thus, that rationality that determines the lack of intrinsically objective status of one's own "I", or "self", or "person", should realize the entire import of the Thatness of personal selflessness, that all persons and their property, from hell-beings up to Buddhas, have no intrinsic reality as the same or as different from their designative bases, whether they be contaminated or uncontaminated aggregates. And thereby one should also understand the method of establishing the lack of intrinsic reality of all those beings' Property.

How the Person Arises as Illusion
Meaning of the Statement of Illusoriness
Unerring Meaning of Arising as Illusion

The Buddha stated in the *Kind of Samadhis,* "Meditate all signs as like mirages, fairy cities, illusory, and dream-like—all objectively empty; you should understand all things in the same way"; and in the *Mother of the Victors*[65], "All things from form to omniscience are like illusions and like dreams." Now there are two meanings in such statements of illusoriness, the ultimate reality's illusoriness in that it merely exists but its truth is negated, and the appearance of an appearance that is actually empty. Here it is the latter (we are concerned with). For this two things are required, that (something) appears, and that it is empty of its apparent objectivity. The meaning of "illusory" will not arise in the mind from something's utter non-existence and mere appearance like a rabbit's horn and the son of a barren woman (appearing merely conceptually), and from (something's) appearing and not turning out to be empty of its apparent objectivity.

Therefore, the method of understanding other things as like the example of illusion is as follows: for example, when a magician manifests an illusion, although there never was any horse or ox there, the appearance of horse and ox undeniably arises. In the same way, things such as persons, although they were always empty of any objectively established intrinsic reality as objects, are understood as undeniably appearing to have that status. Thus, the appearances of gods and humans are represented as persons, and the appearances of forms and sounds etc. are represented as phenomena, and although not even an atom in persons and phenomena has intrinsically identifiable intrinsic reality, all the functions of relativities such as accumulation of evolutionary actions and seeing and hearing etc. are viable. It is not a nihilistic emptiness, since all functions are viable, and since one simply comes to be aware of emptiness, things having always and ever been empty, neither is it a mentally made-up emptiness. Since all things knowable are accepted in that way, it is not a partial emptiness, and when one meditates upon it, it serves as the remedy for all the habitual reifications of the truth-habits.

That profound import is not at all objectively inaccessible to any sort of cognition, but can be determined by the authentic view and can be taken as object by meditation on the meaning of reality, so it is not an emptiness that cannot be cultivated in the context of the path and that cannot be known and cannot be realized, a complete nothingness.[66]

Here one may object, "If this certainty that reflections etc. are empty of what they appear to have is the realization of intrinsic realitylessness, it would follow that a common individual's direct perception would realize intrinsic realitylessness, and he would become a holy person. If it is not so, then how can these examples be suitable for intrinsic realitylessness?"

Aryadeva states in the *Four Hundred*, "The witness of a single thing is said to be the witness of everything. The emptiness of one thing is the emptiness of everything." Thus he explains that the witness or realizer of the emptiness of one thing can realize the emptiness of all other things as well. By understanding that a mirror-image of an object is empty of that object, no damage will be done to the object of the truth-habit that holds the mirror-image to have objectively real status, and one does not understand the emptiness which is the mirror image's emptiness of intrinsic reality without refuting the object (of that truth-habit). Therefore, that cognition does not understand the reality of the mirror-image. This type of cognition, although it understands that the illusion is empty of horse and ox and that the dream-appearance is empty of what appears there, does not discover the middle way view that realizes illusoriness and dream-likeness. However, these are used as examples for the reason that their intrinsic realitylessness is easier to understand than that of other things such as forms and sounds. As for their emptiness of objectively established intrinsic reality, it is established, since if an object is truly established, it is impossible for it to appear to cognition in some other way than it really is itself, by showing the contradiction between those two facts, (truth-status and false appearance). So, these examples of well-known falsities in the world first introduce one to the understanding of nonreality, but from there it is necessary to generate understanding of other things not well known as falsities to the world. These two steps have a necessary temporal sequence, and therefore it is not intended here that when one realizes the emptiness of one thing one (simultaneously) realizes directly the emptiness of all other things; it only means that one becomes capable of understanding that, since one's mind becomes oriented towards the lack of true existence of other things. Thus, the two statements, one, that knowing one is in a dream, one understands that appearances therein of males and females etc. are empty, and two, in the *Ornament of Realization*[67], that "even in a dream one sees all things as dreamlike,"—these two are different in meaning (i.e., one being the dreamer's understanding of being in a dream, the other referring to an advanced state where one's waking insight carries over into the dream).

Thus, to the perception of one experienced in meditating in samadhi, there is an understanding that apparent things such as pots and cloths are empty of what they appear to have; but this is not the same as the understanding of their illusoriness and dreamlikeness which is their lack of intrinsically real status. Therefore, one must investigate thoroughly the distinctive mode of arisal as illusory stated in the definitive meaning Scriptures and the scientific treatises in order to generate realization of illusoriness and dreamlikeness. The cases are similar when uneducated children hold a mirror- image as the object reflected, or when an audience inexperienced in magic perceives a magical illusion as a horse or an ox, or when a person in a dream perceives as real the apparent mountains, houses, and rooms etc. And the cases are likewise similar for the older, educated person, or the magician himself, or the person who knows he is dreaming, all these know that the appearances are untrue. But none of these types of persons have discovered the view of reality.

False Mode or Arising as Illusory

When one has not properly identified the measure of the negatee as explained above, when one's analysis of the object cools down, one first begins to imagine that the object does not exist, then one comes to experience the analyzer also as likewise (non-existent), then even the ascertainer of the non-existence ceases to have existence, and one comes into a state wherein there is no ground of ascertaining anything at all as "this is it" or "this is not it." There then arises perception of a fuzzy, foggy appearance, occurring from the failure to distinguish between intrinsically real existence/non-existence and mere existence/non-existence. Such an emptiness is the kind of emptiness that destroys relativity, and therefore the arisal of such a fuzzy, foggy appearance derived from such a realization is definitely not the meaning of illusoriness.

Therefore, when one analyzes rationally and one comes to consider that such a person is not present even in the slightest upon its intrinsically established object, depending on which (consideration) these appearances arise in a fuzzy, foggy manner—just this is not very difficult. Such experiences occur for all those who admire the Middle Way theories and have a casual learning of the teachings that demonstrate intrinsic realitylessness. But the real difficulty is to completely negate any objectively established intrinsic reality and yet develop a deep certainty about the representation of how that intrinsically unreal person himself is the accumulator of evolutionary actions and the experiencer of evolutionary effects etc. When the combination of those two facts (realitylessness and) the ability to represent those things, is carried to the extreme limit of existence, that is the view of the middle way, so extremely difficult to discover.

Therefore, when one investigates with the rationality analytic of reality, (one must understand that) the failure to discover any sort of production etc. negates intrinsically real production etc., and does not negate every sort of production and cessation. Otherwise, if one negates (every form of production etc.) (reality) becomes like a rabbit's horn and the son of a barren woman, devoid of all functional efficiency, and there is the fault that in the remaining merely illusory appearance the functions of relativity are no longer viable. Chandrakirti discusses this in his *Four Hundred Commentary*, commenting on the words, "That being so, how is existence not like an illusion?" (as follows): "When you experience relativity rightly, it is like an illusory creation, and it is not like the son of a barren woman. If you should negate all forms of production through this analytic investigation, and assert that this is what is taught as the non-production of creations, then this is not illusoriness, but rather corresponds to the son of a barren woman and so forth. So, from fear of getting stuck in the extreme consequence of the non-existence of relativity, do not act like that, but treat (reality) as illusory, without contradicting that (function of relativity)". And further: "Therefore, when you investigate analytically, since phenomena will fail to maintain intrinsically real status, still each individual phenomenon will remain in an illusory manner." Therefore, the holding of appearance as precisely illusory yet existent relativity is not the faulty holding of illusoriness, although if you hold illusory appearance as having objective status or truth status, it is a fault.

Buddha stated in the *King of Samadhis*, "The states of existence are like a dream; herein there is no birth nor any death. Living beings, humans, or even life are not discovered. These things are like foam, like a plantain tree, like an illusion, like a flash of lightning, like the refection of the moon in water, like a mirage. Although no person dies from this world and goes through transmigration into any other (ultimately), still actions committed never lose their evolutionary effect, and good and bad evolutionary effects mature in this cyclic life." When one investigates with the rationality analytic of ultimate reality, nothing whatever is discovered that can withstand analysis such as a person who is born, dies, and transmigrates. Nevertheless, illusory things occur as the evolutionary effects of good and bad (actions). One must develop one's understanding according to this statement (of the Buddha).

Furthermore, when one does not practice in equipoise by concentrating upon the view that has decisively penetrated into reality, but merely finds stability in one-pointedness on not holding anything at all in one's mind, then, when one arises, from the power of that (samadhi), appearances such as mountains etc. no longer appear solid and substantial but appear indistinct like fine smoke or like a rainbow. But this is not the arisal of illusoriness explained in the Scriptures: because this is an appearance in emptiness with respect to a coarse substantiality, and is not an appearance in emptiness of the intrinsically real status of those apparent things; and also because the absence of solid substantiality is definitely not the meaning of emptiness which is intrinsic realitylessness. Otherwise, there would be the faults that it would be impossible for the truth-habit to arise when perceiving a rainbow as qualified object, and there would be no possibility of generating the wisdom realizing truthlessness when considering substantiality as the qualified object.

The Method Employed for the Arisal of Illusoriness

Well, what should be done for the unerring arisal of the meaning of illusion?

For example, when the visual consciousness sees an illusory horse or ox, one depends on the certainty in mental consciousness that the apparent horse or ox does not exist, and one generates a certainty that that horse or ox appearance does not exist. In the same way, one depends on both the undeniable appearance of person etc. in conventional cognition[68] and the certainty through rational cognition[68] that very thing is empty of an objectively established intrinsic reality, and thereby one generates the certainty that person is an illusory or false appearance. By that key, one reaches the essence of the meditation on emptiness as like space wherein one's concentration allows not even an iota of mental orientations which are substantivistic sign-habits.[69] When one arises from that (concentration), and one regards the arisal of apparent objects, the aftermath illusory emptiness arises. In that manner when one investigates repeatedly with the rationality analytic of the presence or absence of intrinsically objective status in things, after one has generated an intense certitude about intrinsic realitylessness, one's observation of the arisal of appearances is the arisal in illusoriness, and there is no separate method of determination of the emptiness that is illusoriness. Thereupon, when one engages in activities such as prostrations and circumambulations etc., the certitude from the above analysis is taken into account, and the engagement in those activities becomes the training in the arisal of illusoriness. From within the actuality of that, one should perform those (activities). When one purifies that, the mere remembrance of the view causes those things to arise in illusoriness.

To express the method of seeking that certainty in an easily understandable way; having initiated the proper arisal in general of the above explained rational negatee, one should indentify it by considering thoroughly how one's own misknowledge reifies intrinsic realities. Then, considering specifically the pattern wherein if such intrinsic reality exists it will not go beyond sameness or difference (with its basis of designation), and the process wherein devastating refutations accrue to the acceptance of either alternative, one should derive the certainty that is aware of the refutations. Finally, one should confirm the certitude that considers that there is not even the slightest intrinsically real status in the person. And one should cultivate repeatedly such (certainty-derivation) in the emptiness orientation. Then one should become involved in the appearances of the conventional "person" undeniably arising as objects of cognition, and one should cultivate the attitude oriented toward relativity, wherein that (conventional person) is represented as the accumulator of evolutionary actions and the experiencer of evolutionary effects, and one should discover the certitude about the systems wherein relativity is viable without any intrinsic reality. When those two facts (i.e., the viability of relativity and the absence of intrinsic reality) seem contradictory one should consider the pattern of their non-contradiction by using the examples of mirror-images etc. Thus, the mirror image of an object (such as a face), although it is empty of the eyes and ears etc. that appear in it, is still produced depending on the object and the mirror and it is destroyed when either of those conditions are removed. Those two facts (its emptiness of the objects and its being produced depending on them) are undeniably coincident in the same phenomenon. Like that, there is not even an atom of intrinsic reality status in the person, and yet this does not contradict its being the accumulator of evolutionary actions, the experiencer of evolutionary effects, and its being produced depending on the actions and afflictions of previous (lives). One should cultivate this consideration. And so, one should understand (illusoriness) in this way in every such occasion.

Determination of the Phenomenal Selflessness

"Phenomena" are the five aggregates that are the person's designative base, the six elements such as earth, and the six media such as eye and so forth. Their emptiness of objectively established intrinsic reality is the selflessness of those things. There are two parts to the way of determining this; one negating (phenomenal self) by the reasonings mentioned above, and the other negating it by other reasonings previously unmentioned.

Negating the Self Using the above Reasonings

There are two kinds of things among the aggregates, elements, and media,[70] (the physical and the mental). (Their selves) are refuted as above through the analysis of objectively real sameness and difference of parts and wholes, (the parts being) directional, eastern sector, etc., in the case of physical things, and temporal, former and later moments, etc., in the case of mental things. And this is the meaning of the above-cited Sutra: "Just as you understand the self-concept, you should use intellect to apply it to everything."

Refuting the Phenomenal Self with Other New Reasons Showing the Reason of Relativity

The reason of relativity is clearly stated in the *Questions of Sagarmati Sutra*,[71] as logically refuting the intrinsic reality status of things: "Things which occur relativistically do not exist with intrinsic objectivity." In *Questions of Anavatapta Sutra*, Buddha also clearly states, "What is produced from conditions is unproduced, it is not produced through any intrinsic objectivity. I declare that everything conditional is empty. Who knows emptiness, he is consciously aware." This (kind of statement) is extremely common in the precious Scriptures.

In the latter quotation, the "unproduced" in the first line is explained by the "not produced through any intrinsic objectivity," which thus qualifies the negatee in the negation of production. Chandra, in the *Clear Words*, cites the *Visit to Lanka*,[72] "intending the lack of intrinsically real production, I say all things are unproduced!" Thus the Teacher himself explicates his own inner intent in the *Discourses*, explaining for those who worry that perhaps the unqualified statements of productionlessness mean that all things produced do not exist at all, that it rather means that there is no production through any intrinsic reality.

In the third line, the Buddha states that conditionality of dependence on conditions is equivalent to emptiness of intrinsic objectivity, which is tantamount to the equation of emptiness of intrinsic reality with relativity, and shows that the Buddha does not intend an emptiness of functional efficacy, which would be the negation of mere production.

Nagarjana also, in the *Wisdom*, states, "Whatever is relatively occurrent is peace in its objectivity." That is, (things are) peaceful, or empty, with respect to intrinsic objectivity, by the reason of the relativity. Thus, one should understand that these statements clear away the darkness of erroneous opinions such as that the Middle Way system must advocate nonproduction with respect to (even) relative production.

Such a reason of relativity is extremely praiseworthy. The Buddha states in the *Question of Anavatapta Sutra,* " Wise persons will realize the relativity of things, and will no longer entertain any extremist views." That is, one no longer entertains extremist views once one realizes relativity. Furthermore, Chandra declares, in the *Introduction,* "Since things are occurrent in relativity such reifications cannot be attached to them. Hence, this reasoning of relativity cuts open the whole network of bad ideas." This is the unexcelled distinctive specialty of the eminent beings Nagarjuna and his son. Therefore, here, among (all) reasonings we should celebrate the reason of relativity.

Here, there are two chief points of resistance that obstruct the correct view. One is the reficatory view or absolutist view that has a fixed orientation toward truth-habits that hold to the truth status in things. The other is the repudiative view or nihilistic view which goes too far by not appraising the measure of the negatee and becomes unable to incorporate in its system the certitude about cause and effect within relativity, losing all ground of recognition about anything such as "this is it" and "this isn't it." These two views are completely eliminated by the negation of intrinsic reality based on the reason that brings certitude that from such and such a causal condition such and such an effect occurs. For, the ascertainment of the import of the thesis radically refutes absolutism, and the ascertainment of the reason radically refutes nihilism.[73]

Therefore, all things, inner such as creations etc., and outer such as sprouts etc., which occur in dependence on misknowledge etc. (and seeds etc. respectively), being thus (relative) are not correctly established as intrinsically identifiable. For if they were to be intrinsically objectively established, it would be necessary for each to have an independent, self-sufficient reality status, which would preclude their dependence on causes and conditions. As Aryadeva says in the *Four*

Hundred, "What exists relativistically, will never become independent. All this is without independence; hence the self does not exist."

By this, one should realize that persons and (things) such as pots have no intrinsically real status, since they are designated in dependence on their own aggregation (of components); this is the second formulation of the mason of relativity. Since (things) are dependently produced and dependently designated, they are not objectively the same as what they depend upon; for if they were the same all actions and agents would become the same. Neither are those two objectively different; for if they were, any connection could be refuted and that would preclude any dependence.

As Nagarjuna said, in the *Wisdom,* "When one thing depends on another, they are not (objectively) the same, and neither are they different; therefore there is no cessation and no permanence." He also said, in the *Transcendental Praise,*[74] "The sophists believe that suffering is self-created, other-created, created by both, or causelessly created); you declared it is relatively occurrent! Whatever occurs relativistically you proclaim it to be empty—'things have no independence!' This is your matchless lion's roar." That is, the reason of relativity refutes the holding to sameness and difference, the entertaining of the absolutist and nihilist extremisms, and the holding to the four extreme modes of production.

Thus, having derived certitude about emptiness that is the emptiness of all the objectifying attitudes of substantivism, it is extremely praiseworthy to assume responsibility for ethical choice by not abandoning the certitude about the relevance of the evolutionary effects of actions. As Nagarjuna states in the *Disclosure of the Spirit of Enlightenment,*[75] "While knowing this emptiness of things, who is still responsible for evolutionary actions and effects, this one is even more wondrous than wonder, even more miraculous than miracles!"

To achieve this, one must distinguish between intrinsically real existence and mere existence, and between lack of intrinsically identifiable existence and non-existence. As Chandrakirti states in the *Introduction Commentary,* "while understanding how to represent the intrinsically unreal cause and effect of a mirror-image, what intelligent person, perceiving the mere existence of forms and feelings etc., things going not beyond causality, would attribute intrinsic reality to them? Therefore, while existence is perceived, there is no intrinsically real production."

If you do not distinguish these (existences and non-existences), you will not get beyond the two extremisms of reification and repudiation, since as soon as something exists it will have objective existence, and once something lacks objective existence it will become utterly non-existent. As Chandra says in the *Four Hundred Commentary* "according to those who advocate the substantial existence of things, as long as something is actually existent, it must be intrinsically objectively existent. If it ever loses its intrinsic objectivity, it becomes completely nonexistent, like the horn of a rabbit. These persons thus never get beyond dualistic positions, and hence they have a difficult time making their various claims consistent."

Therefore, (in our system), we are free from all absolutisms by the absence of intrinsic objectivity, and we are freed from all nihilisms by our ability to present an intrinsically unreal causality in that very actuality (of emptiness of objectivity).

As for "extreme," Vasubandhu defines it in his *Methodology of Elucidation*[76], "extreme" means terminus, conclusion, proximity, direction, and contempt. Granted that these "extremes" are even accepted in our own system, nevertheless, the "extreme" that is a resistance to the view that is called "extreme-free," (is something different). Now Kamalashila, in his *Middle Way Illumination*,[77] (criticizes an exaggerated notion of extremism), saying, "If there is some sort of existence in the ultimate of something whose objective nature is purely mental, then, just because it existed, how would adherence to its permanence or impermanence become an extremism? It is not logical to consider a proper attitude that accords with the true nature of things a downfall." What he says here is correct, that a correct mental attitude according with reality is not a downfall, hence not extremism. Rather it is as in common parlance, where the edge of a cliff is called the "extreme", and falling off it "falling to an extreme." Just so holding things to have truth-status and bolding them to have no status at all or not to exist at all; these are falling to extremes of permanence and annihilation which are the precise opposite of objective reality. And holding things not to exist ultimately and holding evolutionary causality to exist conventionally, these are not extremisms; since the objects so held do in fact exist as they are held; and since Nagarjuna says in the *Rebuttal of Objections,*[78] that things which are ultimately non-existent do exist there (conventionally), "if you get rid of actual realitylessness, actual reality will be established," and in his *Emptiness Seventy,* "we do not negate this way of the world, that "this occurs relative to this.""

Therefore, to differentiate between saying something "is not existent" and "exists" and saying it "does not exist" and "is not non-existent," is merely to discern a difference in the mode of expression, for there is not the slightest difference in the meanings that arise in the mind, no matter how much you analyze them. So to say that such difference in expressions constitutes the difference between extremism and non-extremism is just to prattle nonsense about mere words.

How the above Reasonings Prove the Truthlessness of the Untreated

Nagarjuna, thinking that the truthlessness of untreated things such as space, calculated cessation, uncalculated cessation, and Suchness could be easily proved once the truthlessness of persons and created things was proved by the above-explained reasonings, stated in the Wisdom, "If created things are utterly unestablished, how can untreated things be established?"

As for the way in which it is easy to prove: once intrinsic reality in created things is negated as above, their nonreality is established as sufficient for the presentation of all functions such as bondage and liberation, cause and effect, and objects and means of knowledge. That being established, then untreated things also, such as Reality and calculated cessation, even though also lacking truth-status, can still be well represented as the goals of the paths, objects of knowledge, and as the Dharma-Jewel, refuge of disciples. It is never said that "if one does not maintain these things as truths, the systems which must present those things are invalid." Therefore there is no point in maintaining the truth-status of these (untreated) things, (since truth-status is not required for conventional, viability).

Even if one did claim their truth-status, one would still be required to maintain their presentability as characterized by such and such characteristics, as (their being) disconnected causes and disconnected effects and as their being cognized by such and such validating cognitions. And in that case, if they are (claimed to be) not connected with their own means of attainment, characteristics, and means of cognition, then one cannot avoid the fault of all unconnected things being characteristic and characterized (to each other) and so forth. And if it is claimed that they are connected, then, since it is impossible for a true, intrinsically real thing to depend on anything else, the claim of connection cannot be sustained.

Thus one should negate (truth-status) Through the analysis of sameness and difference. If this rational analysis cannot refute the truth-status of these (uncreated things), then one cannot refute even in the slightest the truth-status of anything, since created things are completely similar.

Here, some may imagine that, since the meaning of created things' emptiness of intrinsically real intrinsic objectivity is that there is no objective reality in that kind of thing and that it has a nihilistic emptiness; whereas Suchness has its own intrinsic objectivity, and thus truly exists. This is the view that repudiates the relativity of created things, the ultimate resistance that misconceives the determination of created things' emptiness of intrinsic reality. And the latter (idea that the uncreated absolute) has intrinsic objectivity amounts to the intolerable absolutism which reifies truth-status (in the absolute), and is a misunderstanding of the authentic import of emptiness.

Now there are some people who insist that there must be something with truth-states, since a thing's being empty of intrinsically real objectivity means that it does not exist in itself, and once not existent in itself it is impossible for it to exist anywhere else. They then carry on and present a theory that something must have truth-status, since if everything were truthless, the reasons and references proving that (truthlessness) themselves would be devoid of intrinsically real objectivity, and the proofs would have an unestablished subject. But these are just irresponsible statements arising from a failure of investigation.

If the logical implications of this are thoroughly understood, it becomes apparent that the fact that the Indian Buddhist schools, once they assert the truth-status of things, definitely maintain the truth-status of all things, even calling themselves "philosophical realists," and once they assert truthlessness, no longer assert anything at all to have truth-status; this fact is a sign of their utterly distinctive superiority to the babbling philosophers of this area around here![79]

Here, those who say two inconsistent things about Suchness, agreeing about the above pattern of emptiness of intrinsically real objectivity of superficial things, yet getting into various ways of argument about whether or not the ultimate is ultimately, established or not—these persons should be clearly recognized from the above explanations. For, the non-assertion of the truth of all phenomena and things through the logical negation of the truth in things, and the advocacy of the truthlessness of all phenomena and things based on a nihilistic emptiness from a flawed grasp of emptiness are two absolutely dissimilar positions.

Here one may object, that if the meaning of Nagarjuna's statement, "If created things are utterly unestablished then how can uncreated things be established...", is as explained above, then how does this not contradict his statement from the *Philosophical Sixty*, "the Victors declare that Nirvana is the only truth; thus what wise person would imagine that therein some residue is not eliminated", i.e., that only Nirvana is truth and others are not true; and also his statement from the *Ultimate Realm Praise*, "all of the Victor's Discourses wherein he teaches emptiness are for the sake of eliminating afflictions, and not to cause the destruction of this realm", i.e. that the Discourses teaching emptiness which is intrinsic nonreality are for the sake of eliminating afflictions and do not show that there is no realm whose nature is purity.

These (assertions) actually refute the meaning of the references. The meaning of the first reference is the same as that of the passage,

"The Lord (said): Monks! This supreme truth is unique. It has a non-deceptive nature. It is Nirvana. All creations are deceptive and false in nature." This Sutra teaches that Nirvana is truth and all creations are false. It clearly shows that the meaning of "truth" here is "non-deceptive" and the meaning of "falsehood" is "deceptive." Now, since "Nirvana" here means "ultimate reality" according to Chandra's *Philosophical Sixty Commentary*, the cognition that directly experiences it is undeceived by any appearance of intrinsic objectivity where there actually is none. On the other hand, the remaining creations are deceptive in that they appear intrinsically real to cognitions perceiving them when they actually are not intrinsically real. Hence, the "truth" here is not a truth-status that withstands analysis by the rationality analyzing for ultimate truth-status or its lack. Still, what can one do when people do not carefully think over the meaning but merely fasten on the mere name?

Furthermore, since Nagarjuna explains, in his *Philosophical Sixty*, that " 'Existence' and 'Nirvana', these two do not exist; the very knowledge of existence itself is that which is called 'Nirvana'." That is, neither existence nor peace exist by virtue of any intrinsic reality, and the very object of the knowledge of the intrinsic non-reality of existence is itself Nirvana. So how can this be the philosophical position that claims that the emptiness that is the truthlessness of the samsaric life-cycle is a nihilistic emptiness?

As for the meaning of the reference from the *Ultimate Realm Praise*, it shows that Sutras teaching emptiness which is intrinsic nonreality, in order to get rid of the root of all other afflictions, i.e., the truth-habit about phenomena, teach the nonexistence of its reified object, and do not teach that there is no emptiness which is the naturally pure realm wherein the two selves, objects of the truth-habits, are negated.

Therefore, this reference becomes standard to refute ideas such as that "this reference teaches there is no voidness which is the negation of the negatee, truth, since though there is emptiness it is not truly established" and that "it is not necessary to realize the emptiness which is the Suchness of the ultimate in order to exhaustively eliminate the afflictions." Therefore, Nagarjuna, from the very same *Praise*, says,

"The mind can be cultivated by the three ideas 'impermanence, emptiness, and suffering', but the supreme cultivator of the mind is the intrinsic nonreality of things"; and "One should meditate on the very lack of intrinsic reality of things as the Ultimate Realm", i.e., that the Ultimate Realm to be contemplated is the very intrinsic nonreality of all things, and that such contemplation is the supreme cultivator of the mind.

Thus, how can it be proper to quote this (in support of) the position that, since the emptiness which is intrinsic realitylessness of things is a nihilistic emptiness, one must employ some different, truly established emptiness as the emptiness to be contemplated? This would be like saying that, to dispel the pain of terror from mistakenly thinking there is a snake to the east, "Showing there is no snake there would not serve as remedy, so one must show that there is a tree to the west!" For, what one is saying here is that the realization of the truthlessness of the objects of truth-habits is no remedy to cure beings' suffering from truth notions about such apparent things, and that rather one must show that some other irrelevant object truly exists.

Presentation of the Two Realities
The Ground Differentiated into the Two Realities

Former scholars held many opinions about the grounds of differentiation into the two realities. Here, knowable objects are the ground of differentiation, following (Shantideva's) statement in the *Education Manual*.[80] "Knowable objects are comprised by the superficial and ultimate realities."

The Number into Which They are Differentiated

They are divided into the two realities, superficial and ultimate, according to Nagarjuna's statement in the *Wisdom*: "The reality of the social superficial and the reality of the ultimate object."[81]

The Purpose of Such Differentiation

Here we might wonder, since the "two" in a dual differentiation must involve difference, what is the mode of difference? Here many former scholars, out of the three types of difference—actuality-difference, where both things have different real causes, as in the case of pot and cloth; differential difference, where actualities are the same and the cause of one or the other thing is unreal, as in the case of production and impermanence; and exclusive difference, where one thing negates the other—claimed that the two realities were exclusively different, a few of them maintaining they are the same in actuality but differentially different. According to the correct statement of Kamalashila in the *Illumination of the Middle Way*, that "the relation of identity is not precluded even when (one of the relata) is unreal," the (relation of) actual sameness and differential difference is not precluded in either the case where both causes of difference are unreal or the case where one or the other is unreal. Chandrakirti states in the *Introduction Commentary:* "This indicates that the intrinsic actuality of all things has two forms—superficial and ultimate." So each thing considered has two actualities, superficial and ultimate. It would be extremely irrational for the two realities (therefore) to be two different actualities, were they not the same actuality. And if there was no actuality to those two, they would become non-existent. For being existent is concomitant with having either one actuality or many actualities.

Also, Nagarjuna states in the *Disclosure of the Spirit of Enlightenment* that "The superficial is explained as emptiness; and emptiness itself is superficial, because it is definite that they are mutually indispensible, like production and impermanence." If such things as sprouts were different actualities from their own ultimate realities, they would also be different actualities from their own emptiness of truth (status), and hence would possess truth-status. Thus, as the (two, sprout and its truthlessness) are not actually different, they are the same in actuality. A sprout (on the other hand), though it is its own emptiness of truth, is not its own ultimate reality.

Now some treatises say that the two realities are neither the same nor different. Some interpret this as intending that they lack any intrinsically real sameness or difference. Some interpret this as intending that they have neither different actualities nor identical differentials.[82]

Explaining the Meaning of Each Type
The Superficial Reality
Verbal Meaning of "Superficial" and "Reality"

In the *Clear Words*, Chandrakirti explains "superficial" in three ways, as "a covering over reality," as "mutual dependence," and as "social convention." The latter of these is explained as having the nature of the expressed and its expression, the knowable and its knowledge and so forth, but by this the superficial reality is not to be understood as including all expressibles and knowables whatsoever, and not merely the expression and cognition of subjective conventions. Now the first of the above three is the superficial represented as reality in superficial cognitions of forms etc. This is also the misknowledge which reifies existence of intrinsic reality in things lacking in any intrinsically real objective status. For, truth-status being objectively impossible, truth is (merely) represented in cognition, and there is no representation of truth in a cognition free of truth-habits.

Thus Chandrakirti states in the *Introduction*: "It is superficial because delusion obscures its nature; and what artificially appears therein as real was termed a 'superficial reality' by the Sage; since an artifical phenomenon is 'superficial.' "In the *Commentary*, he explains that "thus what is included in the branches of existence is represented as a superficial reality by the force of afflictive misknowledge. For Disciples, Self-Enlightened Sages, and Bodhisattvas who have abandoned afflictive misknowledge make no presumption of the reality of things which appear to them as existent such as creations and reflections and so on which (they know) are not real but have an artificial nature. So, while they delude the naive, others understand them as superficial, merely like illusions, through the fact of their relativity."

Therefore, while things represented as existent according to the superficial reality are so presented by misknowledge, he does not indicate there is no representation of superficial reality at all for Disciples, Sages, and Bodhisattvas who have abandoned afflictive misknowledge. Now the first reason for that is as explained above—that it is because, since afflictive misknowledge is the truth-habit, its perceived object is impossible even conventionally, and superficial reality is concomitant with conventional existence. Therefore, if things are the superficial which is the basis of the presentation of superficial existence, they must not be what is taken as superficial by afflictive misknowledge. The second reason is that according to those who have abandoned afflictive misknowledge there is no superficial which is represented as truth by truth-presumptions, and so those creations are not established as real for them, while still they do not establish the utter lack of any superficial reality. Therefore, the statement that creations are "merely superficial" for them should be understood as intending that, since among "superficial" and "reality," "reality" does not present itself to them, the word "merely" rules out "reality" without ruling out "superficial reality", and this is the intention behind the mention of both "merely superficial" and "superficial reality." The *Clear Words'* statement, "That which is real according to mundane superficialities is the mundane superficial reality", and the *Introduction Commentary* statement, "that superficial whereby reality appears, things each appearing as intrinsically real while actually being devoid of intrinsic reality, is a reality which is superficial, constituted by the errors of the world, and so is the social superficial reality", should both be understood as clearly referring to the reality according to the superficiality of the previously explained misknowledge, and not to the reality which has conventionally real status. For otherwise it would contradict the Dialectical interpretation wherein conventionally intrinsically identifiable status is impossible, and also because both the negations of truth-status and the proofs of truthlessness are accomplished by means of conventions. Along these lines one should understand also the explanation of the status of the superficial Jñana garbha.

Here one might imagine, "Well, since a true reality and a true self are real according to the superficiality maintained by the truth-habit, they become superficially real!" That would certainly be the case, I grant, if something merely true according to the superficiality of the truth-habit were to be represented as a superficial reality, but that is not what I said. I was merely explaining according to what kind of "superficiality" that "superficial reality"'s "reality" was a "real superficiality," as well as the mode of its corresponding "reality!"

The Nature of Superficial Reality

Each of these internal and external phenomena has both ultimate and superficial actualities. If we illustrate this with the case of a sprout (they are respectively) the actuality of the sprout discovered by the rational cognition that sees the object which is the authentic knowable, Thatness, and the actuality of the sprout discovered by the conventional cognition that encounters the delusive objects of false knowables. The former is the actuality of the sprout's ultimate reality, and the latter is the actuality of the sprout's superficial reality. According to Chandrakirti in the *Introduction*, "All things are perceived as having two actualities, each discovered by authentic and spurious perception (respectively); the object of authentic perception is Thatness, and that of spurious perception is said to be the superficial reality." This teaches that the sprout has the two actualities of the two realities, the ultimate being encountered by the former cognition, and the superficial being encountered by the latter cognition, and does not teach that one and the same actuality of the sprout has both realities depending on whichever of the two cognitions. As the *Commentary* states, "The intrinsic actuality of all things is precisely indicated as having two forms, superficial and ultimate"; so, the actuality of each thing is differentiated into two, an ultimate (actuality) which is discovered by the cognition which perceives the authentic object, and the superficial (actuality) which is discovered by the cognition which perceives the false.

The superficial reality is not objectively real, being real only according to the truth-habit, and so to ascertain the elimination of its objects, one must ascertain their falseness. In order to ascertain the delusive status of a superficial object such as an identified "pot", for example, one must find the view which refutes through rational cognition the conceptual object of the truth habit concerning that object, since falsity will not be established by validating cognition without rational negation of truth. Although "pot" and "cloth" and so on are superficial realities, to establish them cognitively it is not necessary that they be established cognitively as objects belonging to the superficial reality; just as, though "pots" and "cloths" are illusory in that they appear (intrinsically real) while lacking intrinsic reality, the cognitions that establish them (as merely present) do not necessarily establish them as illusory objects.

Therefore, to interpret this system as being that, according to the cognition of a common individual with no Middle view, the superficial reality of pots and cloths etc. is presented, and the ultimate reality is presented according to the (cognition of the) holy person, is not correct; for, it is the opposite from (Chandrakirti's) statement in the *Commentary*, that "the very thing that is the ultimate for the common individual is the merely superficial for the holy person who has attained the sphere of illumined perception; for that thing's the ultimate reality for them." Common individuals perceive pots etc. as real, which is the same as holding them to exist ultimately, and therefore those things, pot, etc., have ultimate status according to their cognitions, and are not superficial objects (for them). But such pots etc. which according to them are ultimate in status, are superficial according to the intuitive perception of the holy persons who encounter appearances as illusory. And he mentions "merely superficial" here since such an (exalted) cognition represents nothing as really true). That being the case, furthermore, he says "their intrinsic reality is the ultimate," and therefore one should formulate these, differentiating between "the pots etc. are superficial" and "their intrinsic reality is the holy persons' ultimate"; and one should not say that "pots etc. are ultimate for the holy persons", because the rational cognition that perceives their true objectivity does not encounter any pots etc., and because the meaning of ultimate reality is stated to be that encountered by the rational cognition which perceives the authentic object.

Categories of the Superficial

The Dogmatic Madhyamikas assert that cognition which perceives intrinsically identifiable status (in things) is definite about their existence as they appear, and that there are differentiations about whether objective appearances have or do not have the intrinsically identifiable status they appear to have, without their being any differentiation of subjective cognitions into authentic and spurious; according to Jñana garbha's statement in the *Two Realities,* "Although both appear the same, the authentic and spurious superficial (realities) are differentiated according to whether or not they have functional efficiency." (However), this (Dialectic Madhyamika) system asserts that everything that appears to have intrinsic identifiability to a person endowed with misknowledge is an appearance (only) for that cognition deluded by misknowledge, and therefore they do not differentiate superficial objects into authentic and spurious.

Chandrakirti states in the *Introduction Commentary* that "what is spurious even superficially is not the superficial reality." (But) what he means here is that a mirror-image of an object is not really that object according to the superficial (cognition) of an educated social person, and so it is not a superficial reality according to that person. Nevertheless, since it is an object encountered by perception of delusive objects which are superficial knowables, it is a superficial reality. And just as a cognition which perceives a mirror-image is mistaken in its apparent object, so the appearance of intrinsically identifiable blue etc. to one with misknowledge is also erroneous as an apparent object. If a validated object is presented as true, its being erroneous contradicts its representation, but the same (erroneousness) can accompany the presentation of that validated object as superficial. Otherwise, if there were no conventionally real status (at all), then one could not present any superficial reality, and when the superficial illusory things were presented conventionally, it would be impossible to represent them as superficial realities.

According to the Dialectical Middle Way system, the six cognitions not deceived by any circumstantial causes of error and their six perceived objects, and the six cognitions opposite to them (circumstantially deceived) and their six perceived objects are presented (respectively) as the authentic superficial and as the false superficial, including both subjects and objects together in both cases. They are presented further as true and false superficials depending on social or conventional validating cognition itself, and not in relying on the rational cognition that corresponds' to the perception of the holy persons. Therefore, they do not differentiate true and false superficials (as does the) Dogmatic Middle Way system, since (for the Dialecticians) there is no question of differentiating between an ignorant person's perceptions of mirror images etc. and blue etc. by whether or not they are mistaken concerning their apparent objects. As Chandrakirti says in the *Introduction,* "the social persons recognize what is perceived by the six sense faculties when undamaged, and they are true according to society itself; the rest are represented as false by society itself." The one exception here is the opposite to the holding of the intrinsic identifiability of persons and phenomena, which are habit-patterns arising from such as the circumstantial mental deceptions caused by wrong theories regarding both things, which (opposite tendency, i.e. wisdom of selflessness) is (after all) not (usually) established by conventional validating cognition. Further, although dualistic perception arises in the phenomenally omniscient intuition that is free of all cause of deception by instinctual misknowledge, still it is not mistaken with regard to its perceptual objects; the reasons for this have already been explained elsewhere.[84]

Ultimate Reality
The Meaning of "Ultimate" and "Reality"

Chandrakirti states in the *Clear Words,* "It is an object and it is supreme, therefore it is 'ultimate,' ('supreme object'). The same thing is also 'real', therefore it is called 'ultimate reality'." Thus he asserts that both objectivity and supremacy constitute the "ultimate reality." The mode of reality of ultimate reality lies in its non-deception, since it does not deceive people by appearing in one way while actually being another way. Chandrakirti, however, states in the *Philosophical Sixty Commentary* that (even) this ultimate reality is merely presented as existent in terms of social conventions. Therefore, the verbal meaning of "reality" in "superficial reality" and "ultimate reality" is different, the former being "reality" in terms of the truth habit (only).

The Nature of Ultimate Reality—Actual Meaning

The nature of ultimate reality is as explained above in terms of the *Introduction* statement that it is what is discovered by the perception of the object which is the authentic knowable. Chandrakirti further explains in the *Commentary* that "the ultimate as the very object of the special intuition of those of authentic perception is discovered as the intrinsic actuality of the self, but it (itself) is not established by its own intrinsic nature; it is a single actuality." Thus, he states that, while it is discovered by the uncontaminated intuition that encounters Thatness, it has no intrinsically objective status (itself). Therefore the position that "since it is something discovered by the uncontaminated equipoise, it has truth-status (itself)" is refuted. He calls it "the special intuition" to indicate that it is in adequate to define it as what is discovered by whatever type of holy intuition, but that ultimate reality is what is discovered by the special intuition that is the ontologically omniscient intuition. The meaning of "discovery" here is establishment by that (special) cognition, which is similar to the usage in the case of the superficial.

As for the process whereby that (cognition) discovers that (object), just as someone with distorted vision sees hairs falling in the sky and another without that distortion does not even see such an appearance as hairs falling, so those damaged by the distortion of misknowledge perceive an intrinsic objectivity in the aggregates etc., but those who have completely eliminated the instinct for misknowledge and those who have the intuition of the holy learner's uncontaminated equipoise by way of their perception of Thatness, like the person with undistorted vision, do not perceive in the very same (aggregates etc.) even the slightest dualistic appearance, the reality that they perceive being the ultimate reality. As Chandrakirti states in the *Introduction,* "Those construct a false actuality such as hairs etc. by the power of hallucination, while others, by the purity of their vision see the very same things as Suchness—this should be recognized." Further, from the *Commentary,* he continues, "The Lord Buddhas, free from the instincts for misknowledge, see the ultimate reality in the aggregates etc. in the same manner that the person of undistorted vision does not see hallucinated hairs." Now the ultimate which is thus perceived is the ultimate actuality involved in each thing considered as having two actualities. Further, that (very actuality) is the Nirvana which is the pure intrinsic reality free of intrinsically real status of each thing under consideration, as well as the Nirvana which is the Truth of Cessation free from whatever kind of seed of defilement. Therefore, Chandrakirti makes such statements as, in the *Philosophical Sixty Commentary,* " 'Well then—is Nirvana just the superficial reality after all?' 'Yes, that's just it' " and "therefore, Nirvana is construed as precisely the superficial reality." As for the meaning of such statements, the presentation of Nirvana, ultimate reality, as existent is a presentation merely of existence in terms of the cognition of conventional superficial reality, but it is not that this system asserts that Nirvana is superficial reality.

From the same *Commentary,* Chandrakirti explains that "Three of the Holy Truths are superficial realities while Nirvana is ultimate reality." Here one objects that because he states that the other three Truths are superficial reality and Cessation is ultimate reality, and because he presents Nirvana as superficially existent, his statement that there is an ultimate reality is contradicted. In answer to this objection, it is said that ultimate reality is only mentioned in terms of social conventions. Therefore, all things represented as existent are presented in term of social conventions. Thus, Buddha states, in the *Transcendent Wisdom 100,000,* that "all these things are designated in

dependence on social conventions and not in terms of the ultimate."
Nagarjuna states, in the *Emptiness Seventy*, that "Duration, production,
and destruction, existence and nonexistence, inferiority, equality, and
superiority—the Buddha mentioned these in terms of social
conventions and not in terms of the ultimate." So, all statements of
the Victor which present duration, production, and destruction, or
existence and nonexistence, or inferiority, mediocrity, and
superiority—all these are presented only in terms of social conventions,
and are not presented in terms of any sort of authentic objectivity
which is not just conventionally presented. Therefore, master Jñana
garbha's statement that "there is ultimate reality through reality in the
ultimate" means that, since he explains rational cognition itself as a
kind of ultimate, it is a reality according to it, as it is not deceived, and
he does not intend any sort of truth-status that can withstand critical
analysis, because in his treatise, he refutes the truth-status in all things.

   Thus, if one says that "if the ultimate is not ultimately real, then
the superficial is not superficially real!", we accept that. But, if one
says that "if the former is not established in the former, then the latter
is not established in the latter!", it becomes tantamount to saying that
"if the negation of truth (-status) is without truth-status, then the
negation ground, considered things, becomes truly established!" (and
this is unacceptable), because ultimate reality itself is presented as
precisely the negation of truth in considered things, all considered
things would not be superficially established implies that they would
not be falsely established (even, and not that they would retain truth-
status). But even that (supposed implication) becomes extremely
incoherent, because by the very fact of the lack of truth-status of the
lack of truth-status of all apparent considered things, the negation-
ground necessarily is established as false. Therefore, while ultimacy-
analytic rational cognition need not establish something that is
presented as conventionally existent, it is necessary that such a thing
not be faulted by any sort of validating cognition, either conventional
or rational. Chandrakirti states, in the *Philosophical Sixty Commentary,*
that "the four properties such as impermanence abide in the
appropriative aggregates superficially, and so to hold them is not

mistaken, but the four (opposite) properties such as permanence do not inhere in the aggregates even superficially, and so to hold them there are explained to be erroneous"; and in the *Introduction*, "The inner essence imagined by those Fundamentalists, so much troubled by the sleep of unknowing, and those things imagined as illusions and hallucinations—none of these exist even according to the social world." Thus, the Self and the Principle imagined by these Fundamentalists, and those imaginary objects such as illusions and hallucinations are said not even to be conventionally existent, merely existing according to an erroneous cognition. It is therefore baseless supposition to hold that these things are presented as superficially existent in the Dialectical system; besides which none of the other great Madhyamikas accept them. As for Chandrakirti's assertion in the *Introduction* of the equivalence of subject and object in terms of existing or not existing, it is not merely in terms of general existence and non-existence, but is in terms of intrinsically real existence and non-existence.

Therefore, while things presented as conventionally existent are presented as existent in terms of verbal conventions, all things presented in terms of verbal conventions are not accepted as conventionally existent. And as for the assertion that something is "merely" presented in terms of conventions, the word "merely" definitely does not exclude there being anything other than subjective conventions, nor does it exclude a (conventionally) presented thing's being established by a (conventional) validating cognition. Rather, this system does not present the existence (of anything) through the discovery of a referent object by investigation into the mode of being of that referent out of dissatisfaction with its being presented in terms of conventions, nor does it present (that thing) as non-existent when no (referent) is discovered. It asserts that if anything were to be discovered by investigation through such a type of inquiry it would become endowed with truth-status, and therefore does not accept even conventionally that anything is discovered to exist through such an analytic process. Since it thus formulates the criterion for what constitutes analysis and non-analysis into reality, it considers that if something were to exist by virtue of intrinsic identifiability, it would come to have intrinsically objective existence, not merely being established in subjectively conventional terms, and it does not accept therefore any intrinsically real, intrinsically identifiable, or intrinsically objective existence, even in conventional terms. But I have explained all this extensively elsewhere.[85]

Rebuttle of Debates

Here some argue that if the Buddha's ontologically omniscient intuition discovers ultimate reality, how does it not contradict Chandrakirti's statement in the *Introduction Commentary*, "If one objects that, 'Is not the experience of such an intrinsic reality utterly non-existent? And so how do they perceive it?' We grant that; however, they see by the process of not seeing.,' He explains that the vision of reality is not seeing at all, and he quotes in support of the explanation that ultimate reality is even beyond the sphere of omniscient intuition, the explanation that mind and mental processes do not function at the Buddha-stage. So, if the Buddha does not perceive the aggregates etc., how does this not contradict the explanation that he knows absolutely everything, given in the context of his ten powers?

The statement about "seeing by the process of not seeing" does not mean that he does not see any kind of object at all, but rather it shows that, if these objects (advanced) by the power of the veil of misknowledge were to exist in reality, the holy, uncontaminated, equipoised intuition must perceive them, and so from the perspective of not seeing them at all, it sees their ultimate reality; because it is presented that the realization of the negation of a negatee comes from not perceiving that negatee when it should be perceived if it were to exist.

The meaning of the statement that the "supreme seeing is not seeing" is to be understood in the same way. As the *Encyclopedia* states, "Forms are not seen, sensations are not perceived, concepts are not experienced, and thoughts are not perceived. There is no perception of consciousness, mind, or mentality—this is the experience of the Dharma". This is the teaching of the Transcendent One. Beings say in words 'See the sky!' But how do you see the sky? This you must examine. The seeing of the Dharma is taught by the Transcendent One to be like that. That experience cannot be explained by any other example." Here "not seeing" refers to the five aggregates, and "seeing" to the Dharma, which here has the meaning of Thatness, as in the statement that "who sees relativity, sees the Dharma!" Here, the example is "sky," which is the mere exclusion of tangible obstruction. To see, or to experience that is not to see any obstruction, the negatee in this case, when it could be seen if it was there. In this example, the "not seeing" refers to the obstruction, and the "seeing" refers to the space. As in this example, (the seeing of reality) is not a seeing, and the last two phrases (of the quote) negate the idea that the seeing of reality is like the seeing of blue. And the statement that the five aggregates are not seen teaches that according to the vision of Thatness by uncontaminated equipoise, considered things are not seen.

In the *Entrance into the Two Realities,* it is said that "Gods! The ultimate reality transcends everything including the sphere of the omniscient intuition supreme in all aspects, and it does not correspond to any expressions such as 'Such is the ultimate reality!' " Here, when one expresses "ultimate reality," it is explained that there is no experience in the mind as when subject and object appear to be separate. Therefore, this reference is a source for (the ultimate's being) the elimination of dualistic appearance, and not a source for (the idea that) the Buddha does not experience the ultimate.

In the *Introduction Commentary,* furthermore, Chandrakirti states that "He is called 'Buddha' because he realizes only the intrinsic reality unaffected by any created phenomenon; because he has that experience." Thus, according to the vision of reality by the Buddha's ontologically omniscient intuition, only the ultimate reality of things is experienced without any contact with relative things.

As for the "elimination of the process of mind and mental functions," it means that the process of constructive thought is eliminated at the time of realization of Thatness, and does not show that mind and mental functions are non-existent. As Chandrakirti states in the *Clear Words,* "Thatness is free of constructive thought, since it is free of those mental processes which constitute constructive thought. As the Buddha says in a *Discourse*, 'What is ultimate reality'? Where there are no processes of mind, not to mention any letters.' " Thus he explains the meaning of the "lack of mental processes" as the lack of the constructive thought process. And even that is said not to be definitely eliminated at the time of the holy learner's equipoise, but only at the time of Buddhahood, according to the *Introduction Commentary*.

Furthermore, in the *Introduction Commentary*, Chandrakirti proves that if that (ultimate) intrinsic reality were not to exist, the austerities of the Bodhisattvas would be pointless, and he backs this up with scriptural references. Thus, "What is the intrinsic reality of these things? It is that which does not depend on anything else, the intrinsic actuality realized by the wisdom free of all distortions of misknowledge. Who would ask, 'Does that (itself) exist? Or does it not exist?' If it did not exist, for what purpose would the Bodhisattvas practice the path of the Transcendences? For it is to realize that reality that the Bodhisattvas undertake their hundreds of hardships." To support that, (he quotes) "Noble son! If the ultimate were not to exist, the pure practice would be pointless, the arisal of the Transcendent Ones would be pointless. But because the ultimate reality does exist, Bodhisattvas are said to be expert in the ultimate.' Thus, if the ultimate reality were not to exist, practices for the sake of the purity of ultimate Nirvana would be pointless, as the disciple would be unable to realize it, and the Buddhas' visiting the world in order to cause them to realize that would be pointless, and the great Bodhisattvas would become inexpert in ultimate reality. Therefore, since he quotes such Scriptures to prove the existence of the ultimate reality, to hold that the interpretation of this great Master advocates that the ultimate reality is not a knowable object and that the holy equipoise has no intuition that realizes Thatness, is simply a false speculation.

Further as for the meaning of his statement in the *Introduction Commentary*, that "therefore we represent that 'Thatness is realized' (only) designatively, and actually there is not knowing of a something by a someone, since both the knowable and the knowers are actually unproduced"; first of all, it is that the representation of the realization of Thatness which differentiates between the subject, intuition, and the object, Thatness, is merely according to conventional cognition, and not according to that intuition itself. "The knower is unproduced" means that it is without intrinsically real production, and so the whole process becomes like water being poured into water.

As for the statement that "since mind and mental functions do not penetrate into Thatness, the object of intuition, it is realized only by the Body," it means that the objective to be realized is Thatness, the subjective means of realizing that is the subjective intuition, and the realizer, or knower, is the Body of Perfect Beatitude.[87] As for the way in which that Body realizes that Thatness it is by the process of elimination of the constructive thoughts constituting mind and mental functions, as explained above, which can be known by his statement in the *Commentary* that explains that the Body which realizes Thatness is free of all mind and mental functions, having the intrinsic reality of peace.

(The idea that) the Buddhas does not see the aggregates etc. is a repudiation of phenomenological omniscience and of all phenomenal objects, since "existent" and "not known by the Buddha" are mutually exclusive statements. Therefore, phenomenal objects necessarily appear to phenomenological omniscience, and they do so by arising in that (ultimate) cognition, since the system of this master does not advocate aspectless cognition. Among the apparent phenomenal objects there are two kinds: one kind, such as the Buddha's signs and marks, which is not a deception by the instinctual misknowledge; and a second kind, such as the impure animate and inanimate things, which is a deception by instinctual misknowledge. The first of these kinds is not eliminated on the stage of Buddhahood; the second kind is eliminated, since its cause is eliminated. As for the way in which they appear, when the Buddha's signs and marks appear to a person who has not abandoned misknowledge, they appear to have intrinsic identifiability when they actually do not, but not for the reason that the objects themselves arise by the power of instinctual misknowledge, but they appear so by the power of the subject's being deceived by instinctual misknowledge. And in that case, they do not appear so (intrinsically identifiable) to that subjectivity merely according to the fact that they appear that way to some other person, but from that person's very own point of view. On the other hand, in the phenomenologically omniscient intuition of the Buddha, things appear (also) according to (the cognition of persons) who have not abandoned misknowledge, where forms and sounds etc. appear to be intrinsically identifiable when they are not, but they appear so to the Buddha only from the point of view of their appearance to such persons deceived by misknowledge, and do not appear to the Buddha from his own point of view without depending on their appearing so to other persons. Therefore, the appearance of unreal forms etc. as intrinsically real also arises in the Buddha's omniscience according to their appearance for those subject to misknowledge, but without depending on such an appearance to such a person, they are not cognized as appearing in that way from a Buddha's own point of view. Therefore, there is no fault here that the Buddha's omniscience becomes erroneous by being aware of such appearances, for, even though such intuition does not arise from deception, their awareness is there by the key point of his intuition's necessarily having awareness of all objective knowables. Therefore, according to phenomenal omniscience's own point of view all phenomena appear as selfless and realityless, like false illusions, and do not appear as real; and their appearance in that intuition with the aspect of their appearance to persons subject to misknowledge is merely due to their arisal with a true appearance to other persons.

Nagarjuna states, in the *Philosophical Sixty*, that "Those who are expert in phenomena perceive impermanent phenomena as collections of deceptive things, selfless, empty, and isolated," and Chandrakirti comments that "they see them in such a way since they have accomplished the ultimate." Likewise, Jñana garbha states, in the *Two Realities*, that "The Omniscient One directly sees all relative productions just the way they appear, devoid of any imagined objectivity." Thus, the phenomenological omniscience directly sees things in reality; and again, "When he does not experience subject, object, and essence, because of his firm abiding in the non-arisal of any signs, he does not arise." Thus, (the Buddha) never again arises from the samadhi wherein dualistic appearance is eradicated. Thus he speaks in both ways in these two explanations.

However, although it must appear contradictory to assert both (that he sees only non-dually and that he sees things individually) and not one or the other, as long as one does not understand, they are not in fact contradictory. For, although the vision of Thatness and the intuition aware of all phenomena are one actuality, depending on their respective objects, they can function as rational cognition and as conventional cognition without the slightest contradiction. Understanding this point depends on properly understanding how, although at the time of the elementary view, rational cognition and conventional validating cognition occur with different modes of discovering when operating on a single considered thing, they have not the slightest contradiction to one another. At the time of fruition (in Buddhahood), when the two intuitions encounter their objects, if you understand well not only just that (they are not contradictory), but also how each validating cognition applies to the object, you can also understand how even though the two objects are not separately ascertained, the two subjectivities do not operate on a single basis. And this should be understood as an extremely fine point concerning the identification of the two realities.[88]

The Categories of the Ultimate

The ultimate reality is differentiated according to the *Introduction Commentary's* statement, "If emptiness is extensively differentiated, there are the sixteen emptinesses. Its medium differentiation is into thing-emptiness, nothing-emptiness, self-emptiness, and other-emptiness. And most briefly, (it is differentiated into) the two personal selflessness, and phenomenal selflessness," Other treatises mention two categories, the actual ultimate and the corresponding ultimate. For example, Kamalashila in the *Middle Way Illumination* states that "this non-production is termed 'ultimate' and 'corresponding ultimate'" but it is actually not so, since actually the ultimate transcends all fabrications." And Shantarakshita states in the *Ornament of the Middle Way*[89] that "the ultimate reality is called 'ultimate' and 'corresponding' but really it is free from the whole mass of fabrications." Jñana garbha also speaks the same way in the *Two Realities*. Further, the *Two Realities Commentary* and the *Ornament* explain the negation of production etc. in the ultimate as the superficial reality.

In regard to the meaning of this, many old-time scholars considered this to refer to two ultimate realities, one verbal and one not verbal, the former being the emptiness that is the negation of the production etc. of form etc. ultimately, which is a designative ultimate reality with the nature of the superficial reality; and the latter being not an object of knowledge, since it could not be the object of any sort of cognition whatsoever. But that is not the meaning of these statements; it is rather explained as follows: while it is necessary that the objective reality should be called "ultimate" there are many explanations in which the subjective rational conviction is so termed. For example, in the *Two Realities,* "reason is ultimate, since it is not deceived" and in the *Illumination of the Middle Way,* "those statements that things are utterly unproduced ultimately," have the following meaning; the wisdoms arising from authentic learning, reflection, and meditation, since they are non-erroneous subjectivities are called 'ultimate' because they are the ultimate of this." There are two kinds of rational cognitions the non-conceptual intuition of the holy equipoise, without conceptual thought, and the rational cognition that encounters Thatness depending on a reason, with conceptual thought, and so forth. Bhavaviveka's explanation in *Blaze of Reason* of "ultimate" as both non-conceptual intuition and as the wisdom that corresponds to that, and Kamalashila's explanation, in the *Illumination,* of the two intimates, have the same intention. Therefore, the meaning of these treatises is not a differentiation of the objective ultimate only without differentiating the subjectivities (involved).

Now, the first (of the two kinds) is the penetration into Thatness, and is the actual ultimate, as it can cut off instantaneously with regard to its object mental fabrications both of truth and of dualistic appearance; it is what is meant by "transcending all fabrications." The second one, while it can terminate fabrications of truth with regard to its object, cannot terminate fabrications of dualistic appearance, and it is called "corresponding ultimate" since it corresponds in form to the transcendental ultimate. Similarly, the two modes should be explained with regard to the ultimate which is the object for the negation of ultimate production etc. of form etc. The objective emptiness according to the non-conceptual rational cognition is the actual ultimate free of both kinds of fabrications while (the same thing) according to the conceptual rational cognition being free of only one kind of fabrication, is not the actual ultimate free of both kinds of fabrication, yet it is not said in general not to be the actual ultimate reality. Therefore, except that it is free of all fabrications of dualism according to a certain type of cognition, it is not possible for that truth-emptiness to be free of all fabrications of appearance, and therefore it is not the meaning of the treatises that for it to be ultimate reality it must be free of all fabrications of dualistic appearance.

Therefore, the Illusionists'[90] claim that the coordination of the ground aggregates etc. and the truth-devoid-appearance just the object achieved by inferential rational cognition, is the ultimate reality, refers to the corresponding ultimate and not the (actual) ultimate reality. Although the perception of freedom from true sameness and difference establishes the perception of truthlessness of sprouts etc., that is not the object for such achievement for a thoughtful person who has not (yet) ceased his doubts as to whether that object exists or not in truth, and that reason does not serve as a genuine reason for the termination of his doubts. The *Illumination* states that both reason and probandum of freedom from (true) sameness and difference are merely exclusions, stating that it is the same whatever is taken as reason, either non-sameness, non-difference, or not both of them. This is not interpreting them as implicative negations, as one, can understand from the examples used therein, and as that is certainly not the position of Shantarakshita, Kamalashila, and Haribhadra. In regard to the exclusion of fabrications of the negatee in appearance, taking it as the latter of the two possibilities, exclusion or determination, and asserting that ultimate reality is merely the object encompassed by inference—

none of the great Madhyamikas take this position. You should understand in this way the detailed explanation of the systems of these masters, as I have given it in the extensive *Path of Enlightenment*.

Janagarbha, in the *Two Realities Commentary*, after explaining the negation of production etc. as corresponding ultimate, continues, "When others hold only the 'perfect,' it should be etymologized as 'also pure,' (meaning that this expression for the ultimate is itself but an analogy). If we analyze this, it is merely superficial. Why? Since the negatee (truth-status) is not existent, it is clear that there is no negation ultimately."[91] Here, the "others," that is the Idealists, assert that they have truly established emptiness which is the negation that negates the phenomenal self in the negation ground. But his own system does not consider that the phenomenal self is present as the negatee, and so he says that the negation which negates that is not really achieved. Therefore, his statement that the negation of ultimate production etc. is superficial, means that it is superficially existent, and does not show that it is (itself) the superficial reality.

Further, from the same text, he answers the objection that "true production should actually be perceived, but it is not, and so it is like the false superficial, and so the negation of true production etc. is also the false superficial, since the phenomenon that is the negation ground should be perceived but it is not," by saying that "it is not that it is not perceived, since it is not different from the actuality of the phenomenon." Here, when blue etc. is perceived, its truth-emptiness is explained as being apparent; for, although the mere negative exclusion which is truthlessness does not appear to the visual consciousness etc., he intends it to be an implicative negation, such a thing being superficial by definition, and so it is not prevented from being the ultimate reality which is the emptiness that is the mere exclusion of truth. Shantarakshita, in the *Ornament*, says that the negation of ultimate production etc. is included in the genuine superficial, being explained as there through its correspondence with the ultimate reality. He also mentions that the ultimate is the abandonment of the entire network of fabrications concerning being and nothingness.

In regard to this network of fabrications, Jñana garbha states in his *Two Realities,* that "Therefore, 'it is not empty, it is not non-empty, it neither exists nor does not exist; it is not non-produced and it is not produced,' such things and so forth the Lord proclaimed." And furthermore, "Why? That is free of fabrications. Just that is free of the whole network of constructive thoughts." Here he explains the "network of fabrications" as the network of conceptual thoughts. That is abandoned according to the direct realization of Thatness. That is the actual ultimate. And what is not like that, rational cognition with its object, is the former corresponding (ultimate), as previously explained. Further, in regard to the negation of true production etc., there are both the rational cognition that negates it and the inferential object both, and one should understand the method of including it in the genuine superficial on that basis. And that method of explaining the freedom from the network of assertive fabrications about the two realities is very useful in many contexts.

The Number of the Two Realities

Of necessity, when one determines that something is a false and deceptive thing, one has excluded that thing from being non-deceptive. Deceptive and non-deceptive are therefore mutually exclusive contradictories. Thus they apply to all knowables pervasively through their mutual exclusion, and there is no third option. Thereby one should understand the certification of the number of the two realities.

(The Buddha) stated in the *Meeting of Father and Son,*[92] "Thus the Transcendent One realizes the two realities, the superficial and the ultimate. Knowable objects are all included in these superficial and ultimate realities." He states that all knowable objects comprise the two realities. He also states in the *Holy Thatness-Teaching Samadhi*[93], "other than the superficial and the ultimate, there is no third reality." This is a clear statement of the certification of the number of the two realities. If you understand the differentiation of the two realities, you will not become confused about the Sage's teachings, and if you do not understand them, you will not understand the reality of the Doctrine. Further, you must understand it according to the determinations of the Protector Nagarjuna. Chandrakirti says in the *Introduction* that it is very important for those seeking liberation to be expert in the two realities: "there is no method for (attaining) peace for those who stray from the path of Master Nagarjunapada. They fail in both the superficial and ultimate realities, and failing there, there is no attainment of liberation. Conventional reality serves as the technique, and ultimate reality is the result of that technique. Who does not understand the differentiation between them gets involved in false paths, under the influence of wrong notions."

The Categories of Transcendent Insight

When you discover the view that realizes the two selflessnesses from the above teaching of the necessary conditions for transcendent insight, you should meditate on transcendent insight.

How many transcendent insights are there?

Here, I have not mainly taught the high stages of transcendent insight, but have emphasized the transcendent insight to be meditated by common individuals. To completely analyze that type of transcendent insight, there are the insights of the four realities, the insights of the three doors, and the insights of the six investigations.

The insights of the four realities are stated in the *Elucidation of the Intent* as the four, "discernment" and so forth. Among them, "discernment" takes the contents of reality as its object, and "investigation" takes the nature of reality as its object. The first contains thorough examination and thorough analysis, and the second contains examination and analysis, since they (respectively) discern coarse and subtle objects. The identification of these four is stated in the *Stages of the Disciples* and in the *Instruction in Transcendent Wisdom*.

The insights of the three doors are stated in the *Elucidation of the Intent* as (the insights) arisen from signs, arisen from thorough investigation, and arisen from individual discrimination. As for the description of these three taking the import of selflessness as an example, first selflessness is identified, then taken as object, and then its significance is imprinted in the mind without engaging in repeated determinations. The second (stage of insight) consists of determinations in order to ascertain what was not previously certain. The third (stage of insight) is the analysis as above of the identified import.

The (insights of the) six investigations are the thorough investigations and individual discriminations of meaning, phenomenon, nature, orientation, time, and reason. (Insight) investigating meaning investigates (whether) 'the meaning of this expression is this'; investigating phenomena considers 'this is internal' or 'this is external,' etc.; investigating nature, it investigates whether 'this is a particular nature or a general nature,' or 'this is a common nature or an uncommon nature'; investigating orientation, it investigates the faults and disadvantages of negative orientations and the virtues and benefits of positive orientations; investigating time, it investigates "such happened in the past, such happens in the present, and such will happen in the future." (Insight) investigating reason, investigates through the four types of reasoning; it investigates relational reasoning by viewing how effects occur depending on causes and conditions, considering specifically the objects of superficial and ultimate realities; it investigates functional reasoning by investigating how things perform their specific functions, such as fire by burning, considering "this is the phenomenon, this is the activity, and this is the function it accomplishes"; it investigates logical reasoning by investigating how things are established without contradicting validating cognitions, considering whether "this is supported by perceptual, inferential, or scripturally testimonial validating cognitions or not"; and it investigates natural reasoning by investigating the commonsensical natures, the inconceivable natures, and the ultimate natures of things such as the heat of fire and the wetness of water, respecting those natures and not considering other (possibilities). The presentation of these (investigative insights) as six fold is to be understood by the yogi, but they can definitely be included in three categories, as concerned with verbal meanings, with phenomenal objects, and with ultimate natures. The first investigative (insight) is in terms of the first (concern), phenomenal

investigation and particular nature investigation are concerned with
the second, and general nature investigative (insight) and the other
three are concerned with the third. The first-explained four insights
operate through three doors, and manifest six modes of investigation,
and therefore the (insights of the) three doors and the (insights of the)
six investigations are included in the (insights of the) four realities.

The four attitudes explained above (in the quiescence section)
such as the 'balancing' attitude, are explained in the *Stages of Disciples*
as being common to both quiescence and insight, and thus there are
also four conscious attitudes in insight.

How to Meditate on Transcendent Insight
Meaning of Meditating on Insight Based on Quiescence

Just as (the Buddha) states in the *Elucidation of the Intent* that having
first achieved quiescence one meditates on insight, the treatises of the
Holy Maitreya, Asanga in his *Bodhisattva Stages* and *Disciple Stages*,
Bhavaviveka, Shantideva, Kamalashila in his three *Stage of Meditation*,
and Ratnakarashanti in his *Instruction in Transcendent Wisdom*, and
so on, many treatises also state this. The intention of these statements
is not that first of all one should generate a quiescence that perceives
any kind of object, not oriented to the meaning of selflessness, and
then subsequently one's practice oriented toward selflessness becomes
transcendent insight; because quiescence and insight are not
differentiated by the objects they take up; because Ratnakarashanti
explains in the *Instruction* that one first generates quiescence oriented
toward the reality of emptiness of subject-object-duality and
subsequently one generates insight through analytic meditation on
the same object; and because Arya Asanga, when he explains insight
concerned with the contents of reality, states that after generating
quiescence there is a meditation of insight based on it concerned with
the levels of peace[94] which moreover is said to be a path common to
non-Buddhists and Buddhists as well as to common individuals and
holy persons.

Therefore, when one newly achieves quiescence, not having achieved it previously, it is precisely achieved by placing the mind in one point toward any object whatsoever, and is not properly practiced through repeated analysis of its chosen object. It will be achieved if practiced in the former way, and it is impossible to achieve if practiced in the latter way. However, one who has already achieved quiescence in the former way can certainly continue to practice merely his focused meditation as before, but if he practices an analytic meditation through the specific discrimination of wisdom whether in the context of phenomenological or ontological concerns, he can derive ultimately a distinctive one pointed samadhi. Thus, since that (practice) seems to achieve a specially powerful one pointed samadhi which the former (practice) cannot, analytic meditation is recommended.

As for the way of practice, it is the procedure of first seeking quiescence and then, based on that, subsequently practicing insight, and that is the reason why quiescence and insight are differentiated by their different procedures in practice, even though they may both take the same object such as selflessness. Especially, since the meditation of the two transcendent insights, that concerned with the levels of peace through specific discernment of the faults and virtues of the higher and lower realms, and that concerned with selflessness cultivated through analysis with the wisdom of the specific discrimination of the meaning of selflessness, is (indispensably) necessary to generate a firm and intense certainty, it has the greater power to abandon specific abandonees, (defilements and obscurations). As for the phenomenologically concerned transcendent insight, it is not only the meditation concerned with levels of peace which abandons the manifest afflictions, but is also stated by Ratnakarashanti in the *Instruction* to be the analytic meditation which discerns the nature of the eighteen elements, by which illustration one can understand the other insights which are meditated by distinguishing phenomenal objects.

Although Ratnakarashanti explains in the *Instruction* that one must generate quiescence and insight on the stage of yoga oriented toward the phenomenological before generating quiescence and insight oriented toward the ontological, here, following the view of Shantideva and Kamalashila etc., insight is generated after first generating whatever sort of quiescence, and I mean here the transcendent insight oriented ontologically (toward ultimata reality).

Vehicles in terms of which this System applies

Well, that gradual procedure of generating such quiescence and insight, is it in terms of Individual Vehicle or Universal Vehicle, or in terms of Sutra or Tantra?

This system is common both to the Individual Vehicle of the Disciples and Self-Enlightened Sages and the Universal Vehicle of the Transcendences, also being common to all four of the (main theoretical schools)[95] It also holds likewise for the three (lower) divisions of Tantra Vehicle; I have explained already the positions of the different Tantras and their great elucidators in the *Stages of the Tantric Path.* As for the Unexcelled Yoga (Tantras), the *Secret Union*[96] also uses Ratnakarashanti's statement in the *Instruction,* "if you examine your own mind, all things abide within it. This teaching resides in the Vajra of Space; there is no phenomenon and no reality." The *Union* also explains the orientation toward mind-only, as taught in the *Visit to Lanka:* "depending on mind alone, do not imagine any external objects"; the orientation toward Suchness, and the teaching of the three stages of the yoga of non-appearance. It also appears to explain as above the procedure of practice of quiescence and insight through focused meditation and analytic meditation in the first two stages. Thus it accepts a similar procedure of generating (quiescence and insight) in the mental process oriented toward reality. My own interpretation is that in the context of the Unexcelled Yoga the procedure of generating the understanding of the view must be practiced according to the Middle Way treatises. In practice, however, although there are conscious attitudes analytic of Thatness sometimes during the aftermath (intuitions) of the creation stage and the perfection stage, and although the perfection stage yogi who has achieved the ability to concentrate on the essentials in the body must definitely meditate through concentration on top of his view, when cultivating Thatness in equipoise, there is no practice of the analytic meditation of transcendent insight as explained in other treatises. Therefore, in that context you should not employ one-pointed reality-meditation upon one's view in alternation with employment of analytic meditation. But this is not the context to clearly teach the reasons as to why it is enough to practice in that way (placing one-pointedness upon a correct view), so I have only explained the reasons why one should do the opposite in other paths.

Actual way to Meditate on Insight based on Quiescence

If you do not discover the view of selflessness, no matter what method of meditation you practice, your meditation will not abide on the import of Thatness. So, you must discover that view. And even if you have an understanding of the view, if you do not remember the view when you meditate on Thatness and focus your meditation upon that, you will have no meditation on reality. Further, if after each new session of analysis of the view you focus your mind on not holding anything at all, it is not the cultivation of reality of Thatness. Further, practicing by remembering that view and just focusing upon it is no more than the above practice of quiescence and the meaning of the treatises is not just to practice insight in alternation with that. Therefore, you should practice through the specific analysis by means of wisdom of the impart of selflessness, as explained above.

If you practice analytic meditation by itself, the quiescence you previously generated will decline, so you should practice analytic meditation mounted on the horse of quiescence, now and then blending in periods of focused meditation. Moreover, if you practice analytic meditation often, your focusing decreases, so you should often return to focused meditation, engaging in abiding by itself. If the focused meditation is overdone you, become averse to analysis or you ignore the functioning of your analysis, and your mind becomes obsessed with one-pointed abiding, and so you should often return to analytic meditation. Your meditation has the greatest power if you practice quiescence and insight in balanced proportion, so that is how you should practice.

Kamalashila says in the last *Meditation Stages,* "When you meditate on insight and wisdom comes very strongly, quiescence becomes weaker, and the mind becomes agitated like a candleflame in the wind, so reality will not be experienced very clearly. At that time, you should meditate on quiescence. If quiescence becomes too strong, then, like a man who has fallen asleep, you will not experience reality very clearly; therefore, you should then meditate on insight." Thus, it is not correct to hold that all thoughts occurring in analytic practice are substantivistic sign-habits which are truth-habits, and therefore terminate them; because, as I have repeatedly established, truth-habit-thought is only one tendency of thought. If you decide that rational refutations overwhelm whatever is held by discriminating thought, this becomes the nihilistic repudiation that has overextended the rational negatee, and it is not the meaning of the Scriptures, as I have established. Yet you may still think that, even if you do not assert that with regard to other subjects of concern, whatever is held in cognition regarding ultimate nature is (merely the product of) substantivistic sign-habits which conceptualize truth(-status) in things. In fact, those (sign-habits) are the fault of a defective habit pattern (of mind), and do not (function) with regard to all objects cognized; because it is stated that the egocentric individual desiring liberation must investigate reality from many scriptural and rational perspectives.

Again, you may think that the meditation on Thatness, as it is for the purpose of generating non-discrimination, is not produced by analytic discrimination, since cause and effect must correspond (in their natures). The Lord himself clearly answered this (qualm), in the *Kashyapa Chapter.*[97] "Kashyapa, for example, when you rub two sticks together, they produce fire and are themselves completely consumed in the process. In the same way, Kashyapa, authentic analytic discrimination produces the faculty of holy wisdom, and, being produced, it serves to consume that authentic discrimination itself." Here he clearly states that the holy wisdom is generated by discrimination.

Similarly, Kamalashila states in his middle *Meditation Stages,* "when the yogi analyzes with wisdom and does not cognize as ultimately certain any intrinsic objectivity of anything, he enters the samadhi free of discriminative thought, and he realizes the utter non-existence of the intrinsic objectivity of anything. When someone does not meditate with wisdom by means of specific discrimination concerning the intrinsic objectivity of things, but merely meditates exclusively on the abandonment of all conscious attitudes, he never eliminates that (particular) discrimination of that (absence of mental function), and he will never realize the utter non-existence of intrinsic objectivity, since he is devoid of the illumination of wisdom. Thus, from the authentic specific discrimination arises the fire of the true wisdom of reality, like fire arisen from rubbing-sticks, which then burns the sticks of discrimination. This is what the Lord stated." Otherwise, it would never happen that the uncontaminated would arise from the contaminated, the transcendental from the mundane, a Buddha from a living being, a holy person from an alienated individual and so forth. For in all these cases the effect is dissimilar from the cause.

Nagarjuna states in the *Disclosure of the Spirit of Enlightenment,* that "where discriminations occur, how could there be emptiness? The Transcendent Lords do not perceive any mind in the form of discriminated and discrimination; where there is discrimination and discriminated, there is no enlightenment." But here he is teaching that enlightenment will not be attained when truth-status is perceived in discriminated and discrimination, and does not negate discriminative wisdom nor the mere function of discriminated and discrimination. Otherwise, it would contradict his extensive determination of Thatness through many discriminative analyses in that text, and also (if mere discrimination were meant) their not being seen by Buddha means their nonexistence. Again Nagarjuna states in the same text, "Emptiness, called 'non-production,' 'emptiness,' and 'selflessness,' if it is contemplated as anything less, it does not serve as meditation on that." This does not refute meditation that takes emptiness and selflessness intrinsically unproduced as its object, but refutes meditation on an inferior emptiness, the lesser nature that is conceived by holding those (emptinesses) as having themselves truth-status. As he states in the *Transcendental Praise,* "As you taught the nectar of emptiness to cure all mental constructions, you put down those who adhere to it (as true in itself)." Likewise, he said in the *Jewel Rosary* that "thus neither self nor selflessness is apprehended in reality. Therefore the Great Sage eliminated the views of self and selflessness." Both self and selflessness have no objective status in reality, and so the view that holds both as truly existing is eliminated. But this does not refute the view of selflessness; because, as in the previous quote from the *Rebuttal of Objections,* if it is not the case that there is realitylessness of intrinsically real status, then intrinsically real status would become existent.

Likewise, the Buddha's statements in the *Encyclopedia* that "If the Bodhisattva presumes that 'this aggregate is empty,' then he is involved with sign and has no faith in the unproduced condition," and in the *Great Mother* that "If you treat form as 'empty' and 'selfless,' then you are involved in signs and are not involved in the transcendence of wisdom," are referring to the holding of truth-status in emptiness etc. Otherwise, it would have been illogical to say "no faith in the unproduced condition," because faith also would become involvement in signs, and also because it would contradict the statements in the same Scripture that "things should be understood as lacking intrinsic reality, and this is the engagement in the transcendent wisdom"; and "when wisdom ceases the created, the uncreated, and good and evil, when not even an atom is apprehended, that is considered the transcendence of wisdom throughout the universes"; and from the *King of Samadhis* as well: "Who discerns selflessness in things and meditates on that discernment, that serves as cause for the attainment of the fruit of Nirvana; no other cause will bring forth peace"; and from the *Heart of Transcendent Wisdom,* when Shariputra asks, "when a Bodhisattva wants to engage in the profound transcendent wisdom, how should he educate himself?" Avalokiteshvara replies that "he should truly regard these five aggregates as empty with respect to any intrinsic reality."

Therefore, according to Nagarjuna's statement in the *Ultimate Realm Praise,* "The principle that serves to cultivate the supreme mind is intrinsic realitylessness," and "while the habits of 'I' and 'mine' are constructing the external world, the experiencing of the two forms of selflessness will exterminate the seeds of existence"; and Chandrakirti's statement in the *Introduction,* "thus by the view of the emptiness of self and property, the yogi will become liberated"; so one should understand (the question). And one should cultivate the continuum of the certainty about selflessness and realitylessness.

Kamalashila explains in the first *Meditation Stages* that "the meaning of the statement of the *Spell for Entering Non-Discrimination,*[98] 'through the lack of any thoughtful attitude, the signs of "form" etc. are abandoned,' is intended as being that 'lack of thoughtful attitude' means the non-apprehension through analytic wisdom, and not just the mere absence of any thoughtful attitude, since the substantivistic adherence to form etc. from beginningless time has not been abandoned by mere lack of thoughtful attitudes, as in the case of one absorbed in the trance of unconsciousness." Therefore, the scriptural statements about abandoning substantivistic sign-habits through meditating on the absence of thoughtful attitudes are explained as intending the realization through investigation by proper analytic wisdom that not even an atom is apprehended by the objective orientation of the truth habits. He further explains in the middle *Meditation Stages,* "If one seeks what is the mind, one realizes emptiness. If one investigates thoroughly what is that mind that realizes, one realizes its objective reality is also emptiness. Through such realization, one enters the yoga of signlessness." This teaches that one enters the reality of signlessness by first employing analytic investigation, which very clearly demonstrates that it is impossible to enter the reality of non-discrimination by mere emptiness of thoughtful attitudes and by not analyzing the objectivity of phenomena through wisdom.

Thus that statement from the *Jewel Cloud* (that Kamalashila quoted) explains in that way, and he continues by saying that if the view of Thatness is not found through proper analysis, it is impossible to enter non-discrimination concerning the import of Thatness. He further explains in the final *Stages of Meditation* that "The statements of inconceivability and transcendentality etc. are in order to refute claims of realization of the profound meaning through mere learning and reflection, showing that those (profound imports) are for the discriminating inner realization of holy persons and are inconceivable etc. for others, and also to refute the improper thinking that holds the import of the profound as (itself) having truth-status. They do not refute the proper analytic investigation by discriminating wisdom, since such refutation would contradict a great many references and reasonings. Although that (analysis) is constructive thought in actuality, it is also a proper conscious attitude, and it causes non-discriminating intuition to arise. Thus if you want that intuition, you should rely on that (analytic process)." These statements of his all refute the claim of the Chinese Master that you cannot discover the view that determines Thatness by relying on scriptural references and reasonings, but you will realize Thatness by absorbing yourself in the utter lack of thoughtful attitudes.[99] It is extremely important to understand these well.

These ways of meditation occur also in the old instructions on the stages of the path. Potoba says, in his *Collected Sayings*,[100] that "Some say that you should rationally determine intrinsic realitylessness at the time of study and reflection, but meditate only on non-discrimination at the time of meditation. But such leads to an irrelevant emptiness, which will not serve as a remedy, since it is meditated as something else. Therefore, even at the time of meditation, one should discriminatingly investigate the absence of sameness and difference, or relativity, whatever you are used to, and also fix yourself slightly in non-discrimination. If you meditate like that, it remedies the afflictions. If you want to follow the unique Lord (Atisha) and if you want to engage in transcendent wisdom's method, (you should know) that is the method of meditating on wisdom. Further, if you practice personal selflessness, you should penetrate it by that way." And Atisha said, "Who understood emptiness" Chandrakirti is the disciple of Nagarjuna, who saw the truth of reality, as predicted by the Transcendent Lord. The special instruction descended through him brings one to the realization of the truth of ultimate reality." The way of that teaching was explained by Atisha in the *Instruction in the Middle Way*[101] and, as Master Kamalashila's intention seems similar, this (view) seems widespread. Thus, for the practice of transcendent insight, you should understand from the above the reliance on the six preparatory practices, and the methods of practice in the actual sessions, after the sessions, between the sessions, and especially how to practice free of depression and excitement.

Criterion for Attainment of Insight through Meditation

If you meditate through investigation by discriminating wisdom in that way, until you have achieved the above explained ecstatic adeptness, you have a simulated transcendent insight. Once that ecstatic adeptness is generated, you have the genuine transcendent insight. The actuality and method of generating adeptness is as already explained. Further, this must occur without weakening of quiescence and there is an adeptness developed from that, so merely having adeptness is not enough. Then what is? If you can develop ecstatic adeptness through the power of the practice of analytic meditation itself, that then becomes transcendent insight. This is the same whether it involves the transcendent insight oriented toward the contents of reality or the transcendent insight oriented toward the nature of reality. As Maitreya stated in the *Elucidation of the Intent,* "Lord! Until the Bodhisattva has attained the physical and mental adeptness, what is his thoughtful attitude that focuses thought on those well considered things taken as inner images for his object of samadhi?' 'Maitreya! It is not transcendent insight. It should be called a coordinated attitude that simulates transcendent insight.' "And as Ratnakarashanti says in the *Instruction in Transcendent Wisdom,* "Who has attained that physical and mental adeptness should focus on reality, and should analyze with willed attention on the considered meaning of reality as the object of samadhi (held) as an inner image. As long as physical and mental adeptness has not been generated, it is a thoughtful attitude that simulates transcendent insight, but once they are generated, it becomes transcendent insight."

If (insight) can by its own power develop adeptness, it can also develop one pointedness of mind. But this development of quiescence by the power of discriminating analytic meditation itself is a virtue of having previously achieved quiescence. Thus when one who has (already) thoroughly achieved quiescence practices analytic meditation, his quiescence becomes even more consummately intense, and so you should not think that the practice of analytic meditation through fine discrimination will lead to a lessened share of concentration.

Way of Integration of Quiescence and Insight

As explained in the contexts of the criteria for the achievement of both of them, you cannot integrate quiescence and insight if you have not attained both of them, so both must definitely be attained in order to integrate them. Sometimes it happens that integration is attained from the beginning of the attainment of transcendent insight. The pattern of that is, by the power of practicing analytic meditation relying on previous quiescence, it becomes integration (of quiescence and insight) if one has attained the thoughtful attitude which naturally applies itself without conscious motivation, as explained above in the quiescence section. As Asanga explains in the *Stages of Disciples*, "Just how are quiescence and insight mingled in equal integration and what is the path of the integration of quiescence and insight? To explain, when the nine calm states of mind are attained through equanimity, one strives to discriminate between phenomena with the higher wisdom, stabilizing oneself in that achievement of samadhi. At that time, one enters the path of discrimination between phenomena spontaneously without any effort, and one's transcendent insight becomes like the path of quiescence, without any conscious motivation perfectly pure, and it becomes completely purified, harmonious with quiescence, and combined with blissful experience." Therefore, it is called "entrance into the balanced mingling of quiescence and insight," and the "path penetrating the integration of quiescence and insight." Kamalashila also states in the final *Stages of Meditation*, "when depression and excitement are eliminated, and one is naturally engaged in balanced absorption, the mind emerges with extreme clarity in focus on Thatness—then one relaxes one's effort and stabilizes oneself in equanimity. You should recognize that this is the attainment of the path of integration of quiescence and insight." According to these statements, this (integration) occurs after achieving the actual transcendent insight.

Ratnakarashanti adds from the *Instruction in Transcendent Wisdom*, "after that, one perceives reality as an image occurring in reflective thought. In that very mind, when both (quiescence and insight) are experienced through the continuation of uninterrupted and unobstructed conscious attention, that is called the path of integrated quiescence and insight, Therein, quiescence and insight are combined and connected, mutually embracing each other in function." Here, "unobstructed" indicates that, without needing to concentrate on non-discrimination, that very analytic meditation itself leaves the fabrications of analysis and enters the freedom from discriminative thought by its own force. "Both are experienced" means that one experiences both a quiescence which is the perception of the image of non-discrimination and an insight which is a perception of the images of discriminative thought. "Through the continuation" means that analytic insight and quiescence which focuses on the conclusion of the analysis are not simultaneous, but, at the time of the quiescence, the actual quiescence derived by the force of analysis, both transcendent insight which discerns phenomena apprehended in their real nature, and quiescence which is the samadhi which stays stably in one point on that reality, function in coordination.

At such a time, quiescence and insight function in a balanced combination. For that, one must attain meditative realization, so, from within a state of undisturbed flow of thoughtlessness of firm stability one can gently analyze the import of selflessness, like a minnow parting about on the surface of unruffled still waters. Now, this combination is considered a simulated integration of quiescence and insight, and not the actual integration.

Such a way of the integration of quiescence and insight must be understood according to the teachings of the original treatises, and one should not rely on other explanations that presume it to be otherwise. And you should understand from my extensive *Stages of the Path* the extensive details (of the teachings) of the "stages of the path of enlightenment" (tradition) on the conclusive analyses through reasoning, the supportive scriptural references, and the processes of meditation.

Written by the Easterner Tsongkhapa Losang Drakpae Pal at Ganden Riwo Monastery.

PART IV

Praises, Prayers, and a Mystic Conversation

It is well known that Tsongkhapa had a special connection with Mañjushri, in fact can be thought of as an emanation of that great Boddhisattva. At least, he always salutes Mañjushri as his Special Deity and Guardian Guru, as above in the *Destiny* poem, and his main instructions on the profound emptiness came directly from Mañjushri. The present hymn was composed probably in 1394 during his long retreat at O'de Gungyal hermitage in Ol Kha, some time after he was granted the marvellous vision of Mañjushri sitting before him, with his sword of wisdom connecting them, the handle in Mañjushri's heart and the tip in Tsongkhapas, with the stream of rainbow nectar of the five wisdoms flowing down the blade. Or it is possible that it was written in 1398, when he again returned to this favorite hermitage, the time he wrote the *Praise for Relativity*. It is a valuable work, as inspired by his constant direct visions of the Bodhisattva.

The second chapter is a praise of Maitreya, known as *Brahma's Diadem,* which was written at the behest of both Vajrapani and Mañjushri, with the Great Presence of Maitreya at Dzing Ji in mind. After Tsongkhapa came out of his long retreat with his eight companions in 1395, their first act was to start a movement to refurbish the great statue of Maitreya in that temple. This was one of Tsongkhapa's four major deeds, and the consecration was accompanied by numerous miraculous signs witnessed by the multitudes that attended. Tsongkhapa himself was sometimes considered an emanation of Maitreya as well as Mañjushri, as by the Nyingma Master, Lhobrag Namkha Gyaltsen, who wrote, "Protector Maitreya, the future Captain of living beings, considered the beings of this decadent age with His great compassion, and visited us as Tsongkhapa, the glory of the Land of Snows—I invoke the feet of the glorious Guru." But in this poem, Tsongkhapa writes under the inspiration of Mañjushri, to Maitreya as the future light of the world, presently watching over us from his heavenly eyrie in Tushita.

The third chapter is a *Prayer for Rebirth in Sukhavati* the western pure land of the Buddha Amitabha, so famous especially in Chinese and Japanese Buddhism. It was also written in 1395 and 1396, during the work on the Dzing Ji temple, also under the inspiration of Mañjushri.

After the great dedication at Dzing Ji, Je Tsongkhapa set out with his close followers to the south, thinking strongly of making a pilgrimage to visit the Holy Land of India. On the way, he was invited for a visit by the great Nyingma Master, Lhobrag Khenchen Namkha Gyaltsen, also known as Chagdorpa, due to his special affinity for and mystic communion with the Bodhisattva Vajrapani. Chagdorpa was perceived as Vajrapani himself by Tsongkhapa, when he was teaching Tsongkhapa a number of important teachings on the Tantras, as well as transmitting some important Stages of the Path lineages that had descended through the Kadampas. And Chagdorpa saw Tsongkhapa as Mañjushri himself, when he received some teachings from the younger saint. The *Dialogue* included here is between the Khenchen and the Bodhisattva Vajrapani, in the presence of Tsongkhapa, referred to by a Sanskrit name, Matibhadrashri, although it appears that, as with Mañjushri and Umapa at first, Tsongkhapa cannot see or hear Vajrapani directly. The prophecies are quite interesting, especially as they seem to bear on the present predicament of Tibet.

All these chapters I have translated myself. My thanks to Demo Locho Rinpoche for his invaluable assistance with some difficult passages in this last chapter.

The Ocean of Clouds of Praises of the Guru Manjughosha

'Jam dbyangs bstod sprin rgya mtsho

Je Tsongkhapa (written in 1394)

Who calms the flames of ambitions for one's own pleasure,
   with the waters of long-cultivated compassion,
Who cuts the net of imaginative fabrications,
   by seeing the reality of the profound as it is,
Who carries with tireless heart the responsibility of helping
   others, to reveal to beings what he sees himself,
My mind is aimed at such a tutelary deity as you, O Mañjushri!
Please consider for a moment these flowers of verses of
   praise,
Stirred by the wind of faith, O Mañjughosha, Treasure of
   Wisdom,
O radiant shining mass of rays of saffron light,
Like the great solid golden axial mountain,
Embraced by the rays of the rising sun!

Though one were to seek strenuously everywhere,
One finds no good refuge other than in you,
When my mind thus turns itself toward you,
It is like a sun-burnt elephant plunging in the lotus pond!
Thus, expressing your excellence, when I let my mind go

Toward the means of finding fulfillment of my hopes,
It is like the lowly beggar's pleasure
When he sees the beautiful gift-giver coming!

Praise of Body

Your body is tall and straight like the axial mountain,
Its expanse is handsome as the banyan tree,
The complexion of your skin is pure and clear
Like dust of gold, fine, smooth, and soft.
On your crown, like the tip of a victory standard,
Your coiffe of long, soft, shining black hair,
Is bound in a beautiful turban whose crest
Has five tufts, slightly leaning to the left.
Your head is massive like a shapely parasol dome,
Adorned with a diadem of precious stones,
Your hair-line is high and well-defined,
And the spread of your brow is like the waxing moon.
The mid-brow is adorned by an immaculate *urna*-hair,
As if carved out in pure silver,
Shapely, curling to the right,
Clear white as a lily or as a lotus stalk.
Your eyebrows are long, even, of lustrous soft hairs,
Black in color and slightly arched.
Your eyelashes are attractive as a bull's,
Thick, soft, not bristly, well-proportioned.
Your eyes are long and slightly round,
Like the petals of the blue utpala-lotus,
Beautiful, the pupils and whites unclouded,
Clear as the petals of the white lotus.
Your nose is well proportioned and prominent,
Your lips attractive, red as the bimba fruit,
Your forty teeth white, even, and well-polished.
Cheeks round and full like the king of deer,
Your tongue sensitive to good taste is soft and supple,
And can cover the entire orb of your face.
On the long lobes of your fine ears

Dangle earrings adorned with many gems.
And your immaculate neck is well adorned
With a necklace of sparkling jewels.
The surfaces of your hands, feet, arches, shoulders, and
   neck,
Are broad, round, with the veins not prominent,
Your body completely full, with no imbalance,
Its upper part as broad as Mahadeva,
Your chest as wide at the slope of Meru,
Your arm well rounded at the shoulder,
Long and beautiful like the elephant-king's trunk.
The web of beauty on your fingers and toes
Is well shaped like the king of geese.
Your nails shine with a polished red color,
Their garland adorning your fingers,
Like new shoots on the branches of the wish-granting tree,
Soft, flexible, long, with youthful flesh.
The palms and soles of your hands and feet
Are adorned with the best thousand-spoked golden wheel,
Precise and complete, not jumbled together,
Distinct and regular as if pressed from the same seal.
Adorned with armlet and bracelet,
Your right hand holds the sword
That cuts the root of the tree of materialism,
Shining forth a brilliant net of light.
Your left hand holds at your heart
The stalk of a blue utpala-lotus,
On which rests the supreme volume of exact and full
   teaching
Of the path of relativity, the sole doorway to peace.
Upon your shimmering lower robe of variegated silk
Soft and smooth, dyed with marvellous colors,
The lower hem of golden tinkling bells
Makes a pleasant sound, beautifully draping.
Your organs are retracted like a superb horse,
Your fine and soft body hairs
Grow individually, curling to the right

And grow upwards on your body.
Their skin delicate, your calves are good and round.
Your ankles are without protruding bones.
Your soles are flat like a turtle's belly.
A quarter of the foot turns out, and your heel is broad.
On a seat of a perfectly round moon-disc,
On the saffron center of a six-petalled white lotus,
Ankles adorned with beautiful, tinkling anklets
Your two feet are crossed in the Vajra posture.

Your body is supremely beautiful, supreme body born of
    the superlative cause, ultimate store of merit,
Like an 'illusion before many beings, in all superb lands
    limitless, throughout endless space,
Born on occasion, teaching the path of enlightenment even
    in other lands, your body, O Teacher,
Its superb array here and elsewhere, even if all beings were
    to become omniscient, they could not express it!
As the thousand-rayed sun plunging its seven horses into
    the saffron ocean,
Your body radiates everywhere masses of light of which
    one can never see enough,
By whatever merit I gain by this slight praise,
May the beautiful body of Mañjughosha never leave my
    sight!

When I just have beheld your body,
I weary of my long wandering in existence,
May my troublesome mind always taking the wrong path
Come into the power of the spirit of enlightenment!

Praise of Speech

Further, having attained an infinite store of samadhis,
With retentions, superknowledges, and doors of liberation,
May I manifest limitless physical arrays,
To see the Victors in the million universes!

Then, having reached the limit of wide learning,
Satisfying limitless beings with the Dharma,
May I before too long attain the supreme body
Of the chief of all Victors, the Lord of Speech!
Your saffron body manifesting a thousand light-rays,
As if reflecting in the surface of a polished mirror,
Erect and beautiful as a curving rainbow,
I salute you Mañjughosha, Lord of Speech!

Your voices fill all universes everywhere in every different
    language,
Satisfying the minds of all living beings appropriately,
    eclipsing even the lustre of creators,
Melody of your speech like a sphere of music, which sweet
    speech outlasts the samsara,
Whose ear it enters, it takes away their sickness, their old
    age, and their death.
Your speech is pleasant, gentle, charming, heart-stirring,
Harmonious, its sweetness is pure, stainless clear light,
Worth hearing, taming the wild with sweetness,
Not rough, not coarse, very calm, it pleases the ear.
Satisfying body, mind, and heart, it generates delight,
Painless, all-informing, it is to be understood.
Brilliantly delightful, intensely delightful,
Totally illuminating, enlightening,
Rational, relevant, free of all redundancy,
Its tone is sweet as a lion, elephant, lord of serpents,
Dragon, gandharva, kalavinka, Brahma, Crane, lord of
    swans.
Its drumbeat is not high, not low, penetrating all
    appropriately,
Your phrases are expressive, not incomplete,
Not disheartened, not feeble, pervaded with joy and insight,
Cohesive, relevant, and all conclusive,
Satisfying all senses, not contemptuous, not vacillating,
Renowned throughout the whole thoughtless samsara.
It dispels the three times, punishes the demon hosts,

Emerging with supremacy in all its forms.
Such a voice with sixty-four qualities,
All are present even in a single statement,
It gives happiness to the hearing of the lucky
As far as space can reach.
It does not seem too loud when near, nor faint when far,
But accords with the language of each of countless disciples
    like a crystal prisming various colors,
Manifests as coming from all parts of your body, such as
    crown, urna-hair, and throat,
And yet it pacifies all the notions of all those hearers, just
    as the Brahma-voice can manifest from sky.
Like the deep thunder within the rain-cloud
Girt with its belt of beautiful red lightning.
By this merit of praising the speech of Mañjughosha,
May I never be parted from the hearing of your speech!

Just by hearing your stream of speech,
The lucky accept it, condemning wrong discourse,
May the well-wrought phrases reach the ultimate
In the explaining, writing, and arguing
That fascinate all the intelligent!

Easily obtaining supreme intellectual understanding
Of unhindered linguistic grasp of all languages of beings,
May I achieve the triumph of cutting off all doubts
Of all living beings without exception!

Never transgressing the boundaries
Of the statements of your instructions,
Through devoted single-pointed practice,
May I quickly achieve the mastery of speech!

Praise of Mind

Color of good gold mixed with dyes of coral,
Wisdom certain of the proper color of all knowables,

Lord of Wisdom, Mañjughosha, refuge of beings,
May you as supreme refuge grant superlative wisdom!

Drunk on the ichor of materialism, knowledge of right
and wrong destroyed,
Completely wrecking the tree of virtue, with his trunk
poisoned with afflictions,
The mind dragged by the chains of existence, losing the
female elephant of success,
Such is the elephant of the mind hard to tame, running
amuck in the jungle of unconsciousness!

It should be bound tightly with the rape of conscience,
mindfulness, and awareness,
Driven with the goad of genuine reasoning,
And guided onto the good path of holy relativity,
Praised and trodden by millions of supreme holy ones.

With the powerful force of tireless effort on that way,
By meditating again and again for limitless aeons,
By the Vajra of the illusion-like samadhi,
The mountain of extremisms is rendered merely a name!

Again the innumerable Lord Victors,
Being pleased by oceans of clouds of supreme offerings,
With the sound of the Brahma-voices from their taintless
throats,
Grant supreme instruction taught with one intention.

This food of nectar eradicating the hundred illnesses of
existence,
By constant use increases the strength of the body of
intelligence
Which reaches the transcendences of the energetic deeds
Of the Bodhisattva so very difficult to reach.

The one is no longer oppressed by extremist habits,
False appearances entirely conquered, there arises
The chief of all samadhis without hindrance—
The samadhi renowned as like a Vajra.

By the power of your manifestation of that
Appearance on the part of illusory objects
And the dream-like intelligence, which knows clearly
All experience and appearance, enter the ultimate realm.

Thus, like a tree whose root is destroyed,
Since you have eradicated the seeds of all habits,
How could you, refuge, ever deviate
From the Body of Truth, as long as space shall last!

Thus while you, Protector, never leave the ultimate realm
   at all,
The vivid appearance of the many objects are perfectly
   known individually without mixing,
Though like reflections in a mirror, or like a rainbow in
   the sky,
O Intuitive One, Your wisdom embraces all even in an
   instant!

From generosity comes wealth and not poverty,
From avarice comes poverty and not wealth!
You understand all such points of inexorable relativity,
Therefore, you are the chief of philosophers!

The process of evolution with its fruits of virtue and sin
Of all those who move unchecked through existence,
There is nothing in it that you do not understand;
Therefore, there is never any parting from your speech.

The process of various attitudes such as sticking to desire,
Inclining to hatred, or the reverse of these and so forth;
Since you directly see all this, none of your deeds
Can ever fail to accomplish the aims of beings.

Not a single one of all the categories of the eighteen elements
Are hidden in the slightest from your understanding,
Therefore you never exceed in the slightest
Just proportion in training the faculties of disciples.

Since your understanding is never blocked in application
To the sharpness, dullness, or absence of faculties
Such as faith in those who wander in existence,
You are extremely skillful in the technique of teaching
  Dharma.

Since you know without obscuration entirely
The paths of ascendance and of transcendence
and of going to the wretched states,
You are the excellent spiritual friend of living beings.

Through all samadhis such as those of form and formless,
The lion's stretch and the terrific triumph,
You are not confused in the practice-methods of entrance
  and arisal,
You are consummate in all meditational absorptions.

You are skilled in the limits of the past,
Since you realize in a mere instant
The memory and understanding of former lives of self and
  others
Which have been continuous from beginningless samsara.

You are skilled in the limits of the future,
Since you know very well all the places of rebirth,
Having migrated through death from just this present time
According to one's good and evil actions.

Your direct vision, completely free of blocks,
Sees the Nirvana that is tile termination of defilements
And the eightfold path the means of terminating them;
Thus you are the best of all refuges.

Your knowledge penetrates unhindered the appropriate and
  the inappropriate, the effects of evolution,
Attitudes, the universes, the degree of faculties, the paths
  that lead everywhere,
The afflictions, purifications, the past abodes, death,
  migrations, birth, and termination of defilement,

What point of knowables is not under your command,
not your object?

Those who wander in existence from the beginningless,
Though they frequent with powerful effort
The path of harming others to gain their own happiness,
Are erring as their hardships will prove fruitless.
So you also see that those who for themselves,
Even not harming others even in the slightest,
Day and night strive a hundred ways for liberation,
Have also turned their backs on the true path.
Thus you long practiced the good path of compassion,
The sole path of all the Victors,
The Mother which looks after all beings,
The door for entering the fray of the hero Bodhisattvas.

You, loving one, see the great error of forsaking
Others' happiness, as there's no virtue in all this world,
Not accepting suffering even in your dreams,
And not resting content even with the utmost pleasures,
And so by your primal cultivation
Of the spirit of enlightenment that sees
The equality of self and others,
You hold all living beings as yourself.

Craving one's own happiness blocks the path.
Cherishing others is the treasury of all excellence.
Thus you practice again and again the method of exchange
Of self and others, making all beings yourself.

Thus You, Lord, completely nurse physical strength
Frequently with the mother of compassion,
How can even the culmination of excellence
Be deprived even by the bliss of peace?

Just as the king of birds soars in the heavens
Not falling to the earth, not his proper place,
By praising your mind that stays neither in existence nor
in peace,

May I never be apart from the wisdom and love of Mañjughosha!

The view that removes all occasions for extremism.
And the compassion that sees all beings as one's only child,
Having achieved them easily within my mind,
May I lead all beings onto the supreme vehicle!

The retention that remembers word and meaning of all
teachings,
And supreme eloquence that answers all questions,
Quickly generating these, may I spread out the feast
Of eloquent explanations of the masses of the Dharma!

By the glory of the mind of Mañjughosha
Who, without calculating, fulfills the hopes
Of various disciples according to their inclinations,
May I become beautiful as the autumn moon in sky!

Ceaselessly praised by limitless victors in the universes of
the ten directions,
He is called Mañjughosha, whose sweetness fills the three
realms,
And this ocean of clouds of praises, reverently expressing
just a bit of his excellence,
Who upholds it and reads it, may Mañjughosha quickly
enter his mind!

*Composed by the learned Easterner Losang Drakpae Pal at the hermitage
of O'de Gungyal at the prince of snowy mountains in Tibet, written down
by the Buddhist scholar Bhadrapala.*

Brahma's Diadem
A Praise of Maitreya

Byams pa'i bstod pa

by Je Tsongkhapa (written in 1395)

Reverence to Glorious Guru Mañjughosha !

Ever showering them with tender love,
He yet burns the friends of darkness.
Though He has cut off the toughest bonds
He binds himself tightly with compassion.
Ever possessed of peaceful equanimity
He cherishes others more than Himself.
Bowing humbly at the feet of Mañjughosha,
I praise the Guardian Invincible[1] Maitreya!

Four-faced Brahma praises Him with many mouths,
Thousand-eyed Indra always gazes at Him with devotion,
Rati's Kama drops his pride and bows dawn to Him.
Reverently, I worship the regent's[2] feet!

As sunlight opens lotuses in clear lakes,
As the clear-sky star lord makes lily gardens bloom,
So the sight of His body, wreathed in auspicious signs,
Captivates living beings' hearts, the moment they see it.
May the lotus foot of my Guardian Maitreya
Grace the crown of my head in all my lives!

Devil-beater, free of all fear of life,
Matchless hero, best teacher of the three realms,
Always watching over beings fallen into dangers,
I worship Your feet, O Leader!

With unrestricted access to the totality of facts,
Your power of knowledge conquers the devil army horror,
Whose thunderbolt-weapons fall before You like fresh
    flowers,
You are dazzling with the glory of the ten powers!

You scorch the haughty brains of elephant-rivals,
Sounding the great roars of eloquence amid their congress,
Finishing off the foxes of the false philosophers,
Possessed of four fearlessnesses, You are the Human Lion!

You turn the supreme Wheel of Dharma,
Unturnable even by the proud World-Creator, Lord of
    passions,
Which neither ascetics nor priests can articulate.
You are the Guardian who loves the living beings!

Not even the word "error" affects Your body and speech,
Unfailing in memory, always focused in equality,
Free of discriminations as well as thoughtless trances,
Your activities are always absolutely pure!

You are completely beyond any occasion for failure
Of the will, of energy, or of Your memory,
Of meditative concentration, wisdom, or liberation.
Therefore Your realization is unexcelled!

Your wisdom unblocked and unattached in all three times,
Your physical, verbal, and mental deeds are pure.
Accomplishing beings' aims to the end of samsara,
You are involved joyfully with that responsibility.

Having perfected the mass of magnificent virtues
And conquered susceptibility to the slightest faults,
Please consider for a moment the lamentable plight
Of me who is the object of your compassion!

Though I have this life of leisure and opportunity
Capable of liberation from the great ocean of suffering,
I am defiled by the faults of carelessness. Sloth,
Stupor, frivolity, and desire for gain and fame.

I waste this good body, using it for meaningless pursuits,
When it can easily achieve the supremely meaningful.
I inhabit this human flesh, with the attitude of a beast,
Pray look upon me with your great compassion!

Though I have won the crucial leisure so hard to find,
Though I see the powerful Lord of Death whom no power
    can stop,
Sending forth his messengers who cannot be escaped,
And am already seized by old age and sickness—
Beings do not remember the unsureness of the time of death
Nor that all is lost when death actually comes,
And spend the days and months and years in vain pursuits—
It is time to have mercy on us deluded ones!

What need is there to mention the exaltation of
    transcendence ?
There is no real ambition to reach even mere high estate,
Praised by the Muni as the basis of the spiritual path,
Are You really being indifferent to me?

Though we may have won the body fortunate with high
    estate,
If we do not find the unmistaken path of goodness,
With the wisdom that precisely investigates the teachings,
Once again we will fall into the ocean of cyclic life.
So long enveloped by the dark massive fog of delusion,
Obscuring our right discernment of the ground of ethical
    choice,
Please bestow upon us the lamp of wisdom!

The rain of weapons falls upon the body,
Licked by flames on the ground of molten iron,
Yama's minions impale it on a stake,
And ladle gobs of molten brass upon the tongue.

Frozen in caves of ice in surrounding icy peaks
Lashed by blizzards driven by fierce winds,
Some are covered with blisters, some wounded,
Others torn into many pieces.[3]

Faces covered with hair, with mouths parched,
They see a river and run to drink,
Creatures prevent them, blocking them with swords and
    spears,
And the water seems to turn to blood and pus.

Mouths like a needle's eye, throat choked off by goitres,
Even finding food and drink they cannot enjoy it.
Whatever they do eat or drink burns internally,
They live on excrement and urine, or eat their own flesh.[4]

Enveloped in the great darkness of delusion,
Minds incapable of discerning right and wrong.
One killing another, controlled by gods and men,
They suffer the misery of beating and drudgery.[5]

All peace of mind overcome by the burning fire
Of their consuming jealousy of the glory of the gods,
Bodies slashed and lost from the fighting,
Deceived by trickery, with no fortune to see the truth.[6]

Not to mention the experience, mere hearing about these
    realms
Produces terror in the heart, one shudders in general
At the fall into the great abysses
Of the hells, ghosts, beasts, and titans,
Having accumulated from the beginningless, and still
    doing so,
The unbearable evil action condemned by holy persons,
I quail in the face of this great abyss—
It is time to save me from the terror of bad migrations!

Even in the human abodes, with the high estate
Of power and property, there is the worry of loss,

And the ruin of parting from excellence of fortune.
And the seeking only after the pleasures of desire.
Wanting happiness, one uses means to get it,
But afterwards one will find great suffering
So much more, from the many forms
Of physical pain and mental anxiety.

Even the gods, who sport in the glory of heaven,
With beautiful bodies, adorned with jeweled ornaments,
In fine mansions surrounded by pleasure gardens,
Savouring long the pleasures of desire,
Finally are gripped by the signs of unwanted death.
Then they see they will unwillingly be parted
From the lovely goddesses who captivate their hearts,
From the delightful pleasure gardens,
From the nectar food, fine dress, ornaments of beauty,
And the other youthful gods, so soon!
Then they burn with fiery tongues of sorrow,
Generated by the mental anguish so much more intense
Than all the physical pleasures of that place.
Thus terminates the fruit gained by their striving
In actions of goodness for many lives,
And their carelessness, the cause of bad states, affects them
     finally,
And once again they fall into the hellish realms.

Even those who have gained the form and formless heavens,
Long abiding in pure bliss by power of samadhi,
Without notions longing for desire, without malice,
Beyond sleep and deeds of mental anguish,
Free of suffering from physical and mental harm,
Are not liberated from the bond of cosmic suffering,
And when the impulse of the prior samadhi ends,
Again they fall down and continue their migrations.

Thus even the lords of life, gods and men, are caught
In the ocean of existence by suffering's currents,
Of birth and death and sickness and old age.

So surely it is wrong to love the mundane happiness!
So please save me from the current of existence,
I whose eye of wisdom life obscures,
Mistaking suffering for happiness,
Confused by perverse and foolish notions!
Stuck in the mud of desire, strayed from the path of
    liberation,
Lost in the gloom of nescience, without the eye of wisdom,
Caught in the trap of fabrications, chained in the prison of
    samsara,
Tormented by evolution, I am in need of Your compassion!

To stop at the cliff of the terrible samsara,
One must surely reach the stage of skill
Depending on no other, by discerning rightly
The definitive and interpretable in the boundless teachings,
By the power of pure reason of correct analysis,

Depending on extensive and impeccable learning—
No need to mention the subtle intention of the Victor!
But my intellectual vision becomes not very clear
Even about the crude points of involvement and cessation,
And still this enemy of delusion obscures my heart
And I have no chance for liberation!

Consider this situation, clear the darkness from my heart!
Awaken my instincts left from constant practice
In the ocean of learning over many lives
Of the sciences taught by the Victors and their Sons!
You the sole eye revealing the good path to beings!

I, wretched and without protector,
Abandoned by the holy ones of old,
Like a guest arrived from distant regions, It is time
You cared for me with Your great kindness!

You Maitreya who free all beings with Your love,
Are the refuge served with devotion again and again!
Swiftly, swiftly come and be my spiritual friend
In the Universal Vehicle in all my lives!

Before You, who constantly look out
For all beings with Your great love,
If they remember Your excellence with mind of faith,
Daily You will come to them!

Yet even though one wishes to frequent lonely places
To enjoy the taste of solitude in isolation,
It is physically impossible to go.
Thus, You, to please the holiest of fields of merit,

With pure high resolve filled the realms of space
With jewels, gold nuggets, and heavenly silks,
With the three robes, monk's staffs, and ascetic's bowls,
Recommended by the Sage to the religious seekers,
And also emanated an excellent array of exquisite offerings
From your samadhi and vows,
And offered them all to the Lord of Humans,
With mind detached and free of expectations.

By the mass of pure virtue coming from that
May I become the refuge of all beings
Who have wandered so long in existence
Devoid of joy, tormented by the million pains!
May all beings who are out of contact
With the holy exaltation of the World-Leader,
Take lives as monks with the pure spiritual life,
And awaken their Universal Vehicle genealogies!

May they obtain unwavering honesty and tolerance,
Dauntless heroism and intense powerful faith,
Devotion, and the effort of constant practice,
And the consummate wisdom of discernment!

May the Sugatas be pleased by the ceasing of doubts
Through sustained practice in the ocean of wide learning,
Depending on the spiritual friends, supremely skillful
     teachers,
Kindly leading others with techniques from their own
     insight,

Having discovered the Victor's intention by the power of
pure reason,
And by putting into practice the import of their
understanding!

Not transgressing the regulations of the Muni,
Devoted to the Victor's heir, the spiritual friend,
Extremely sharp of mind, free of faults of wrong practice,
May You have such a retinue of perfect purity!

Disturbed by the mind of dark tendencies,
Obstructed in enjoying the feast of meritorious deeds,
May I never encounter even for an instant,
Such an evil friend, relative of devils!

When I train myself, with proper devotion to Shakyamuni,
May there not even be the name of hindrance,
Blocking the fulfillment of the energetic deeds,
 The demonic action that follows the unlucky ones!

Thus endowed holy and delightful persons
May they achieve without any obstruction
All the favorable circumstances of the deeds of
enlightenment,
Praised by the Leader as the ornament of religious persons!

During the enlightenment deeds, may I establish
All realms of disciples in the renunciation
Bound by the pure precepts, and grant them just with a
thought
All the furnishings appropriate to them!

From now on throughout all my lives,
Whatever I do with body, speech, and mind,
May it all become the cause of benefit
To all beings on all occasions!

Like a mother when her beloved son dies,
Through the love always breaking my heart,
For all beings tormented by all sufferings,
May I give away all my wealth!

When I purify all taints of the stage of deeds in faith,
May I become like Meru amid the golden mountains,
Among the common individual Bodhisattvas
Of the past, present, and future;
And becoming exalted through all the qualities
Of the eyes, superknowledges, and great learning,
May I attain the eloquence not dependent on others!

Training in the stages of the holy Bodhisattvas,
May I become like the eagle among the birds,
Among all the universal beings of three times,
The great heroes abiding on the stages,
And with impeccable intuition penetrating without block,
All the points of knowables extremely vast
Hard to fathom by other Bodhisattvas,
May I become a treasury of energetic deeds!

When I gain the fruit of such practice,
May I perfect through practice of liberative technique,
The very same sum of whatever are the body,
And field and retinue, deeds, lifespan, and vows
Of all the Victors of the three times!
And this world which I contemplate from afar,
May I liberate in a single instant
By the falling of the great rain
Of the nectar of the Holy Dharma.

This "Brahma's Diadem", Praise of the Protector Maitreya, the Victor, sole refuge for the whole world including the gods, was written by the learned Easterner Losang Drakpae Pal at the Retreat House, "Empty Mountain Sunrise," at Lhobrag.

Prayer for Rebirth in Sukhavati

bDe ba can gyi zhing du skye ba 'dzin pa'i smon lam (bDe smon)

by Je Tsongkhapa (written in 1395)

Whose outstanding deeds give endless glory to beings,
Whose mere remembrance banishes the terror of the Lord
of Death,
Who considers every living being as his child with constant
love.
I salute Amitayus, Boundless Life, the Teacher of Gods and
Humans!

Out of love, I will articulate as best I can
This prayer for rebirth in the Sukhavati heaven
Supreme realm highly, excellently praised
Numerous times by the Lord of Sages.

The state of good and evil obscured by the fog of nescience,
Life of ascendance deprived by the weapon of hatred,
Bound in the prison of samsara by chains of lust and craving,
Swept into the ocean of existence by the rivers of evolution,
Tossed by the many billows of miseries of sickness and decay,
Crushed by the burdens of unwanted sufferings,
Mangled in the jaws of the intolerable sharks of the Lord
of Death,

> This is my cry of torment, I who am unprotected.
> If I reverently invoke the Lord as witness to my prayer,
> Amitabha, Boundless Light, Leader, sole friend of the
>   destitute,
> And the Bodhisattvas, Avalokiteshvara
> And Mahasthamaprapta, with their retinues,
> Who have never failed the promise of their conception of
>   the supreme spirit,
> For our sake throughout limitless aeons,
> Like the king of birds swooping through the sky,
> May they come here by their love and their miraculous power!

Depending on the power of the combined focusing of the oceans of the two stores gathered by myself and others in past, present, and future, as I approach the time of death, may I behold directly the Leader Amitabha surrounded by his retinue such as the two powerful sons, and may I feel intense faith directed to the Victor with his retinue!

May I be free of sufferings of torment and being cut off; and may I remember without forgetting my faith and its objects, and so at the moment after death, relying on the miraculous advent of the eight Bodhisattvas to show me the proper path to go to Sukhavati, may I be reborn on a jeweled lotus in the Sukhavati universe just as a person with acute faculties in the Mahayana genealogy!

From the moment of rebirth there, may I attain retentions, samadhis, the unconditional spirit of enlightenment, the inexhaustible eloquence, and the limitless store of such excellences, and pleasing the Unexcelled Teacher Amitabha and the other Buddhas and Bodhisattvas of the ten directions, may I truly be favored with the Holy Teachings of the Mahayana!

May I understand their import correctly, and then in each instant going without hindrance by magic power to the superlative Buddha-universes, may I completely fulfill all the energetic deeds of the Bodhisattvas![7]

Then even though being born in a pure universe, still, motivated by the most intense love, may I mainly proceed to the impure universes by means of unhindered magical powers, and depending on teaching each living being the Dharma according to his special lot, may I be able to establish him on the pure path praised by the Victor!

And by quickly accomplishing those miraculous deeds, may I easily attain the exaltation of Buddhahood for the sake of the infinite beings!

> When the creative energy of life is released,
> May I behold clearly before my eyes,
> Amitabha surrounded by his oceanic hosts,
> And may my being be filled with faith and compassion!

> From the moment when the visions of the Between[8] arise,
> May the eight Bodhisattvas show the unerring path,
> And, being born in Sukhavati, thence by emanations,
> May I lead all beings of the impure worlds!

And in all lives before attaining such supreme exaltation, may I attain only that embodiment fit to practice the perfect learning, thinking, and meditating on the verbal and realizational Teachings of the Victor!

May such embodiments not lack the ornaments of the seven excellences of ascendant status!

And in all those situations, may I attain the memory of lives that remembers accurately all former lives!

And in all those lives, may I experience the hollowness in all existences and be motivated by thoughts captivated by the excellence of liberation, and may I renounce the world in the religious discipline well taught by the Lord!

Having renounced, may I discover the great spirit of enlightenment by ultimately accomplishing the deeds of morality, untainted by even the smallest transgressions, and may I become like an unshakable monk!

Further, in all those lives, understanding the processes of defilement and purification accurately, may I attain the perfect retentions which retain without forgetting all the words and meanings of the Teachings, the factors of perfection!

May I attain the unimpeded pure eloquence that teaches others what I have understood myself! Further, in all those lives may I never lack attainment of the doors of Samadhis such as the "Hero's March," the eyes such as the physical eye, and the superknowledges such as the knowledge of feats of magic!

May I attain the clear wisdom that can distinguish without confusion precisely the subtlest of the subtle facets of defilement and purification!

May I quickly attain the wisdom that can completely cease at the moment of arisal all non-understanding, misunderstanding, and doubting considerations!

May I attain the profound wisdom that mysteriously penetrates the words and meanings of the Scriptures whose measure cannot be taken by any other!

In short, may I become like the Holy Mañjughosha who consummates all the deeds of the Bodhisattvas through his wisdom of skill in liberative technique which discerns the words and meanings of the teachings, a wisdom free of all the faults of pretended wisdom!

Thus having easily found the deep, swift, clear, and great wisdom, may I attain transcendent skill in explanation, argument and composition concerning all the Victor's teachings, which are, respectively, the factors of sustaining the fortunate, chastizing the false philosophers, and gladdening the wise!

Further, in all lives stopping all attitudes that hold my own purposes most important and all feelings of laziness and discouragement about the energetic deeds of the Bodhisattvas, while reaching the ultimate of the supreme powerful heart that undertakes the purposes of others, may I become like the Holy Avalokiteshvara, who consummates all Bodhisattva deeds through the spirit of enlightenment which is skill in liberative technique!

Further, may I reach the ultimate in the deeds of the Bodhisattva by competent skill in liberative technique in conquering all demons, fundamentalists, and antagonists, while I am engaged in the purposes of myself and others, becoming like the Holy Lord of the Esoteric, Vajrapani!

In all my lives, may I find the great enlightenment through the massive effort that never deviates an instant from the moment of the spiritual conception to perfect the Bodhisattva deeds whose energy abandons all laziness, and may I become like the incomparable King of the Shakyas!

May I become in all my lives like the Buddha Medicine-King, Bhaishajya Guru, able to heal all pains of body, speech, and mind, just by having His name pronounced, by conquering all ills of mind and body that obstruct the achievement of enlightenment!

May I become in all my lives like the Victor Amitayus, able to overcome all untimely deaths just by having His name pronounced, having reached the ultimate in voluntary control of the lifespan!

When an obstacle to life is approaching, may I behold my refuge Amitayus' manifestation of the vision of his body which conforms to the *Discipline* by means of his four activities, and may all such obstacles be eradicated the moment I see that body!

As for that manifestation of the vision of his body according to the Discipline, may I recognize it as the protector Amitayus and generate a firm and non-artificial faith, and by the power of that, may I never fail to have the Victor Amitayus work openly as my spiritual friend in all my lives!

Furthermore, may the full-fledged spiritual friends of the Mahayana, the root of all mundane and transcendent virtues, be pleased with me and look after me throughout all of my lives!

While he looks after me, may I attain unbreakable faith in that spiritual friend and may I only please him through all doors of activity! May I not bring about even an instant of his displeasure!

May I be not incompletely instructed by all the advice and instructions of the spiritual friend!

May I be able to understand correctly all the meanings of those teachings and to perfect them through practice!

May I not go under the influence of the non-spiritual and sinful friends even for an instant!

In all my lives, may I realize faith of confidence in the effects of evolution, the mind of renunciation, the spirit of enlightenment, and the perfected view, and may I enter uninterruptedly into the experience of effortlessness!

Whatever root of virtue I have made through my physical, verbal, and mental actions throughout all my lives, may it all serve as the cause of only the purposes of others and the pure enlightenment!

Written by the learned Easterner, Tsongkhapa Losang Drakpae Pal, at Dzing-ji Temple, in 1395.

Garland of Supremely Healing Nectars

A Dialogue between
Karmavajra, The Nyingma Master Lhobrag Khenchen and
Bodhisattva Vajrapani in the Presence of Je Tsongkhapa
(At Lhobrag in 1396)

Reverence to Vajrapani, Lord of the Esoteric!

"You who are the actuality of the mind of all the Buddhas of past, present, and future, who are the great Vajradhara, Lord of the Esoteric, who are blessed by Buddhas as numerous as the Ganges River's sands, since Your memory[9] is like an elephant's, please teach the uttermost pinnacle of all vehicles!

Since You have the ornament of goodness, please teach the authentic view that abandons all abrasive and disagreeable views!

Since You are all-triumphant, please give a teaching that cuts wide open the net of doubts regarding view, contemplation, and action!

Since You are a mine of precious gems, please give a teaching that generates in our life the inconceivable samadhi of integrated quiescence and insight!

Since You have the message of truth, please teach the instruction that pours down the great rain of Dharma that puts out the blazing fire of afflictive thoughts!

Since You are ablaze with flames of wisdom, please teach the profound precept that burns the kindling of materialism and substantivism !

Since You are all beauty of form, please teach the instruction that fills the eyes with tears born of the vision of the precept that generates uncontaminated bliss!

Since You are the precious wish-granting gem, please give the extraordinary instruction that brings swift realization of the Buddhas' Body of Truth, concise in expression yet extensive in meaning, and so clear that the person of acute intelligence ceases his doubts and realizes the meaning, and the dumb cowherd can also get the words and understand the meaning—for the sake of this request of Matibhadrashri and for the sake of this prayer of mine, I, Karmavajra!"

When I had so petitioned, an extraordinary taste came from between my teeth and coiled around my tongue until I felt completely ecstatic! It must be thanks to You, O Guru! Then without manifesting His body, His unconquerable voice spoke as follows:

"Karmavajra! Bring these esoteric words of mine to the ear of Matibhadrashri![10] It is the intimation of Father Samantabhadra, the heart's message of Mother Samantabhadri—this esoteric speech of mine, I Vajradhara! To achieve the great supreme medicine, the uttermost pinnacle of all vehicles, seek out the clear light of the mind itself!"

I, Karmavajra, asked: "What is the actuality of the clear light?"

He said, "Karmavajra! The clear light (is explained by) three; actuality, nature, and compassion."

Karmavajra asked, "When one meditates on the clear light, are there pitfalls? Or not?"

He said, "Your question is extremely good! If someone does not understand, there are pitfalls. I will explain four points: the pattern of error, the sign of error, its faults, and the effect of error. First, the pattern of mistaking the actuality; in general, what we call 'actuality' is the introspectively known reality which exists just like this, free from the adulteration of present artificial consciousness, originally clear emptiness wherein nothing is (intrinsically) established. When a person meditates on emptiness without focusing just on that, he falls into the error of cutting off enlightenment at emptiness, by not freeing his mind from the holding of emptiness. The sign of error is that thoughts arise such as that 'above there is no Buddha, below there is no hell, the utter lack of establishment of anything is emptiness.' The fault of the error is that the mind that thinks 'everything is empty,' on the positive side, abandons all religious practice such as devotion, purification of perception, refuge-taking, spiritual conception, love, and compassion, and engages in the enterprises of this life, and on the negative side, all his practice is contaminated in the activities of sin. For one who thus engages in such perversion of the truth, there is no place to go but the Vajra hell. The fruit of such evil activities is that, on the positive side, since such a one has distorted the truth of the virtuous orientation, he conceives the nihilistic view of the fundamentalists, and on the negative side, by distorting the orientation toward causality, he wanders in the ocean of suffering. Karmavajra! There are many who say they realize emptiness, but there are very few who actually realize the real condition of ultimate reality!

"Karmavajra! There are four (points) to the pitfalls concerning nature. First, the pattern of error concerning nature; in this clarity where in body and intuition have the intrinsic brilliance of empty awareness, faces and arms have no categorical (intrinsic) status in the body, and colors and signs have no categorical (intrinsic) status in intuition. When a person settles upon the indivisibility of clarity and emptiness as merely the clarity aspect which is the intrinsic brilliance of emptiness, and does not know the integration of the indivisibility of clarity and emptiness, it is the mistaking of awareness as illumination. The sign of this error is that all Dharma teachings go their separate ways. When you teach such a person the expression of 'integration,' it does not fit into his mind. The fault of this error is that the mind that thinks 'universal illumination is substantial' does not aspire to engage in any Dharma practice, and, being too extreme in verbal adherence to theories, it departs from the path of omniscience. There is no way this person will become liberated, since his illumination has become fixated. The effect of this error is that such a person becomes attached to a clear light that appears externally and therefore is reborn in the realm of form. Not knowing his inner awareness as clarity-emptiness, he migrates with his mind fixed in one orientation, and has no occasion for liberation. Karmavajra! There are many who say they perceive the clear light, but there are few who cultivate illumination-emptiness as integration!

"Karmavajra! There are also four (points) in the pitfall concerning compassion. The pattern of error; this constructive thought that arises as variety, not arising as the intrinsic brilliance of clear empty awareness, no matter how it arises, never exceeds awareness-emptiness (indivisible). A person who does not understand that, is said to mistake awareness as emptiness. The sign of error is that he engages exclusively in the physical, verbal, and mental activities of this life. The fault of this error is that his attitude that constructive thought does not arise in the Body of Truth causes everything that arises to be bound by the net of constructive thought; he becomes arrogant, and his virtuous exertions are dissipated. Since his practice emphasizes bad instincts, he only achieves (the aims of) this life. Bound by the chains of dualistic suspicions and doubts, he himself binds himself. The effect of this error; not knowing the pitfalls of constructive thought, he becomes fixated in his instincts. Not knowing the evils of causality, he ends his life while still on the path of vacillation, and after death he gets lost again in the three realms. Karmavajra! There are many who say they have no constructive thoughts, but there are few who understand the criterion for the liberation (of whatever) arises."

I, Karmavajra, asked, "There is no point in not avoiding those three pitfalls; how are those three pitfalls avoided'?"

The Lord of the Esoteric said, "Karmavajra! This emptiness, the actuality of awareness, is not contrived by anyone, has no cause, no condition, but has been there from before the very beginning. It has no infraction or observance, it cannot be focussed on or mistaken—it is Buddhahood in the realm of primal perfection. Likewise, this natural clear light is effortlessly indivisible from beginningless emptiness. Its exercise is ceaseless compassion. Whatever arises lacks intrinsically real status, so you must understand all three as the great integration, Buddhahood in indivisibility!"

I, Karmavajra, again asked, "What are the pitfalls in view, meditation, and action?"

The Esoteric Lord said, "Listen, Karmavajra! First, there are the five pitfalls with regard to view; the pitfall of view itself, the pitfall of place, the pitfall of companion, the pitfall of affliction, and the pitfall of partiality. First, the pitfall of view itself: the yogi in this esoteric Tantric system prefers naked direct perception to the view generally taught, accepted as emptiness devoid of extremes. But there is no difference between those two if the ultimate is realized. If it is not realized, then the general view is a verbal view held in the analytic mind and does not hit upon the actual import; it is an erroneous view. Not trusting in the view which is direct perception, but placing confidence in the verbal, analytic view, one thinks that there is nothing to aim at, and that freedom from extremes is inactivity, and then one's actions are corrupted with regard to the principles of virtue and sin. Thinking that there is no good and bad evolution, virtue has no reward, sin brings no harm, everything is straightforward equality, one stays content with ordinariness. This is called the "view that dallies with evil," and is the root of all erroneous views. Matibhadrashri must act in the profound integration of the view, which is intrinsic clarity of non-dual direct perception, with evolutionary cause and effect.

"The pitfall of place: in general, one who realizes the temporary view should go to a clear and solitary place such as a hermitage in order to enter the realm of the ultimate view. Even though one has a temporary view one needs the discipline of retreat to cultivate it. Bad places distort one's view. Tell Matibhadrashri! The temporary view must be cultivated in retreat.

"The pitfall of friends: one who has the temporary view should associate with friends who agree with the Dharma and do not increase afflictions. It is impossible not to be infected by bad actions if one associates with bad friends. They lead one into (the concerns of) this life and leave no room to cultivate the view. They are the root of the pitfall of increasing the afflictions. Karmavajra and Matibhadrashri! If you do not want to fall into this error, cut off all attachment to unwanted friends and stay in solitude.

"Fourth, the pitfall of afflictions: that person who has the temporary view, if he is not motivated to overcome the arisal of afflictions, will be motivated into afflictions by whatever external circumstance. Gathering evolutionary action even in an instant, he will engage in bad evolutionary action for a long time. Bad evolutionary action will be gathered through the influence of the five poisons with regard to all six kinds of apparent objects. The evolutionary effect of that will emerge both temporarily and ultimately, and when afflictions are generated, though mindfulness of instantaneity may hold them, a loose awareness will let them go. Meditate on love and compassion for all living beings controlled by such afflictions. Pray for blessings that they may be motivated into the path of overcoming those afflictions. Especially, invoke the Guru from the depths of your heart. Purify the seed of afflictions with mantras, and consider it essential to meditate in the Mystic Deity. Afterwards, when you are naturally released in the view, make extensive dedicatory prayers. If you move on such a path, you will attain virtues as a result, both temporarily and ultimately. If you do not employ such a path, you will become stuck in the mud of afflictions and your view will not become actuality. It is the great root of pitfalls. Karmavajra and Matibhadrashri! If you do not want to fall into such error, employ the remedies for whatever afflictions are generated. Put them into practice.

"Fifth, the pitfall of partiality: all persons who have the temporary view take refuge erroneously in Scriptures (by fastening upon) the view given in the treatises of their own schools exclusively, and divide things into 'self' and 'other', 'higher' and 'lower factions,' and 'good' and 'bad', and they make Buddha's great extreme free view into something to be grasped at and presumed upon by (ordinary) persons. This is the root of errors. Karmavajra and Matibhadrashri! If you do not want to fall into such error, you must realize the extreme free view is a great vast emptiness!

"Now for the second point, there are five errors with regard to meditation: the error of actual meditation, the error of place, the error of friends, the error of faults, and the error of passions.

"First, the error of the actuality of meditation: although the Guru nakedly identifies actuality, nature, and compassion, the disciple does not understand, and cannot decide about actuality, nature and compassion. He falls into error by not understanding the indivisibility of clarity and emptiness. Then, when he practices according to the method of his Guru, he falls into the state of a human of the desire realm through his attachment to the merest particle of physical and mental bliss; he falls into the state of the deities of the pure abodes through his attachment to the mere absence of thoughts in his mind; he falls into the state of the deities of the form realm through his attachment to mere thoughtlessness in clarity; he falls into the state of desire realm deities through his attachment to thoughtlessness in regard to bliss; and he falls into the state of the formless realm deities through his attachment to thoughtlessness in regard to emptiness. These are the pitfalls in the three realms. If he continuously ceases sense-objects, he falls into the realm of infinite space. If he ceases, without sensations, even the feeling of falling into deep sleep he falls into the realm of absolute nothingness. If he ceases all clear illumination in his consciousness, he falls into the realm of infinite consciousness. If he generates continuously the mere shine of bliss in his clarity-awareness and utter nothingness in his perceptual awareness, he falls into the realm beyond consciousness and unconsciousness. These are called the "falling into one-sided quiescence." When one migrates via death from these, one migrates throughout the three realms and the six species. Karmavajra and Matibhadrashri! If you do not know how to eliminate the errors of meditation, (meditation) is unnecessary, since you will just return to migration when the realms of dumb meditation are lost.

"Furthermore, if you accept body and mind as (really being) the way they are experienced by the alienated individual, you fall into the error of the ordinariness of your own being. If you adhere one-sidedly either to being or nothingness, you fall into the spiritualism or the nihilism of the fundamentalists. If you accept the repudiation of all objects except for the mind, you fall into the state of the Disciples and Self-Enlightened Sages. If you accept appearance as mind, you fall into the error of the Idealists. If you accept animate and inanimate things as divine, you fall into the error of the Tantrics. What is the use of meditation when you cannot avoid the extremes of errors?"

I then asked for some method to avoid these pitfalls.

The Esoteric Lord said, "If you want to avoid these pitfalls, then, like Matibhadrashri, first broaden yourself by learning, then in the middle concentrate (the teachings) into the essentials by means of the personal instructions identifying (realities), and finally, at the time of practice, do not fall into the above errors, and, in spite of the fact that longing and attachment arise in meditation, meditate like a rabbit lying in an eagle's nest or like an archer (waiting for his prey). And you will not fall into any pitfalls, if you relax with regard to whatever appearance arises in your experience, not negating or establishing any infraction or observance or doubts or worries about whatever arises, and if you do not cling to any of it.

"Second, to show the pitfall of place and friends: the person who is meditating should meditate in a solitary and suitable place. If he stays in a crowded monastery or a place that arouses the passions, he will fall into error by the force of defilements, possessions, attachment and aversion. If he associates with bad friends, his meditative growth and enthusiasm will be disturbed, and he is buying his own suffering. Karmavajra and Matibhadrashri! If you practice a pure teaching, it is urgent that you use forceful means to abandon the negative influence of bad friends and bad places.

"Third, to show the pitfalls of meditation: when you cultivate your meditation, there are three (faults), depression, excitement, and distraction. There are (six) kinds of depression: because of place, because of friends, because of time, because of food, because of posture, and because of meditation. First, depression on account of place; if one stays in a forest in a low or sunken place, or in a country where solitude is disturbed or where defilements are prevalent, one's consciousness will grow stupefied, one's subtle drop becomes unclear, one's awareness dull, sleep too long, body heavy. One should perform ablutions and confessions and go to a high and clear place, and meditate in an open place or let the wind blow in the window. Contemplate snowy peaks, and meditate naked, and this (type of depression) will be dispelled.

"Second, depression on account of friends arises by staying with defiled persons. Make purifications and ablutions, and this will be dispelled by protecting yourself from people who have broken their commitments and are full of defilements. Third, seasonal depressions, which come in spring and summer when you feel oppressive and depressed, are dispelled when you meditate in high places as in the snowy mountains. Fourth, depressions caused by food and clothing come from using the defiled food and clothing of people, and are dispelled by avoiding such food and clothing. Fifth, depressions caused by posture occur for beginners from meditating while walking, sitting, lying down, etc., and are dispelled by meditating using the three postures or the Vajra posture, bringing intensity to the awareness and brightness to the faculties by sitting erect and alert. Sixth, depression caused by meditation: when one meditates, by meditating with one's consciousness (focussed) in the lower body, one becomes sunken down in one's physical being. That is depression, and it is dispelled by carrying one's senses, imagined as having the clarity of a lamp, through the sky, strengthening the awareness by the intense brilliance of mind itself. Karmavajra! As for the dispelling of obstacles of meditation, it is not accomplished by anyone without strong energy.

As for the pitfall of passions, there are many thieving enemies of one who practices meditation. Generated by the root five poisons, 84,000 passions arise, which leave no room for meditation and lead him into cyclic life. One should be undistracted concerning them, by imagining one is like a mother fearing loss of her only son; one should abandon them as if they were a snake suddenly appearing in one's lap. One should hold them with mindfulness which is vigilance, practicing as in the path application (mentioned above) in the context of the view. Otherwise, in an instant, bad evolutionary action is accumulated. If you do not want to fall into such error, you should exert yourself in careful choice of action, never apart from the watchman of alertness. Again, until view and meditation are stable, practice alone like a wounded deer. Especially, it is of the utmost importance to flee from the passions, seeing them like poisonous snakes.

"There are two (points) to explain the faults of excitement, excitement on account of place and excitement on account of conditions. Excitement on account of place: when one meditates in a high and clear place, one's awareness becomes clear, one's consciousness will not stay still, and constructive thoughts become excited and spread out everywhere. If one lets them loose to spread as they will, they become influenced by passions, so awareness should be settled in between tightness and looseness. If you cannot overcome it, subdue it by the gaze of the disciples. Sometimes, it can be subdued by aiming one's consciousness toward one's sitting mat. In the evening, lie down placing the mind within a black drop within an intestine like vein in the center of the soles of the feet. When the vapor of thoughts emerges, identify it and (seal it) with PHAT. Hold the breath, and afterwards let it go in relaxation. Or else, it is dispelled by leaving thought to run its natural course, leaving it to proceed on its familiar path.

"Second, excitement on account of conditions: thought picks up on any sort of external circumstance, and spreads the mind excitedly in the direction of the passions. Generate a will, thinking, "What's the use, it is unnecessary," and practice with love, compassion, aversion, technique, wisdom, respect, and devotion. Thereby, compel oneself along the path motivation (mentioned above) in the context of the view.

"Third, there are two points in the fault of distraction: distraction through misunderstanding, and distraction on account of circumstances. First, distraction from failure to understand: not knowing how to delimit the session of meditation, as much as one meditates there is no impact. Wrong views are generated toward the Guru and the instructions. Not distinguishing between realization and (superficial) understanding, one's meditation becomes dumb. For that, one should invoke the Guru, generate certainty about the instructions, often delimit the sessions of meditation, meditate powerfully without involvement in other affairs, and meditate by cutting off fabrications at the times of clarity. Then, distraction is cut off, and one's experience will increase from culmination to culmination. Second, distraction due to circumstances: here one becomes distracted by external circumstances, becoming involved in the six kinds of objects mixed with the five poisons, and one's vacillations cannot be contained by mindfulness. As a remedy for that, if one applies it suddenly, one should cut off as a whole the perception of appearances, realizing them as illusory. Karmavajra! If you want to eliminate those pitfalls, whack the pig on the snout with a club!"

Again, I Karmavajra asked the Esoteric Lord, "Do not the Tantras harness the passions to the path?"

The Esoteric Lord said, "Of course they harness passions to the path. But none but the peacock can make a diet of poison. That person who is able to harness passion to the path, without abandoning them, is more rare than the Udumvara flower. Even the keenest person experiences passions as friends, but in the end they will become poison for him, so it is important he abandon them. If, however, he first enters the realm of their abandonment as much as possible, then all passions and objects of desire arise as illusions, and lust and attachment for them do not arise. If some emerge, it is not necessary to stop them, they cause no harm. If they do not emerge, the mind to achieve them does not arise, there is no wishing. Just that is the criterion for their becoming motivations of the path. If one harnesses passions to the path before getting rid of intense attachments, it is like a fly flying around honey and becoming stuck in it. Karmavajra and Matibhadrashri! That is how you should take the measure of the stages and paths!

"Third, there are two pitfalls on the path of action, the pitfall of action at the wrong time, and the pitfall of action in general. First, the pitfall of action at the wrong time: bee-like action precedes learning, thinking, and meditation, it is action of a beginner, and goes wrong when engaged in, during the time properly spent under discipline. Deer-like action is action at the time of practice and goes wrong when engaged in at the time of discipline, as one's samadhi come under other influences. Dumb-like action is action when practice gets down to essentials, and, if engaged in at the bee-like time, goes wrong when the verbal meanings are not discerned. Actions like a dove entering its nest are actions at the time one's inner experience is generated, and become obstacles to samadhi, and go wrong when there is no intensity.

Madman-actions are actions demonstrating one's experience and when engaged in at the time of partial experience, being generated go wrong because the ultimate aim is not discovered. Lion-like actions are actions when the view has become experiential and go wrong if engaged in at a time (more suited) for (further) practice, because they do not occur on the basis of reality but go wrong by being diverted through extraneous appearances. Dog-pig-like actions are actions at the time of initiation and if engaged in at the wrong time go wrong because of the interference of one's Daka. If your actions do not go wrong, as one's inner perceptions arise as reality, external appearances are transformed into inconceivability, and one can err in regard to the esoteric. One can achieve any kind of miraculous feat, since one can master any kind of appearance that arises. To eliminate the above types of actions, you should understand the pitfalls of action, (or else) the effect will not come forth. Karmavajra and Matibhadrashri! You should act in accordance with the treatises on the general Dharma!

"Second, the pitfalls of action in the context of the Dharma in general: although you may be conscious about incidental acts, if they do not accord with the Dharma they do not contribute to the path of Buddha and are called 'artificial,' being erroneous actions. Karmavajra! If you do not want to err at the time of actions, you should do whatever action in such a way that it contributes to the path of enlightenment!

"Third, there are two types of pitfalls in regard to the final fruit, a temporary one and a final one. First, the temporary pitfall: if you hold the ordinary fruit of the practice of the profound instructions as supreme, your pride and arrogance are generated, and that is the error that impedes the ultimate fruit. Although you have achieved a fruit, if you do not terminate doubts, it is to mistake the fruit for a cause. Karmavajra and Matibhadrashri! You should recognize that the cause of doubts is baseless!"

Again, I Karmavajra asked, "If this pith teaching about awareness is intuitively realized, is the conception of the loving spirit of enlightenment necessary still? Or not?"

The Esoteric Lord said, "The Tantras of the Mahayana are very much distinguished by the conception of the loving spirit of enlightenment. Still, if you do not remember at all four times the evils of the life-cycle of cause and effect such as death and impermanence, everything naturally becomes a concern of this life (only). If you do not meditate on love and compassion toward all living beings at all times, although you may nominally acclaim the Mahayana, you have already fallen into the error of the Disciples and Self-Enlightened Sages. If you do not understand the moment by moment crisis of ethical choice concerning the subtlest aspect of cause and effect, various sins will accrue, even though your realization may be advanced. Karmavajra! If you want to live up to the Dharma honestly, you must always relate those above (spiritual conceptions) to your realization!"

Again, I Karmavajra asked, "What is the greatest obstacle to the practice of the path?"

The Esoteric Lord said, "When you first enter the path, the obstacle is whatever circumstance leads your mind in the wrong way. Especially, for a man, women are most demonic. For a woman, men are the most demonic. For both, food and clothing are very demonic."

Again I asked, "Most Tantrics nowadays say that the use of a consort has a tremendous impact. How is it in fact?"

The Esoteric Lord said, "The consort who can elicit the impact of the path is more rare than gold. Obsession with an inferior woman makes you into a sex-fiend! Purifying your perception (in regard to such a woman) makes your heart suffer. Your accumulated stores of merit and wisdom) are offered to the sex-fiend. Your perverted lust is made into a divine quality. If you can, you will unite even with a dog. Faith is generated from your mouth, but abandoned from your heart. Your avarice and envy become enormous. You accumulate no exalting evolutionary action, but it drags you down like an iron hook. Any impact that increases the Dharma is not brought forth, and you are led by the nose of lust and suffering. You practice with the hope of liberation through desire, but it only becomes a cause of increasing your passions. You hope it will be a basis of expanding your scope, but you get carried off in a bag of loss and defilement. A consort who keeps no spiritual commitment is a demoness!"

I asked, "Who then is the only one fit to consort with?"

The Esoteric Lord said, "Someone who has none of the above faults. Especially, one who is respectful to the Dharma, great-minded, persevering, great in faith and compassion completely endowed with the six transcendences, obedient of the advice of the Guru, devoted to the practitioner, who holds the Tantric vows as dearly as the apple of her eye, with no urge for sex at times that are not times of power, and who observes the rules of purity. If you find such a (consort), she can serve as a friend of the path. As such is extremely rare, and as such has the purpose of developing a desirous person, it is the especial fortune in Dharma of the keenest practitioner. Ordinary persons, since their passions go their own way, must abandon any (such ideas). If you enter the door of Tantra yet do not keep your vows, better not have any hopes about Buddhahood!"

Again, I Karmavajra asked "Since this kind of addiction about food, clothing, and body harms one's Dharma practice, please give men an instruction for getting the mind free of these three!"

The Esoteric Lord said, "Karmavajra! These bodies are (soon) destroyed. The length of life has been determined long ago. There is no certainty, whether you are old or young. No one gets out of death. I never saw anyone who failed to die because of their attachment to their body, no matter how beautiful. Let go of all cherishing of the body and discipline yourself in retreat. As for clothing, it is sufficient to wear even the poorest. As for food, grain and water is enough. Human beings are not capable of (much) practice of Dharma. Now, if, motivated by the spirit of enlightenment of love and compassion, you accomplish some virtue, it has great power. But it is extremely rare.

"These teachings of my esoteric words are the heart's message of the Dakinis. This esotric speech of mine, I, Vajradhara have taught to Matibhadrashri who is blessed externally by the Goddess Sarasvati, and internally by the Goddess Guhya jñaneshvari. And I seal this instruction for three years, that it not be taught to anyone else. The name of this instruction is "The Dialogue Garland of Supremely Healing Nectars." This medicine is as if unpalatable in the mouth of faith of the beginning disciple; even if it goes in their mouth of faith, it is as if vomited out. The application of this medicine has no superior in curing the plague of cyclic life. Having first requested this medicine, digest it without vomiting it out. If you can, you will become liberated from the fierce plague of cyclic life."

Again, Karmavajra asked the Esoteric Lord, "What is the character of this Matibhadrashri? Will he attain Buddhahood? Which Mystic Deity looks after him? Where was he born in his former lives?"

The Esoteric Lord said, "This Losang·Drakpa is a person who has extensively gathered the two stores. For seven precious lives he manifested the form of a Pandit and accomplished the aims of living beings. In his just previous life, he was born in Kashmir near Shrinagar as the Pandit Matibhadrashri, and he gathered an excellent circle of five hundred disciples. According to the perception of ordinary people, he was renowned as having attained the path of application. But even I Vajrapani cannot measure his excellences. He is looked after by the special deities which are outer and inner Goddesses, as well as by the Protectors of the three types (i.e., Avalokiteshvara, Mañjushri, and Vajrapani); these are his Mystic Deities. As to his Buddhahood, I do not show that, it will be predicted by Avalokiteshvara and Mañjushri. He is a person who benefits when contacted by seeing, hearing, or remembering. Other persons cannot take the measure of his character."

Again Karmavajra asked the Esoteric Lord, "How long will the Teaching remain in the Land of Snow"?

(The Lord said), "From now on, the present is the time of Scriptures, and within that the time of Sutras. Along with the Discipline it will remain for thirteen hundred years."

Again Karmavajra asked the Esoteric Lord, "What will be the state of suffering or happiness in this Tibet, the Land of Snows?"

(The Lord said), "The evil side will grow and defeat the side of good, and people from the frontiers will come into the center. On the strength of that, the frontier gods and demons will also come into the center. Then all the people in the center will go into foreign lands, and the central deities and demons will also go into foreign lands. On the strength of that, the gods and demons will not be at peace with the other gods and demons. Plagues and famines will afflict many people, and living beings will have no happiness. You, the responsible preserving teachers must be compassionate. Now is the time when war comes from outside and overcomes. The teaching can be restored by the scholars and monks even performing the merest portion of the necessary service. It is still possible to restore it if the techniques of reversing (the evil process) are employed. By the power of the evolutionary action of living beings, this cannot be delayed more than ten years. If the Community becomes divisive, it is a sign that the worst will happen sooner. If one cultivates the samadhis of the supreme vehicle, such as non discrimination, the experience of transcendent insight will be generated, arising even more quickly if distinguished by the profound technique of compassion. If you get to the essentials in the body through the profound techniques of reciting mantras, realization will inevitably spring up in the mind, which means that the great compassion will arise, through the presence of the inconceivable, supreme principle of profound technique. If there is no learning, then only erroneous Tantras will multiply, so learning is extremely important at the beginning stages.

However, nowadays, the method of spiritual conception through the blessing of contemporary meditators, of what worth is it beyond generating the merest fraction of the experience of transcendend insight? When they recite the mantras and spells of the profound Tantras, they only get a few ordinary accomplishments. Rather than that, you should generate a deep adherence to the supreme accomplishment. Thus, you must generate a purified perception toward everything. And, to generate an experience of perfect transcendent insight, you must rely on a Guru who has himself generate a perfect transcendent insight. If you do not generate a perfect transcendent insight, you should study my esoteric teaching, for you will need to eliminate (innumerable) pitfalls. Since the view is impeded in its range of understanding for those who have no quiescence, the Victors did not say that transcendent insight by itself is sufficient. It simply does not happen. The most excellent technique to elicit the experience of transcendent insight consists of the Six Yogas and the Great Perfection, the extraordinary instruction of the Tantra. While it is true that in general there are inconceivable various categories of causes of liberation and Omniscience, they can be condensed into three types. Among my esoteric teachings, there are many. Whether or not Dharma practice serves as the path depends on the extent of the extraordinary spirit of enlightenment. The actuality of the spirit of enlightenment is great compassion. Its function is to accomplish the aims of living beings. It is extraordinary. The criterion for the perfect generation of the understanding and experience of those three (spirit, compassion, and activity) is whether all selfish motivations have ceased and exclusive thinking of altruistic concerns has been achieved."

I, Karmavajra, asked, "Is this Great Perfection the perfect view?"

The Esoteric Lord said, "The Great Perfection is an exalted view, and also the elucidation of the view by Masters Nagarjuna and Chandrakirti is without error. It is impossible to generate transcendent insight without relying on them. Nowadays, in dBus and Ü-Tsang, there are inconceivable numbers of people who are able to terminate reifications about the path of Buddhahood through the power of unerring references and reasonings, and then to teach others the correct path. But there is no certainty that those who can teach this are in fact the ones called upon to teach. If those who cannot teach this do the teaching, everyone including the teacher go to the bad migrations! One has to feel compassion for them!"

Again, Karmavajra asked the Esoteric Lord, "What will be the length of life of this Losang Drakpa? What kind of followers will he have? Going where will his accomplishments increase? In his future lives, where will he accomplish beings' aims? Please tell me."

The Esoteric Lord said, "His accomplishment of beings' aims will increase if he does not stay in one place. His life span can be no more than forty five, although if he spends his time exclusively in practice, he can stay seventy one years, or maybe seventy three. To accomplish beings' aims, his life will become that long if he practices the meditations of White Tara, Amitayus, and Mañjushri Raktayamari, since he has connection with Mañjushri. If he does not do that, there is the danger that the evil side will interfere with him. The above practices are extremely precious. Of his followers there will be three who will be outstanding, and many who will enter the path of accumulation. As for his path, even the holy persons cannot measure it from the predictions already made in his former lives. He will soon behold the faces of the above mentioned Mystic Deities. There are three ways in which he will have these visions: the best is seeing them directly; the medium is seeing them mentally in meditation practice; and the worst is when he beholds them in dreams. Before seeing the faces of Mystic Deities, there will occur terrible miraculous events. Beings who are types of great demons will emerge, manifesting as Mystic Deities. Confronting them then, stabilize your samadhi, invite the Intuition-Hero and merge into the (apparent Deity). If it is a (real) Mystic Deity, an intense brilliance is generated. If it is a demon, it disappears. Although there will be inconceivable things such as this, that is all I can easily and understandably explain. I am not inspired to discuss how he will have visions of the Mystic Deities. If I do, the demons will carry it away!"

Again I asked, "This Losang Drakpa, where will he be reborn in the next life?"

(The Lord said), "He will be born in Tushita, in the presence of Maitreya, as the Bodhisattva Mañjushri garbha. Then from Tushita, he will wish to accomplish beings' aims in another human universe, and he will be reborn there in the form of a Dharmaraja, an Enlightened King, from which immeasurable benefit will emerge for the beings there. Third, in this universe's human realm, he will be reborn in the Licchavi community in Eastern India as the Pandit Jñanashri, where he will gather a following of two thousand, all of whom will attain the great accumulation path and the application path."

(Thus spake Vajrapani). Then Karmavajra said to Losang Drakpa, "The words spoken by the Esoteric Lord might not suit others' minds, so you should hide them. The greatness of your body and your virtues, though I could extol them at length, you would not have time to write them down, so I have only partly transmitted them; and the questions as I asked them, and also what he said extensively on his own, as there is no more than this little bit, that I have recorded."

Note: Here it is to be stated that in general there are many forms of correct interpretation of the Great Adepts'[12] deeds and instructions. Likewise, among the revelations of this Holy Master, in the context of the view there are three different systems of interpretation: one according to the Great Seal; one according to the Great Central Way; and one according to the Great Perfection. Each has a definite intention according to the (needs of) the disciples. Especially, this *Supremely Healing Nectar* is the best instruction given to Master Tsongkhapa himself. Even the Dakinis said "The Supremely Healing Nectar is the Supreme Medicine." And Tsongkhapa himself said that "The secret speech of Holy Vajrapani, free of faults of excess, omission, and error that is the Supremely Healing Nectar." He often praised it in this way.[13]

PART V

Praises and an Invocation

The anthology concludes with a number of poems praising and invoking Tsongkhapa, written by a number of different authors.

The first work, *Song of the Tricosmic Master,* was written by Khaydrub Je Rinpoche. In the early part of his life, he was a bitter opponent of the eclectic innovations of Je Rinpoche, but later became a chief Tantric disciple and a major elucidator of Je Rinpoche's making it even more widely accessible to and popular among Tibetans of the time. When Je Rinpoche went to Tushita, he left his throne to Gyaltsap Je, who in turn handed it on to the much younger Kaydrub Je.

The *Song Rapidly Invoking Blessings* is from a collection of thirty seven songs found in the first volume of the *Collected Works* of the Seventh Dalai Lama. The first Dalai Lama was a direct disciple of Je Tsongkhapa, and attained enlightenment under his tutelage. As a result, all the Dalai Lamas wrote a number of works about Je Rinpoche. This particular text is intended for recitation prior to meditation.

The *Praise of the Incomparable Tsongkhapa* is one of the several poems about Je Rinpoche written by the Eighth Karmapa, Mikyo Dorje, an extremely comprehensive scholar as well as a great leader of the Karma Kargyu Order.

These three poems are translated by Glenn H. Mullin and Losang N. Tsonawa, with the assistance of Geshe Ngawang Dhargye on the first, and of Geshe Losang Tenpa of Ganden Monastery on the second and third.

The fourth chapter, translated by myself, is a famous invocation of Tsongkhapa used for several centuries by those meditating on his teachings at the beginning of a session of practice, to invoke his presence and blessings.

Song of the Tricosmic Master

dPal Idan sa gsum ma

by Khaydrub Choeje Gelek Pal Zangpo (1385-1438)

O Je Tsongkhapa, master of the three worlds,
Who surpasses all others in compassion,
The eye through whom all beings
Can receive ultimate vision,
Peerless Refuge of liberation seekers,
To you, a supreme and incomparable Lama,
I offer my spiritual aspirations.

In the very presence of the Victorious One
You entered the ways of enlightenment;
Here in this Land of Snow Mountains
You were renowned as Losang Drakpa;
Now in Tushita Pure Land you abide,
Famed as Wisdom Essence;
To you, mightiest of Bodhisattvas,
I offer my spiritual aspirations.

By the force of ripening merits
You read the teachings and, without study,
Understood texts even in the language of mystics.
To you of naturally perfect excellence
I offer my spiritual aspirations.

From the time your sun-like body
Slipped radiantly from your mother's cloud,
You ever shunned the dancing lights
Of the world and its vain fortunes;
To you I offer my spiritual aspirations.

From very youth you held no distaste
Toward the austerities of Buddhadharma
But secured yourself in perfect discipline.
To you who for countless lifetimes knew
The power of familiarity with meditation,
I offer my spiritual aspirations.

Having unrelentingly examined in depth
The words and meanings of Buddha's teachings,
Constantly and with spontaneity you practised
The guidelines discovered therein.
To you, a treasury of vast knowledge,
I offer my spiritual aspirations.

Not satisfied with strings of empty words,
With subtle reason you fathomed that point
Not perceived by the millions of scholars;
To you who beheld reality itself
I offer my spiritual aspirations.

Were all logicians to analyse
Your teachings a hundred times,
Not even a fraction's fraction
Of your words would prove wrong.
To you of flawless mind
I offer my spiritual aspirations.

Who but you has seen as they are
All the concepts contained
In the texts of the ancient masters?
To you in whom all teachings
Arose as practical advice[1]
I offer my spiritual aspirations.

When the dust clothing the earth
Is inscribed by your lotus feet
Which always rests on the crowns of sages,
That dust becomes an object
Well worthy of worship by men; to you
I offer my spiritual aspirations.

Although a fully omniscient one
Were to challenge your ethical temper,
Not a hint of a flaw
Could ever be discovered:
To you, a perfect renunciate,
I offer my spiritual aspirations.

Like an ocean of wish-fulfilling gems
Is the immeasurable depth of your love,
Beyond even the bounds of clairvoyance.
To you, a mine of benevolence,
I offer my spiritual aspirations.

What load of benefit to beings
Is not carried by your mind so mighty,
For did you not reach the zenith
Of deeds sending endless waves?
To you of miraculous compassion
I offer my spiritual aspirations.

If each breath you release
Acts only as medicine to beings,
Why try to describe the effect
Of your stores of merit and wisdom?
To you, friend of the three worlds,
I offer my spiritual aspirations.

Mañjushri, the Bodhisattva of Wisdom,
Daily appeared directly to you
And rained ambrosial streams of teachings,
The synthesis of the minds of Buddhas
Past, present and future;
To you I offer my spiritual aspirations.

"In the lotus garden of the Muni's teachings
You are likened to a sun amongst Buddhas;"
With these very words Maitreya Buddha
Praised you when in a vision he appeared;
To you I offer my spiritual aspirations.

Beholding the sublime forms of countless Buddhas,
You directly received the transforming powers
Of Saraha, Luipa and the other mahasiddhas;
To you, a supreme and perfected being,
I offer my spiritual aspirations.

Having in a dream been given the blessings of
Nagarjuna, Aryadeva, Buddhapalita and Chandrakirti,
Experience of the Very Dharma, profound emptiness,
Arose within you; to you, who has abandoned
Even the imprints of confusion,
I offer my spiritual aspirations.

With subtle meditation in samadhi centred
Upon reality itself, clear like the sky,
You moved not for a moment
Even in post mediation
From viewing mind as illusory;
To you I offer my spiritual aspirations.

Having mastered the oceans of tantras,
Pinnacle of all Buddhas teachings,
You indeed are a perfect Lama
Inseparable from All-pervading Vajradhara;
To you I offer my spiritual aspirations.

Master who practised exactly as taught
The essential profundities of tantra's two stages,[2]
The ultimate paths, as never before
Shown by another in this land,
And then accomplished their purpose,
I offer you my spiritual aspirations.

By perfecting the coarse and subtle deity yogas,
You eliminated the habitual thought patterns
That conceive existence as profane.
To you whose mind never stirs
From the blissful flow of mystic mandalas,
I offer my spiritual aspirations.

Coasting in the central nadi on a current of air,
You perceived the quintessence of emptiness,
The clear light itself, mahamudra,
Experiencing the summit of great bliss;
To you, the one of vajra mind,
I offer my spiritual aspirations.

Due to the force of your infinite prayers,
Countless disciples spontaneously were drawn
To the path that pleases all Buddhas;
To you, Refuge of all the world,
I offer my spiritual aspirations.

In an era when nothing but the empty name
of "Doctrine" was upheld by teachers and trainees,
You brought into light the three higher trainings[3]
To you, the Great Reviver,
I offer my spiritual aspirations.

When you determined consciously to pass away,
Hosts of Dakas and Dakinis beyond imagination
Making offerings filled the skies.
To you I offer my spiritual aspirations.

Mind focussed on the clear light of Dharmakaya,
Your body transformed into a luminous sphere and,
In the bardo, illusory body yoga fulfilled Sambhogakaya.
To you who gained supreme siddhi
I offer my spiritual aspirations.

From this moment onward in all future lives,
May I sit before your lotus feet

And, hearing your teachings,
Practise only as delights you.

May I be blessed to abandon both
Viewing this life as something to crave
And yearning for happiness for myself alone.
And may I never abandon the bodhimind,
The wish to attain Buddhahood for all[4].

With clear wisdom focussing on the subtle,
May I fathom the perfect words of Buddha
And ascend the path of knowledge.
Thus may I arise to dispel the darkness
Of the ignorance pervading beings' minds.

May I have power to discover
The import of the many tantras
And to practise single-pointedly
The profound significance of their two stages,
Unhindered by inner or outer obstacles,

In brief, may I receive grace to understand
All the teachings of Buddha Shakyamuni,
Especially those of the peerless Vajrayana,
Just as do the Awakened Ones.
Thus may I bring light to the world.

By the virtue of this aspiration,
May I in all future lives never be
Parted from you, a perfect Lama,
And may I dwell with the taste of the teachings
That arose from the depths of your experience.

Because of whatever goodness
I have done or will do,
May you gaze upon me with pleasure,
And may I always unwaveringly practise
Precisely in accord with your advice.

By the power of the mighty deeds
Of Lama Je Tsongkhapa, the tantric Guru,
Until enlightenment may I never fall
From the good path praised by all Buddhas.

The colophon: Written by Khaydrub Choeje Gelek Pal Zangpo, who learned a great deal by sitting for many years at the lotus feet of Je Rinpoche.

A Song Rapidly Invoking Blessings

rGyal ba gnyis pa rje btsun Tsongkhapa-chen-po-la
thugs-rje-bskul-ba'i gsol-'debs-byin-rlabs myur-'jug

by Gyalwa Kalsang Gyatso, the VII Dalai Lama (1708-1757)

Above, in actuality pristine awareness
Manifest as a radiant Buddha mandala,
The pure land of Tushita, the Joyous Abode
Blessed by Buddhas past, present and future.

Mountains of herbs blanketed in sweet aromas.
Flowers blossoming morning, noon and night,
A forest of trees with turquoise leaves
Reminders of the splendid body of Je Rinpoche.

The murmur of a river swiftly flowing,
The stirring songs of birds,
The majestic sound of a Dharma teaching:
Reminder of the gentle voice of Je Rinpoche

The blue sky freely hovering,
Clear, white clouds scattered abstractly,
The young sun casting beams everywhere
The wisdom, compassion and power of Je Rinpoche.

Body adorned with the marks of a Buddha,
Speech raining down vast and profound Dharma,

Mind seeing all things in the sphere of clear light:
I recollect Je Rinpoche, Losang Drakpa

Fulfill your vow to benefit beings;
Descend, grant protection and power.
To you I offer an ocean of all-good things.
Enjoy them within your great bliss.

On the Mighty Nomad Mountain, quiet, easy,
A land made pure with goodness and strength,
Stands your Ganden Monastery[5], prophesied by Buddha:
A monastery producing limitless Awakened Ones.

Your mind on bliss and void inseparable,
The flow of events appeared as a rainbow.
One body sends endless clouds of emanations
To set this world ablaze with joy.

Your profound teachings bridging sutra and tantra
Are jewels for those truly seeking liberation.
Even the words you used are perfect,
Nakedly pointing the way for the ripe.

O Je Lama, because of your infinite kindness
We can understand all sutras and tantras as precepts,
Can see the entire path leading to perfection
And can correct all delusions and mistaken concepts.

O Master, merely hearing legends of your deeds
Can place a man on the enlightening path;
With thoughts of your greatness, with heart
Trembling, I fix mind upon you.

Invisible father gone to bliss,
Listen to this plaintive song
Of a boy still in samsara's quicksands,
Of an ill-fated son cut off from his Refuge.

In terms of extenal appearances,
A monk is easily proud of his robes,

But if his thoughts fall only on the transient
Are his lusts not worse than a layman's?

The masses revel in black actions
And through evil gain their ends.
Flashes of a degenerate age
Crash in the depths of my heart.

How glamorous and exciting to go
Through the motions of practising Dharma,
And to hear the profound teachings;
But the mind, hard as wood, is slow to change.

The spirit, weak and uncontrolled,
Staggers under the three psychic poison[6]
Whenever an object appears to it
A golden vessel filled with urine

Precious humanity, the chance to be a Buddha;
But we create only misery with it
And throw away all hope of actually
Benefitting either ourselves or others.

I, born so late, unfortunate,
Pass my time amid negativity and confusion.
Father Lama, look upon me;
Hold me with hooks of compassion.

In this life, the bardo and future lives,
Pray, be my guide.
My Refuge, forsake me not.
Omniscient One, be with me always.

Care for all beings as a mother for her son.
Spiritual Father, to us who are children,
Reveal visibly the mandala of your body
Magnificent with every mark of perfection.

Bestow upon us the oral teachings
Which render every experience meaningful.

Bless us to make our minds at one taste
With great bliss and unapprehendable wisdom.

Life is impermanent like the setting sun.
Wealth is like dew on morning grass,
Praise is like wind in a mountain pass,
A youthful body is an autumn flower.

Bless me to understand the shortcomings
Of constantly turning on the wheel of becoming
And to fix the depths of my mind
On the path leading to ultimate knowledge.

Bestow upon me transforming powers to fill
My mental continuum with love and compassion,
To see the beings of samsara's six realms[7]
As mothers who have forever helped me.

Bestow upon me transforming powers
Quickly to realize the way things are,
To understand images viewed by the mind
As paintings created by the mind itself.

Help me attain enlightenment in this very life
Through the yogic methods of tantra's two stages,
To see external events as the sport of Buddhas
And the mind as satiated with bliss and emptiness.

And when, to fight delusion, meditation's enemy,
I retreat to a cave on a distant mountain,
A place to give birth to serenity and joy,
Bless me to penetrate the innermost profundity.

Grant me powers swiftly to annihilate
All inner and outer negative forces,
And power to cleanse the stains of having dwelt
For from the limits of Dharma's three bonds[8].

O Mañjushri, who reveals himself magically
In peaceful, wrathful and protective forms,

May your auspicious deeds reach fruition
And you remain a constant Refuge to the world.

Bestow upon me the powerful blessings
Of your mysterious body, speech and mind,
That my every physical, verbal and mental
Movement may benefit beings and the teachings.

May the thunder of the sutras and tantras shake the earth,
May the sun of Tsongkhapa's "Practice Lineage" rage,
May all practitioners attain to power
And all sentient beings realize their wishes.

The colophon: In the year of the Water Dog, Lama Gyalwa Kalsang Gyatso visited Ganden Monastery. Inspired by the extraordinary vibration pervading the place and filled with marvel at the strength and kindness of Omniscient Tsongkhapa, who had founded Ganden, Kalsang Gyatso was moved to write this song.

In Praise of the Incomparable Tsongkhapa

mNyam med Tsong kha pa'i bstod pa

by Gyalwa Mikyo Dorje, The Eighth Karmapa
(1507-1554)

At a time when nearly all in this Northern Land
Were living in utter contradiction to Dharma,
Without illusion, O Tsongkhapa, you polished the
  teachings.
Hence I sing this praise to you of Ganden Mountain[9].

When the teachings of the Sakya, Kargu, Kadam
And Nyingma sects in Tibet were declining,
You, O Tsongkhapa, revived Buddha's Doctrine,
Hence I sing this praise to you of Ganden Mountain.

Mañjushri, the Bodhisattva of Wisdom, gave to you
Special instructions on the thought of Nagarjuna.
O Tsongkhapa, upholder of the Middle Way,
I sing this praise to you of Ganden Mountain.

"Mind and form are not empty of their own natures
But are empty of truly existent mind and form",[10]
You, O Tsongkhapa, are Tibet's chief exponent of voidness,
Hence I sing this praise to you of Ganden Mountain.

In merely a few years you filled
The land from China to India
With peerless holders of the saffron robes.
Hence I sing this praise to you of Ganden Mountain.

Those who become your followers
And look to you and your teachings
Are never again disappointed or forsaken.
Hence I sing this praise to you of Ganden Mountain.

The trainees who walk in your footsteps
Breath the fresh air of the Great Way.
They would die for the good of the world.
Hence I sing this praise to you of Ganden Mountain.

Anyone who disparages your doctrine must face
The terrible wrath of the Dharma protectors.
O Tsongkhapa, who abides in truth's power,
I sing this praise to you of Ganden Mountain.

In person and in dreams you come to those
Who but once recollect your image.
O Tsongkhapa, who watches with compassionate eyes.
I sing this praise to you of Ganden Mountain.

In order to civilize men and spirits you spread
Your teachings through Kham, Mongolia and Turkestan:
O Tsongkhapa, subduer of savages,
I sing this praise to you of Ganden Mountain.

For men coarse and far from the Way, you dispel
Mental clouds, evils and bad karma.
O Tsongkhapa, who bestows quick progress,
I sing this praise to you of Ganden Mountain.

Those who take heartfelt Refuge in you,
Even those with no hope for now or hereafter,
O Tsongkhapa, have their every wish fulfilled.
Hence I sing this praise to you of Ganden Mountain.

Having exposed false teachings transgressing
The excellent ways well shown by Buddha,
You firmly established your Bold Doctrine.
Hence I sing this praise to you of Ganden Mountain.

Manifesting sublime austerity and discipline,
The form and fragrance of your life was incomparable.
O Tsongkhapa, controlled one pleasing to the Buddhas,
I sing this praise to you of Ganden Mountain.

By the strength of the sons of your lineage
And by my having faithfully offered this praise,
May the enlightened activity of Buddha Shakyamuni
Pervade the earth for ages to come.

The colophon : Once when Gyalwa Mikyo Dorje was travelling through the Charida Pass, thoughts of the incomparable Tsongkhapa welled up within him. Overcome by profound faith, he was moved to compose the above poem.

The Tushita's Hundred Gods

dGa' ldan lha brgya ma

An Invocation of Je Tsongkhapa

From the heart of the Lord Protector of Tushita's hundred
    gods,
Floating on fluffy white clouds, piled up like fresh curds,
Here comes the Omniscient Lord of Dharma, Losang
    Drakpa!
Please come down to us, together with Your Sons!

In the sky before me, on a lion throne with lotus and moon
    seat,
Sits the Holy Guru with his beautiful smiling face,
Supreme field of merit for my mind of faith;
Please stay one hundred aeons to spread the Teachings!

I bow to You so beneficial to see, hear, and remember
Your Body of beauty, resplendent with the glory of fame,
Your Speech of eloquence, jewel ornament for the lucky
    ear,
Your Mind of pure genius that spans the whole range of
    knowledge!

Various delightful offerings of flowers, perfumes,
Incenses, lights, and pure sweet waters, these actually
    presented,

And this ocean of offering-clouds created by my
   imagination,
I offer to You, O highest field of merit!

All the sins I have committed with body, speech, and mind,
Accumulated through evolution from beginningless time,
And especially all transgressions of the three vows,
I confess each one with strong regret from depth of heart!

In this dark age, You worked for broad learning and
   accomplishment
Abandoning the eight mundane concerns to realize the great
   value
Of leisure and opportunity; sincerely, O Lord Protector,
We congratulate You for all Your prodigious deeds!

In the sky of the Body of Truth. You Holy Supreme Guru,
Build up the massive clouds of Your wisdom and Your love.
And please pour down on the earth of the deserving disciples
The great rains of the profound and magnificent Dharma!

Whatever virtue I may have gathered here,
May it long make shine the essence of the Buddha Teaching,
Make manifest whatever benefits the living beings,
And especially the Teaching of the Holy Losang Drakpa!

Notes

Part I

1. The *Sukhavati Prayer* is included in part IV below, along with a praise of Maitreya written a bit later from the same inspiration.
2. Part of the instructions given by Vajrapani to Tsongkhapa through the Nyingma Master Lhobrag Khenchen is included in the *Nectar Garland* in part IV below, wherein the Khenchen is referred to by his Tantric name, Karmavajra, and Tsongkhapa by his name in Sanskrit, Matibhadrashri (one way to translate Losang Drakpa).
3. This eulogy is included in part III below.
4. See illustration given on page facing part III.
5. See the Insight part of this work in part III below.
6. See part V below.
7. This direct form of address to Mañjushri reflects Tsongkhapa's constant mystic conversational communication with the Bodhisattva, while his use of the epithet 'Wisdom-Treasure,' indicates his awe, making him hesitate to call his Guru by his personal name. See *Song of Mystic Experiences* in part V.
8. The great Pandits of Buddhist India, Nagarjuna (c. 1-6), Asanga (c. 4-5), Dignaga (c. 5-6), Dharmakirti (c. 7), Aryadeva (c. 2-3) and Vasubandhu (c. 4-5), along with the two Vinaya masters Gunaprabha and Shilaprabha.
9. All these works are found in the Kanjur collection. The scholarly reader will please forgive our omission of precise references, and consult the Suzuki Research Foundation catalogue.
10. Various methods of interpretation used in elucidating the scientific treatises on Tantra. The six limits are *neyārtha, nitārtha, sābhiprāyika, nirabhiprāyika, yathāruta,* and *ayathāruta*. The four ways, *samtāna samaya, samvara, hetu*.

11. Tib. *ji ltar* and *ji snyed*. The former term, lit. "like whatever," is synonymous with "ultimate truth," "emptiness," "thatness," "suchness," etc. The latter, lit. "whatever findable," is synonymous with "conventional truth," etc. The former is also the same as *gnas lugs*, "the way things are," and the latter with *snang lugs*, "the way things appear."

12. The *vast* teachings on the far-reaching activities of the conventional bodhi mind and the profound teachings on the depths of emptiness, the ultimate bodhi-mind.

13. Vajrasana, modern day Bodh Gaya, Bihar, North India.

14. The perfect view; the understanding that everything is empty of true existence.

15. Skt. *Prajña pāramitā* and *Guhyasamaja*.

16. Many beings attain Buddhahood, but only one thousand each aeon manifest the twelve deeds of a universal Teacher. Buddha Shakyamuni was the fourth this aeon, and Je Tsongkhapa will be the eleventh.

17. The lineage Gurus of emptiness meditation that Tsongkhapa received from Mañjushri, who in turn received it from Shakyamuni. See G. Wangyal, *Door of Liberation,* pp. 45-52.

18. Ibid. pp. 52-54. The lineage gurus of bodhimind meditation that Asanga received from Maitreya, who had received it from Shakyamuni.

19. The eighty-four Mahasiddhas, Great Adepts. Tsongkhapa's school, later known as Geluk, synthesizes three Indian lineages, the wisdom lineage of Mañjushri, Nagarjuna, etc.; the method lineage of Maitreya, Asanga, etc., and the practice lineage of the eighty four Mahasiddhas, such as Saraha, Tilopa, Naropa, Maitripa, etc.

20. The Terrific embodiment of the wisdom of emptiness.

21. *bDe ba can du skye ba'i smon lam* and *Mi pham mgon gyi yang dag don bstod*. See part IV below.

22. Skt. *ārya*.

23. The Great Adept to whom Shakyamuni originally gave the Kalachakra Tantra teaching at Dhanyakataka Stupa in South India. Suchandra was King of Shambhala at the time and immediately took the Tantra back there with him. Thus, the Tantra did not appear in India until over one thousand years later.

24. The Great Prayer Festival of Lhasa, conceived and founded by Je Tsongkhapa, continues to the present day. During the first fortnight of the lunar new year more than twenty thousand monks would assemble to commemorate Shakyamuni's miracles at Shravasti. The tradition continues in the free Tibetan communities in India, though of course on a much smaller scale Cf. *The Great Prayer,* Tangent Records, London.

25. Skt. *Mañjushri garbha*. Tib. *'Jam dpal snying po*.

Part II

1. *samsāra*. Sometimes, "life cycle," "cyclic existence."
2. *nges 'byung. niryāna.*
3. *las kyi 'bras bu. karmaphala.*
4. *byang chub kyi sems. bodhicitta.*
5. *rten 'brel, rten 'byung. pratityasamutpāda.*

Lines Of Experience

1. The perfect accomplishments are the realisation of an Enlightened Motive of Bodhichitta and a correct view of Voidness.
2. The Three Realms are the Desire, Form and Formless Realms in which consciousness is preoccupied in turn with either desirable sensory objects or meditative absorptions while either possessing a physical form or not. The Desire Realm is inhabited by hell creatures, hungry ghosts, animals, humans, anti-gods and the first six classes of gods, the Form Realm by the next seventeen classes of and the Formless by the top four classes of gods.
3. The "Mother of the Buddhas" refers to *The Sutras on the Perfection of Discriminating Awareness (Prajñā pāramitā Sūtras)* delivered by Buddha on Vulture's Peak and in which are begun the two Mahayana lineages of the teachings of the profound insight of Voidness and the widespread action of Bodhichitta.
4. *The Lamp for the Pathway to Enlightenment (Bodhipāthapradīpa)* by Atisha is the forerunner for the "Lam-rim" or "Graded Path" literature. In it the two lineages begun with the *prajñā pāramitā Sūtras* are recombined.
5. Tsongkhapa refers here specifically to two of his forty-five spiritual masters, namely the Kargyu Lama Choekyob Zangpo, Most Learned Among the Monks, and the Nyingma Lama Namkha Gyaltsen from Lhobrag, through whom he received and recombined the three strands of Atisha's "Lam-rim" lineage.
6. There are two desirable aims either for higher status with rebirth as a human or a god, or for the definite goodness of either Liberation, from suffering or Full Enlightenment as a Buddha.
7. The nine kinds of beings are derived from the fact that beings may be reborn from any one to any other of the Three Realms, for example from the Desire into the Desire, Form or Formless Realm and so forth.
8. The power-granting king is an epithet of the wish-granting gem, a fabulous jewel which grants all worldly wishes.

9. Buddha's intended themes are renunciation., the Enlightened Motive of Bodhichitta and a correct view of Voidness.

10. The great mistake is to advance sectarian views, to discredit any of the Buddhist Schools, Vehicles or texts, and to disclaim the validity of Buddha's teachings.

11. The initial level motivation is to work for a better rebirth as a human, or a god, out of fear of a lower rebirth. The intermediate level is to work for Liberation from cyclic existence, out of renunciation of your own suffering. The advanced levels to work for achieving the Full Enlightenment of a Buddha in order to be able to liberate all others from their suffering. This highest level, then, is the Bodhichitta motivation.

12. A yogi is someone who has joined himself to actual paths, here specifically ones that lead to Enlightenment.

13. The eight liberties for Dharma study are defined as freedom from the eight states of no leisure. Four of these are non-human states, namely birth in one of the hells, as a hungry ghost, an animal or as a long-lived god. The four human states of no leisure are birth in an uncivilised border region or among barbarians, birth where the words of Buddha are not present, or as a deaf and dumb cretin or instinctively holding distorted views.

14. The three unfortunate states of rebirth are as a hell creature, hungry ghost or animal.

15. The Three Jewels of Refuge are the Buddhas, their Dharma teachings and the Sangha assembly of those who realise them.

16. The eight ripened favourable qualities of a human rebirth most conducive for Dharma study and practice are having a long life, a handsome and healthy body, a good reputable family, with prosperity, honesty and credibility of speech, a strong influence on others, as a male and with a powerful body and mind.

17. The four opponent powers for cleansing yourself of black karmic debts are feeling sincere regret about your previously committed non-virtue and, secondly, invoking what you must rely on, namely the Three Jewels of Refuge and a Bodhichitta motivation. Third is your promise to turn away from ever committing such non-virtue again and fourth is the power of whatever virtuous actions you do to oppose your non-virtue.

18. The two collections are of merit and of insight, the former resulting in your attainment of the Form Bodies of a Buddha and the latter in the Wisdom Bodies or Dharmakaya.

19. The causal Mahayana Vehicle is that of Sutrayana.

20. The resultant Mahayana Vehicle is that of Tantrayana.

A Letter of Practical Advice on Sutra and Tantra

1. Maitreya, *Mahāyānasūtrālaṁkāra.*
2. Nagarjuna, *Suhṛllekha,* 117.
3. Aryadeva, *Mādhyamikacatuḥsataka,* V 4.
4. Kamalasila, *Mādhyamikāloka.*
5. Nagarjuna, *Pañcakrama.*
6. Nagarjuna, *Prajñāmula-nāma-mādhyamikakārikā, Yaidalya Sūtra, Vigrahavyāvartanī, Sunyatasaptati, Yuktisāstika* and *Ratnāvalī.*
7. *Mahāsmrtyupasthānasūtra.*
8. Nagarjuna, *Ratnāvali,* IV 71.
9. *Ibid,* II 19-20.
10. Nagarjuna, *Bodhicittāvivarana,* 85.
11. Mātṛceṭa/Asvaghośa *Varnanārhavarnanastolra.*
12. Nagarjuna, *Prajñāmula-nāma-madhyāmikakārikā,* XXIV 1.
13. *Ibid,* XXIV 20.
14. *Ibid,* XXIV 14.
15. *Ibid,* XXIV 9.
16. Jñana garbha, *Satyadvayavibhāngā.*
17. *Ratnagunasaṁcayagāthā.*
18. Nagarjuna, *Ratnāvalī,* II 16-18.
19. Tsongkhapa, *gSung thor bu,* vol. *Kha,* folios 160A3—169B3.

The Prayer of the Virtuous Beginning, Middle and End

1. Sadaprarudita searched far and wide to find a master who could teach him Voidness and the perfection of discriminating awareness. When he finally located such a Guru, namely Dharmodgata, Sadaprarudita was so poor that he cut off and sold some flesh from his body in order to obtain an offering for requesting these teachings. This account is related in *The Sutra on the Perfection of Discriminating Awareness in Eight Thousand Stanzas (Aṣṭasāhasrikā Prajñā pāramitā Sūtra),* Part 30-2.

2. Once a set of teachings about a certain phenomenon has been understood intellectually, it should be subjected for validation to the four kinds of logic or reasoning in examination meditation. These four are (1) contextual reasoning, looking at the causes and circumstances or at the supporting factors for a certain phenomenon in order to see if they can in fact produce or serve as a basis or context to account for it, (2) functional reasoning, checking if a phenomenon or practice actually does produce its claimed effects, (3) logical reasoning, ensuring that the

teaching is not contradicted by either valid bare perception, inference or scriptural authority, and (4) common-sense reasoning, ascertaining whether or not something fits into what is commonly accepted as the nature of things.

3. The three types of laziness are procrastination, being attached to trivial matters and delusions of incapability. With joyous effort and enthusiasm for virtue, these can be overcome and a state of Enlightenment gradually attained.

Part III

1. Skt. Prasangikāmadhyamika and Svatantrikāmadhyamika.
2. Tib. *rten 'byung*. Skt. *pratityasamutpada*, also translatable as "dependent origination," "relativistic occurrence," etc.
3. Tib. *ma rig pa.* Skt. *avidya*. Not merely a failure to know something, which we mean by ignorance', but a knowing something wrongly, a thinking we know rightly when we mis-know.
4. *blo dung ldan pa*, i.e. Bodhisattvas.
5. *rang bzhin. svabhāva.*
6. *mu stegs pa. tīrthika. A* somewhat derogatory term for non-Buddhists, as referring to those who seek salvation by frequenting holy places, bathing in sacred waters, and invoking various outside agencies to solve their problems.
7. *sgro 'dogs pa* and *skur 'debs pa. samaropa* and *apavāda.* i.e. the mental reification of merely relative things as intrinsically real things, and the repudiation of even the relative reality of absolutely realityless things; i.e. a way of describing the two extremisms of absolutism and nihilism.
8. The Kumuda lily blooms at night, opening its bright white petals for the moon's rays, as most flowers bloom in sunlight, at least according to Indian literary convention. This is the key to this exquisite metaphor, where the white lilies of Nagarjuna's teachings need the moon-rays of Chandra's elucidation to bloom in all their beauty in the mind, as Tsongkhapa attains the complete relief of perfect enlightenment.
9. Tib. *chung ngu.* lit. "lesser," but the *bsdus don* (above as *Lines of Experience*) is really the "lesser," and this the "medium."
10. *Samdhinirmocana Sūtra, The Elucidation of Intent.*
11. Hinayana and Mahayana.
12. *Prajña pāramitopadesha.*
13. *Ratnamegha Sūtra.*

14. Maitreya is here speaking in dialogue with the Buddha, as recorded in the *Elucidation of the Intent.*

15. *Bodhisattva bhūmi* (Asanga, c. 400).

16. *Madhyamā bhāvanakrama,* by Kamalashila, 8th century. During his debates with the Chinese Hvashang Mahayana at Samyas Monastery, Kamalashila composed three texts on the *Stages of Meditation.*

17. Skt. *prāṇa.*

18. *Candrapradīpa Sūtra.*

19. *Dharmasaṃgraha.*

20. *karma.*

21. *saṃsara.*

22. *bodhicitta.*

23. *Bodhicāryavatāra.*

24. Tib. *chos nyid* and *chos can.*

25. This being the context of the Unexcelled Yoga Tantras, the distinctive subjectivity is the great bliss inuition itself.

26. This passage is abstruse, but we assume that adeptness can only arise through the fitness of the neural wind energies brought about by quiescence. Hence, adeptness implies the combination of quiescence with discriminating wisdom.

27. *Shravakabhūmi.*

28. *Madhyamikahṛdaya,* the first great work on comparative ideologies *(grub mtha)* in history, in which Bhavya covers all major schools of philosophy in the 500's in India.

29. Jñana kirti, author of the *Tattvavatara.*

30. Shing rta chen po. maharatha. common epic epithet for a warrior in the *Mahabharata* etc., used in the later Indo-Tibetan literature for the great warriors of philosophy, Nagarjuna and Asanga, and sometimes more extensively.

31. *Abhidharmasamuccaya.*

32. *Bhūmivastu.*

33. Aryadeva was Nagarjuna's closest disciple and Dharma-heir, which means his dates are as confused as his Master's. His *Four Hundred on Yoga Practice* is of the same importance as Nagarjuna's *Wisdom,* and his *Lamp of Integrated Practice* is fundamental for *Guhyasamāja* studies after Nagarjuna's *Five Stages.* Buddhapalita is usually placed in the fifth century, contemporary of Bhavaviveka, both from South India, in the days when Kanci was a major Buddhist center. Buddhapalita elucidated the *Wisdom* from a dialectical point of view, and Bhavya criticized that method, providing a more systematic, dogmatic approach. Chandrakirti (c. 600)

then rebutted Bhavya's critique, and the formal Dialectical school was founded. Shantarakshita (9th century) then came along and continued Bhavaviveka's Dogmatic approach, while relating more closely with the Idealists' positions on the status of external objects, at least conventionally.

34. The expression "Grandmother Treatise" is interesting, since the *Transcendent Wisdom Scripture* herself is known as the *Mother of all Victors* (Sarvajinamata). Thus, since the works of Nagarjuna and Aryadeva, the Holy Father and Son, give birth to transcendent wisdom who gives birth to Buddhahood, they are like the mothers of the mother, i.e. "grandmothers."

35. Sautrantika.

36. Yogacāra.

37. Mayanyāyasiddhi (sGyu ma rigs grub pa).

38. Apratishthitavadi.

39. rNgog blo ldan shes rab, great translator of *Entrance to the Middle Way* and many other works (1059-1109).

40. Jñana sena,

41. Atisha (eleventh century) was the great Bengali Master who spent twelve years in Tibet, starting a tradition of Teaching and Practice that was Tsongkhapa's own central inspiration.

42. People tend to refer to Nagarjuna's basic work as the *Basic Middle Way Stanzas*, which is the translation of the works subtitle, *Mūlamadhyamaka kārika*. Its actual name is simply *Prajña, Wisdom*.

43. Vaibhashika.

44. Respectively, *svarūpasiddha (rang gi ngo bos grub pa), svalakshaṇasiddha (rang mtshan gyis grub pa)*, and *svabhāvasiddha (rang bzhin gyis garb pa)*.

45. *Upāliparipṛccha Sūtra* from the *Ratnakuṭa* Collection.

46. *Yuktiṣaṣṭika.*

47. *Catuhshataka.*

48. *dgag bya (nishedhya)*, the "to-be-negated."

49. *Madhyamakāvatara.*

50. *Vijñānavāda.*

51. *'Jig lta lhan skyes.*

52. i.e. in the *Essence of the Eloquent.*

53. *bdag gir 'dzin pa.*

54. *nyon mongs can gyi ma rig pa.*

55. *bden 'dzin.*

56. *kleshajñeyavaraṇa.*

57. *Shunyatasaptati.*

58. *svasamvṛtti;* a self aware cognition, aware of itself at the same time as it cognizes other objects, posited by Idealists.

59. In the part of the *Path of Enlightenment* above on the Individual Vehicle practitioner, considered the mediocre person, better than the self-seeking worldling, and worse than the altruistic Bodhisattva.

60. *Pramāṇavārtika.*

61. *Āryatathagata gūhyaka Sūtra.*

62. This remarkable finding is further elaborated in the *Essence of the Eloquent*, providing extraordinary insight into the relationship between enlightened and unenlightened mind, as Tsongkhapa says there that the unenlightened person has only the first and third of the three types of cognitions, whereas the enlightened person has all three types. This is very thought provoking.

63. *Samādhiraja Sūtra.*

64. In the *Great Stages of the Path* and elsewhere. Basically, it involves learning to observe the false sense of "I",. "I" that dominates one's experience, which becomes most evident in moments of righteous indignation, when one is falsely accused, for example, and "Why, I am not...'.", "I", "I", "I", rises up powerfully from the heart. This is the time to catch the sense of real "I", and see how it organizes our lives. It is the first key, since we have to identify the negatee before we can negate it.

65. Jinamata, i.e. the 100,000 *Prajñā pāramitā Sūtra.*

66. The big difference between western transcendent noumena and Buddhist transcendent ultimates, such as emptiness and nirvana, is that the former are in principle inaccessible to human cognition, while the latter are the proper objects of human transcendent wisdom *(prajña pāramitā).*

67. *Abhisamayalaṃkāra* by Maitreyanatha.

68. *tha snyad shes pa (vyavaharikajñāna)* and *rigs shes (yukti jñāna).*

69. *mtshan 'dzin (ṇimittagraha),* the holding of things as having intrinsic identity or significance, seizing them as signs. This way of describing the concept dominated naive realist experience of the work has no parallel in western epistemology until the work of Wittgenstein who first clearly described how we project our concepts on the world and then "read them off" it, as if they were really objectively embedded there. He calls this deep mental habit, "substantivism."

70. *skye mched, āyatana.*

71. *Sagaramatipariprccha Sūtra.*

72. *Laṇkāvatāra.*

73. Thesis—emptiness of intrinsic reality (this refutes absolutism), and reason—because of relativity (this refutes nihilism).

74. *Lokatitāstava.*

75. *Bodhicittavivaraṇa.*

76. *Vyākhyayukti.*

77. *Madhyamakāloka.*

78. *Vigrahavyavartāni.*
79. Tsongkhapa is especially critical of the Jonangpa school here.
80. *Shikshasamuccaya.*
81. *lokasamvṛti* and *paramārtha.*
82. *ldog pa, vyavṛtti,* term describing conceptualization as differential, i.e. differentiating its designandum from everything else that it; used by Dignaga to safeguard against the tendency to substantivism, i.e., reifying linguistic categories in reality.
83. Jñana garbha, author of the *Satyadvayavibhanga.*
84. In the *Essence of the Eloquent* and in the *Brilliant Clarification of the Intent,* his commentary on the *Entrance to the Middle Way.*
85. Especially in the *Essence of the Eloquent,* where Je Rinpoche gives his most concise definition of intrinsic identity as involved in the presentation of the radical conventionality of the superficial reality, wherein all intrinsic identities are absent.
86. *Satyadvayāvatāra.*
87. *Sambhogakāya.*
88. I must confess this passage still seems to elude my grasp, though my translation follows my best guess, that the Buddha's absolute and relative intuitions can operate simultaneously on one object, while never confusing that object's emptiness and its appearance in conventional cognition.
89. *Madhyamakālaṃkāra.*
90. These sGyu ma rigs grub-pa's assert that the ultimate is the coordination of considered phenomena and truthless appearance.
91. Bracket required here because of difficulty of conveying the etymology of Skt. *samyak* and Tib. *yang dag.*
92. *Pitaputrasamāgama Sūtra* of the *Ratnakuṭa* collection.
93. *Āryatattvanirdeshasamādhi.*
94. *zhi rags kyi rnam pa can.*
95. Analysts, Traditionists, Idealists, Centrists.
96. *Gūhyasamāja.*
97. *Kashyapaparivārta* of the *Ratnakuṭa.*
98. *Nirvikalpāvatāradhāraṇi.*
99. Kamalashila's opponent at the Samye debate was a renegade Ch'an teacher who taught a simplistic meditation of mere thoughtlessness as the ultimate practice. His view is just as incorrect in terms of the critical sayings of the great Ch'an Masters, such as Ma Tzu, Pai Chang, Huang Po, Lin Chi etc., as it was for Kamalashila. Thus the Hvashang's position should not be considered as typical of all Ch'an Zen.

100. Geshe Potoba of the Kadampa lineage (1031-1105).
101. Atisha's *Madhyamakopadesha*.

Part IV

1. Ajitanatha.
2. i.e. Regent of Shakyamuni in Tushita until he descends to earth and leaves the next Buddha as his Regent.
3. Images of the hells.
4. Preta realms, little better than hells, where beings languish tormented by unsatisfied desires.
5. Beasts, dumb animals.
6. Asuras, or anti-gods, or titans.
7. Note how the Buddhist attainment of heaven is not an end in itself, but involves even from the wish the aspiration to use the heavenly favorable circumstances to learn, contemplate, and meditate, thereby achieving exalted accomplishments and then re-emanating back into the realms of suffering sentient beings throughout the universes in order to benefit them.
8. *bar do.*
9. lit. "ear", referring to the fact that Vajrapani has heard every esoteric teaching from all Buddhas, never forgetting a single one.
10. It seems that Tsongkhapa cannot himself directly see Vajrapani at this point in his life.
11. Naropa's *Six Yogas* and Padmasambhava's *Great Perfection*.
12. The Great Adepts, or Mahasiddhas.
13. There is a note appended in the Tashi Lhunpo edition which purports to soothe anyone who might have been offended by Vajrapani's equation of the Great Perfection with the Great Middle Way of Nagarjuna and Chandrakirti. I have omitted it here, as it seems rather to have the opposite effect, not helpful to contemporary readers.

Part V

1. This line touches upon the spearhead of the Geluk approach to Buddhism: learning as much as possible, but doing so in terms of one's own personal practice. The Geluk Tradition has been condemned by a

number of Western scholars as being overly intellectual. Rather, it would be more accurate to say that the Gelukpas make maximum use of the intellect. Although their intellectual discipline is extremely vigorous—top scholars may study twenty hours a day for forty years—this discipline is never allowed to deviate from actual practice. Tsongkhapa dedicates many pages in the opening part of his *Lam rim chen mo* to this theme. In fact "taking all teachings as personal advice" is one of the four great qualifications of Tsongkhapa's lineage. Cf. the Third Dalai Lama (trans. Glenn H. Mullin), *Essence of Refined Gold*, Vagabond Books Inc., Delhi, 1978.

2. The two stages of tantra: the generation stage (sKyes rim), wherein one generates pride of being a deity, samadhi upon the supporting and supported mandalas, and the eight siddhis; and the perfection stage (rDzogs rim), wherein one practises with the perfect base generated previously and attains the perfect siddhi of mahamudra.

3. The higher trainings in ethics, meditation and wisdom. Perhaps Tsongkhapa's greatest contribution to Tibetan Buddhism was his emphasis on using the three higher trainings—the essence of the Hinayana—as bases and supplements to tantric practice. Of course these three were known in Tibet before Tsongkhapa's time but only in words. Therefore the great translator Taktzang Lotsawa wrote: "Some, clinging to the Hinayana doctrines, abandoned the tantras. Others, loving the tantric system , disparaged the Hinayana. But you, Tsongkhapa, are the sage who saw how to put every teaching given by Buddha perfectly into practice." (See Thub bstan mdzes pa'i gyan, Sarnath Edition, page 618.) Taktzang Lotsawa continues: "You practised all sutras and tantras, but specialised in Vajrayana; you practised all tantric systems, but specialised in Highest Tantra; you practised all stages of Highest Tantra, but placed special emphasis upon the peerless illusory body yoga. O Tsongkhapa, unmatched treasury of teachings, I bow to you."

4. The bodhimind, or Mahayana attitude, is of two types; conventional and ultimate. Conventional bodhimind is also subdivided into two: the wishing bodhimind, which yearns for enlightenment as the most practical way to benefit all sentient beings, and the venturing bodhimind, which ventures into the practices of the six perfections and four ways of amassing trainees. Ultimate bodhimind is the bodhimind which understands emptiness.

5. The monastery built by Tsongkhapa. The Ganden Throne Holder is the official head of the Geluk Sect. Kyabje Ling Rinpoche, Senior Tutor to His Holiness the Fourteenth Dalai Lama, presently holds this position.

6. Attachment, hostility and ignorance.
7. The realms of hell beings, ghosts, animals, humans, antigods and gods.
8. Tibetan: *sDom pa gsum*. The three bonds are those of the Hinayana, Mahayana and Vajrayana, or the pratimoksha vows, the Bodhisattva vows and the tantric vows.
9. The first, third and fourth verses of this song were quoted in my "A Cooling Raindrop," a biography of Tsongkhapa published in the British journal *Vajra*, issue number three, September, 1976. They appear here in a revised form.
10. It seems that during the time of Tsongkhapa many Tibetans were mistaking emptiness, or shunyata, for a type of vaccum-like object somewhat similar to that experienced by gods of the formless realms. Tsongkhapa asserted that such an "emptiness" was not the real thought of Buddha, Nagarjuna, Aryadeva or Chandrakirti, and that the liberation achieved by cognizing it was a short-lived freedom. This sentence, quoted from Je Rinpoche, points to the true emptiness.